T0312179

BEHAVIOURAL ECONOMICS AND TERRORISM

Behavioural Economics and Terrorism can be used as a guide to help us think about thinking and, in doing so, to appreciate the deep quirkiness of human behaviour. Each day, people draw on their understanding of human behaviour. This takes place subconsciously for the most part but as situations become more complex it becomes necessary to think more deliberately about how people make their decisions. This book can be used to better understand human action in such contexts.

In the high-stakes world of counter-terrorism, every angle of advantage is critical. From terrorists' operational choices to the way that information flows through intelligence agencies, the book explains the patterns of behaviour that systematically shape human decision-making, for good and for bad.

Decision-makers' use of reference points, their loss aversion, overconfidence, goals and aspirations all shape their choices under conditions of risk and uncertainty. This book helps to shed light on how to use these concepts (and more) to develop deeper insights into the way in which terrorists think about their attack methods and targets.

Peter J. Phillips is Associate Professor (Finance) at the University of Southern Queensland, Australia. He applies decision theory, including orthodox and behavioural economics, to problem solving in counter-terrorism, intelligence, counterintelligence and law enforcement. He is particularly interested in showing how decision theory can be used to predict patterns of behaviour and in explaining how information (and disinformation) flows can be structured and organised.

Gabriela Pohl is Lecturer (Social Science) at the University of Southern Queensland, Australia. She uses decision theory to help people make better decisions, in law enforcement, counter-terrorism and intelligence contexts. Her work emphasises the importance of 'thinking about thinking' and she strives to show how decision-makers can use behavioural economics to simplify decision tasks and identify the systematic patterns of behaviour displayed by friend and foe alike.

BEHAVIOURAL ECONOMICS AND TERRORISM

Law Enforcement and Patterns of Behaviour

Peter J. Phillips and Gabriela Pohl

Routledge
Taylor & Francis Group

LONDON AND NEW YORK

First published 2021
by Routledge
2 Park Square, Milton Park, Abingdon, Oxon OX14 4RN

and by Routledge
52 Vanderbilt Avenue, New York, NY 10017

Routledge is an imprint of the Taylor & Francis Group, an informa business

© 2021 Peter J. Phillips and Gabriela Pohl

British Library Cataloguing-in-Publication Data
A catalogue record for this book is available from the British Library

Library of Congress Cataloging-in-Publication Data
A catalog record has been requested for this book

ISBN: 978-0-367-70048-5 (hbk)
ISBN: 978-0-367-70046-1 (pbk)
ISBN: 978-1-003-14437-3 (ebk)

Typeset in Bembo
by Newgen Publishing UK

CONTENTS

ILLUSTRATIONS

Figures

Tables

CHAPTER OUTLINES

Chapter 1 Blindfold chess and terrorism

Alexander Alekhine is famous for playing more than 20 simultaneous games of chess without even looking at a single board. He visualised the playing surfaces, the moves, the pieces and, most importantly, the patterns. Patterns are essential building blocks for human thought and decision processes. We can use both orthodox and behavioural economics to tap into these patterns, identify them and use them to study decision-making.

Chapter 2 Patterns of reason and unreasonableness

The Unabomber, Theordore Kaczynski, would disappear for long stretches of time. The Red Army Faction in Germany found itself competing for attention with rival groups such as the 2nd of June Movement. And airplane hijackings in the United States surged and then suddenly dissipated in the 1960s and 1970s. A mixture of orthodox and behavioural economics can help us think more deeply about the decisions that produced these patterns.

Chapter 3 Bounded by rationality

When attacks on the embassies of Western nations became more and more difficult due to increased fortification and security, terrorist groups switched to attacks outside of the embassies, including kidnapping embassy staff. These types of patterns, including the gradual transition towards mass casualty bombings in the early 1980s, can be encompassed, to some extent, by even the most orthodox of economic models.

Chapter 4 Loss aversion and terrorist identity

Terrorists form an identity that they do not want to lose and this makes their choices rigid and insensitive to changing conditions. In economics, this rigidity is explained as a manifestation of the endowment effect, which in turn is explained by loss aversion. The endowment effect, loss aversion and identity combine to explain patterns of engagement in terrorism, attack method choices and a general reluctance to give up any concessions at all during negotiation.

Chapter 5 Prospect theory as a descriptive theory of terrorist choice

The choices of copycat terrorists depend on the outcomes achieved by their predecessors, rivals or idols. The predecessors' outcomes are the reference point against which the outcomes of prospective actions are evaluated. Depending on the position of the reference point, the copycat takes more or less risk in selecting attack methods and targets. The reference point, perhaps one of the most important concepts in behavioural economics, is also central to explaining rivalries between terrorist groups and the choices that they make in trying to assert their ascendancy.

Chapter 6 The hidden side of attack method combinations and international terrorism

Terrorist groups usually combine attack methods and we use modern portfolio theory and behavioural portfolio theory to provide a rationale for this behaviour and a way to analyse what it means for terrorists' risks, rewards and international activities. Combining different attack methods and diversifying across geographical locations reduces the risks that terrorist groups must bear in pursuing their goals.

Chapter 7 Cycles in terrorism and evolutionary stability

A tree, needing light to survive, grows upwards towards the forest canopy. But the tree does not need to grow as tall as it possibly can. It only needs to grow marginally taller than its competitors to shade them out and win the contest for survival. Likewise, to survive, a terrorist group does not need to maximise, in some absolute sense, the number of its supporters, its financial resources, its attacks, its recruits or its media attention. Fitness and survival depend on the growth rate of the group's relative share of all these things. Applying insights from evolutionary game theory allows us to better understand the terrorist group's life cycle and the cycles in terrorist violence that have been observed since 1970.

Chapter 8 Overconfidence, gender differences and terrorist choice

Overconfidence turns up again and again in every setting that psychologists have investigated. Overconfidence leads to risk seeking and too much risky activity. Too much terrorism, from the terrorist's point of view, is terrorism beyond the point at which expected payoffs begin to decline. One possible reason for the difference in the outcomes achieved by the Zebra Killers on the one hand and the Black Liberation Army on the other is their relative degrees of overconfidence.

Chapter 9 Expected utility as a measurement tool in the terrorism context

Expected utility theory can be used to measure the satisfaction a terrorist decision-maker expects to garner from using different attack methods or from attacking different targets. We measure the utility garnered from a series of attacks perpetrated by Carlos the Jackal. Measurements produced by expected utility theory are compared with prospect theory to show how much (or how little) the two models diverge.

Chapter 10 Decision-making with more than one reference point

Multiple reference points, including organisational or career aspiration reference points, can shape risk preferences and decision-making. Prospect theory can be extended so that it can treat situations where decision-makers navigate a status quo reference point while keeping their eye on an aspirational reference point. The amount of 'slack' in the organisation (i.e. the amount of extra resources that can be allocated to tasks) can focus decision-makers' attention on different reference points and encourage more or less risk taking.

Chapter 11 A guide to the terrorism studies conversation

All academic research is an ongoing conversation. The people contributing to it are unique individuals from all backgrounds, each with their own individual perspective. And when a newcomer picks up the conversation and engages with it, he or she brings his or her own unique interpretation of it. We present a guide to the conversation (how to access it, how to use it etc.). The past two decades have revolutionised the way in which the conversation is stored and accessed. The volume of published research has expanded exponentially. A strategic approach to using this research is more essential than ever.

Chapter 12 Information cascades and the prioritisation of suspects

Mistakes such as wrongful convictions have bothered researchers and practitioners for years. One explanation is confirmation bias. We discuss the deeper roots of confirmation bias (in Bayesian updating) before going even deeper to look at the fascinating phenomenon of information cascades. How easily can a cascade start? How many decision-makers does it take? If investigators are prioritising suspects, can a cascade sweep through an investigative team or even across jurisdictions? The answer is that it can. Easily.

Chapter 13 Everyday decision-making

The economic analysis of terrorism has usually focused on extraordinary events such as hostage taking situations, sieges or large-scale assaults on important targets. What about the everyday of counter-terrorism and law enforcement? The relentless grind of information gathering, assessments, surveillance, interviews. And let's not forget the ever present danger. We explore this overlooked side of the story and end with a discussion of one of the more controversial developments in contemporary policing: predictive policing.

Chapter 14 Reason, strategy and discovery

There is a mainstream within behavioural economics, even though the whole field sits outside the mainstream of orthodox economics. To help people to go off the beaten track and find some more amazing and thought-provoking patterns of human decision-making, we end with a road map or guide to behavioural economics that can be used by someone wishing to take up some of the leads we have identified but haven't had the time to explore.

PREFACE

Thinking about thinking

In this book, we present the science of quirky human decision-making and its implications for terrorism and law enforcement decision-making. We believe that behavioural economics, along with other parts of decision theory, gives us the frameworks we need for thinking about thinking. Our goal is to explain the ideas as clearly as possible so that everyone can use them. We aim to show how behavioural economics can be used to explore various scenarios populated by various foes (or friends) who have various characteristics and, in a relatively structured way, it is possible to think about how these foes (or friends) might approach a problem, how they might solve it and how they might choose from the alternatives that they confront. We don't expect an exact, one-hundred percent correct prediction of the precise course of action they will choose to take. Such predictions are called *point predictions*. Rather, we hope to help people to use behavioural economics to develop *pattern predictions*.

Given that counter-terrorism and, for that matter, other fields of national security, including intelligence and counter-intelligence, involves a lot of thinking about both foes' and friends' decision-making, there is room for a set of ideas that can stimulate and guide such thinking without imposing itself as 'the way' to think. Also, while many of the popular books that have been published about behavioural economics tend to be somewhat critical of human rationality and somewhat negative about the way that people make decisions, we prefer to be much more optimistic and much more positive. Things get done. People are making good decisions in the face of risk and uncertainty. A surprisingly high percentage of people are making decisions in accordance with rational choice theory. But there is a deepness to human decision-making that is being revealed by fields of study like behavioural economics. In this deepness, there is structure. There are patterns of behaviour that can be useful to know and useful to think about.

Along the way, we introduce readers to some of the most significant findings in behavioural economics. From terrorists' decisions about attack methods and targets to the choices that shape the Central Intelligence Agency's (CIA) use of information to the relentless grind of everyday policing and counter-terrorism, observed patterns of behaviour are placed in the context of established research findings that identify the deep quirkiness of human decision-making processes. We think about the Unabomber, the Red Army Faction (RAF), airplane hijacking in the 1970s, embassy bombings, mass casualty attacks, Carlos the Jackal, Sam Melville, the 2nd of June Movement, Brenton Tarrant, Black September, Al-Qaeda, Earth Liberation Front (ELF), the IRA, the Zebra Killers, Black Liberation Army (BLA), Ulrike Meinhof and Greece's Revolutionary Struggle. We think about counter-terrorism, the CIA, the Federal Bureau of Investigation (FBI) and other agencies and the role of information, how it flows, how we deal with it and how human decision-making shapes the ways we search for it.

Peter J. Phillips and Gabriela Pohl
University of Southern Queensland,
Toowoomba, Queensland, Australia
October 2020

1

BLINDFOLD CHESS AND TERRORISM

The main C.I.A. [Central Intelligence Agency] unit tasked to capture or disrupt Osama Bin Laden and other Al Qaeda leaders was called ALEC Station…On September 11 2001, ALEC Station held down a small area of the D.C.I. [Director of Central Intelligence] Counterterrorist Centre [C.T.C.], a windowless expanse of cubicles and computers on the ground floor of the New Headquarters building. It was the worst office space at the C.I.A., in the opinion of some who worked there. It felt like a bunker. During the last days of the Cold War, the Soviet-East Europe Division had occupied the floor; its impermeability would thwart the K.G.B.'s eavesdroppers, the thinking went. The C.I.A.'s Russia hands eventually found better quarters and the C.T.C. moved in. The centre was a bureaucratic stepchild. It had been founded in 1986 as an experiment, a place where analysts—typically, writers and researchers with graduate degrees but no operating experience on the street—might work alongside or even supervise case officers, also known as operations officers, the career spies who recruited agents and stole secrets. The C.I.A.'s case officer cadre enjoyed the greatest power and prestige at the agency. It was not natural for them to collaborate with analysts. It was akin to creating teams of detectives and college professors to solve crimes.[1]

Human decision-making is very quirky. While economics has traditionally been associated with purely rational choice, it is within a part of economics called 'behavioural economics' that some of the quirkiest discoveries have been made about how humans think. Together with psychologists, a new vanguard of economists have helped return economics to its roots as a decision science. In high stakes contexts such as terrorism and law enforcement, the findings have significant implications. Although detectives and college professors might make for an odd pairing, the gains from sharing practice and theory and new insights from the lab and from the field have long been recognised. As we shall see, there are things that can be done to get more from this relationship. We think that as far as economics and behavioural economics is concerned, the key lies in patterns of behaviour expressed by verbal arguments supported by data rather than quantitative modelling expressed by formal statistical analysis. Despite outward appearances, this approach is the essence of economic analysis.[2]

In the past 20 or 30 years, economics has changed. A lot. The economics talked about in everyday situations is the economics of money and markets. Traditional economics. If you were to say that you study the economics of defence, people would naturally assume that you study defence spending and military budgets. Although money and markets remain a core part of economics, it is the discipline's roots as a decision science or a science of choice that run much deeper. Consider Lionel Robbins' (1932, p.15) famous definition of economics: Economics is the science which studies human behaviour as a relationship between ends and scarce means which have alternative uses. This definition characterises economics as a science of choice under conditions of scarcity. Of course, many of these choices involve market behaviour but there are broader implications that stretch beyond markets to virtually every decision that people make. Because psychology was not considered a rigorous field of study in the early days, economists took steps to distance themselves and their work from too much psychological speculation. In fact, some of the key models in economics were developed precisely in an attempt to remove psychological factors from the situation. Consumers are less satisfied with additional units of a good, say coffee, not because their taste for coffee wears thin after so many cups—a psychological phenomenon but because additional units of coffee satisfy needs of decreasing importance. Once you have enough coffee, you are better off spending your next dollar on something else (usually).

Later, in the 1940s and 1950s, the invention of game theory took economics further in the direction of studying individual decision-making processes. Game theory was the brainchild of the superb Hungarian mathematician, computer pioneer and genius with a round angelic face, John von Neumann. Von Neumann started by proving his 'minimax theorem' in the later 1920s. When playing a zero-sum game where somebody wins and somebody loses, von Neumann proved that each player would do best by following the strategy of minimising his maximum losses (minimax). The initial proof was for two-player zero-sum games where each player knows the history of 'moves'. Extensions on this original scenario have been the subject of analysis ever since, with von Neumann & Morgenstern (1944) developing solutions for games with more than two players and less than perfect knowledge about the history of moves.[3]

It was not too long before economists and others interested in human decision processes began to experiment by having subjects participate in different types of games to see whether their choices aligned with the solutions (optimal strategies) determined by the mathematicians. This was a major factor in reconnecting economics and psychology. Psychology, by the mid-1950s, was now a much more established discipline than it had been at the turn of the century and although many economists were still suspicious, bold innovators like Reinhard Selten[4] pushed forward with a study of just how well the mathematicians' theories about optimal solutions to games aligned with the strategies chosen by human players. These were early economics experiments and the precursor to modern experimental economics. Over the decades to come, economists would replicate market scenarios and other choice problems in controlled experimental settings, giving their subjects the chance to earn real money and seeing how well the theories of economics held up.

Game theory is a mathematical theory. It is not directly a theory of human behaviour. In the 1947 edition of their book, *Theory of Games and Economic Behaviour*, von Neumann & Morgenstern (1947) worked out what might be called a 'prescriptive' theory of decision-making under conditions of risk. They called it expected utility theory. Being a mathematical theory of measurement, it is based on certain axioms or rules. The rules are simple. For example, if you prefer apples to oranges and you prefer oranges to pears then you must prefer apples to pears. These rules have become the standard depiction of rational behaviour in economics. If you break a rule, you choose irrationally. If you choose irrationally, you won't choose the right strategy for the game you are playing. If a decision-maker follows the rules, he will choose among alternative risky prospects (gambles) in such a way that his choice is optimal. The optimal choice maximises his expected utility. This theory certainly works as a prescriptive model. If you are making choices under risk, you should do what it says. The challenge remained, though, to build a model that *describes*, rather than prescribes, human decision-making in risky situations. For this, we would have to wait.

Bounded rationality

Herbert Simon was raised in Milwaukee, Wisconsin. He later attended the University of Chicago. After early stints at other universities, Simon settled into Carnegie Mellon where he worked from 1949 until his death in 2001. His 1947 book, *Administrative Behaviour*, became a classic in the field of organisational decision-making and human problem solving. In his work, the theme of 'bounded rationality' looms large.[5] Simon realised that the types of problems that people face are often clouded by patches of uncertainty, incomplete information and complexity that render computational efforts difficult and time consuming. These are in addition to the limited cognitive capabilities of the decision-maker. These limitations are magnified by time constraints. Even if a person or group of people could solve a problem, they will not usually have lots of time to spend doing so. Rather than display utility maximising behaviour, Simon argued that people exhibit 'satisficing' behaviour. They try to find the best solution they can within the time allowed and given the information to hand. This will probably not be the absolutely best solution.

Simon was thinking about the possibility that people might not even try to maximise utility. It's not that they can't, it's just that there are too many complexities, too many constraints and not enough time to do so. As such, could a model of human behaviour be built where the decision-maker tried to achieve something other than utility maximisation? Where could one start in order to build such a model? Just as Reinhard Selten realised he could learn a lot about human behaviour through experimenting with game theory, Herbert Simon thought that chess held some of the keys to understanding decision-making processes. At the time, there had already been some research undertaken in the choice processes used by chess players. For example, Adriaan de Groot's *Thought and Choice in Chess* (1965) is an extensive analysis of the psychology of decision-making in chess. Simon was interested because de Groot reported that chess players do not consider all possibilities and then pick the best move. In fact, they consider about 100 possibilities out of around 10^{120} alternatives (i.e. 10 with 120 zeroes). Could this be a case of satisficing?

The study of chess decision-making is important for many reasons. Most people would agree that, as far as the game itself goes, chess players are far from irrational. Their mental feats are lauded. In 1924, Alexander Alekhine, the reigning world champion, played 26 simultaneous blindfold games of chess against strong opponents, including a grandmaster. He won 16 of the games and drew five more. In 1934, he bettered the feat by playing 34 simultaneous games 'blindfolded'. Others have since done better still. The way that chess players structure information and, in the case of blindfold chess, visualise the board and pieces has been the subject of ongoing investigation (Campitelli & Gobet 2005). One thing is clear; they do not assess all of the alternatives and choose the best one. They do not compute and then choose the minimax strategy. But this is not because chess players are irrational. Their rationality is bounded by the complexity of the context, something that even computers could not overcome until relatively recently. The only way to proceed is by replacing an optimisation problem with a satisficing problem.

Heuristics and biases

In case anybody thinks that economics was oblivious to all of this or that economists would choose to ignore it in order to focus on unbounded rationality instead, Herbert Simon was awarded the Nobel Prize for economics in 1978. While producing a tour de force of analysis of human problem solving, Simon did not develop a clearly demarcated descriptive model of choice that could fill the gaps not covered by the prescriptive expected utility theory. That task would fall to others. During the 1960s and 1970s, two Israeli psychologists were at work on what would become a major research program in psychology, the decision sciences and, ultimately, economics. Daniel Kahneman and Amos Tversky started by wondering whether people were good intuitive statisticians. They then started testing, in laboratory situations similar to Selten's game theory experiments, whether certain laws of logic, probability and statistics were obeyed during the decision-making process. They reported that, on the contrary, people routinely violated these laws.

Tversky & Kahneman (1974)[6] found that people appear to use mental shortcuts or heuristics when making decisions. This 'fast thinking' leads to biases. That is, divergences from those laws of logic, probability and statistics. Most of these heuristics have to do with judging likelihoods (probability). In judging the likelihood that a person with particular characteristics holds a particular occupation, people use a 'representativeness heuristic' and judge the probability on how well that occupation represents the person. This might lead the decision-maker to overlook the fact that very few people hold such an occupation and that, despite the narrative, it is more likely that the person is employed somewhere else. Another heuristic is the 'availability heuristic'. Here, the decision-maker bases a probability estimate on how easily he or she can recall instances of the event in question. For example, if we ask someone how likely is it that he or she will be killed by terrorists they might base their assessment on how easily they can recall examples of people being killed by terrorists. This can lead to substantial divergences between the perceived probability and the actuarial odds.

Kahneman and Tversky recognised the implications of their findings for rational choice and expected utility theory. If people could not correctly assess the odds of particular outcomes, there is no way that they could arrive at an accurate assessment of the expected utility of a particular risky prospect. Where would they arrive instead? And, more to the point, how would they get there? Kahneman and Tversky set out to develop a model to describe the decision-making process that people use when choosing from among alternative risky prospects. They called this model prospect theory. Prospect theory describes a decision-maker whose choices are shaped by reference points, fear of losses, alternating risk preferences and strangely weighted probabilities. An expected utility decision-maker assesses the absolute value of an outcome. If a gamble promises a chance of $1000, the decision-maker considers the chance of receiving this $1000 'gain'. A prospect theory decision-maker, though, considers such things as his neighbour having recently boasted about winning $2000. The prospect theory decision-maker views a $1000 prize as a $1000 'loss' because it is less than his $2000 reference point that was influenced by his braggart neighbour.

Behavioural economics

Kahneman & Tversky (1979) published their prospect theory at the same time that other economists were also working on generalisations of expected utility theory. There was something different about Kahneman and Tversky's theory. There was something very eye-catching about it. And it caught the eye of Richard Thaler, the person who more than anyone else would be responsible for turning behavioural economics into a distinct field within economics (Barberis 2018). According to Thaler's (2016) account of the early history of behavioural economics, Kahneman and Tversky's 'stunning graph' was the thing that he first noticed when reading some of their early work. The stunning graph he refers to is the S-shaped utility function.

In economics, a utility function plots the relationship between utility (satisfaction) and goods or money. Orthodox utility functions are concave to depict

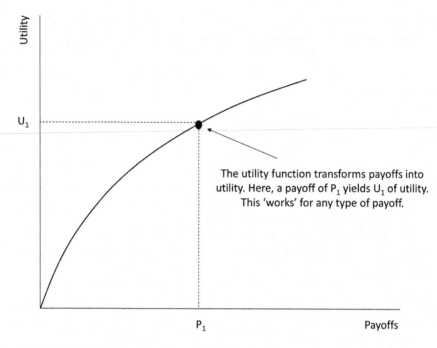

The utility function transforms payoffs into utility. Here, a payoff of P_1 yields U_1 of utility. This 'works' for any type of payoff.

FIGURE 1.1 A regular shaped concave utility function.

risk aversion and diminishing marginal utility. One of these ordinary functions is shown in Figure 1.1. The details are not important for now. What is important is how interesting the S-shaped function looks when compared to the regular shaped utility function. There is something about the S-shape that is much more intriguing.

Kahneman & Tversky (1979) drew an S-shaped utility function inflecting about a reference point. This S-shaped utility function was something entirely new to this part of economics, though undulating utility functions had been used much earlier by Friedman & Savage (1948) and Markowitz (1952). We have drawn an S-shaped utility function in Figure 1.2.

Kahneman & Tversky's (1979) prospect theory could have been just one of many generalisations of expected utility published during the late 1970s and early 1980s (Schoemaker 1982; Machina 1987). Richard Thaler was persistent. Throughout the 1980s and 1990s, he gradually built behavioural economics by enticing new researchers into the field and by teaming up with established researchers who held similar interests in human behaviour (Thaler 2016; Barberis 2018). He used prospect theory and Kahneman and Tversky's heuristics and biases research as a core theoretical foundation to provide deeper explanations for puzzling pieces of human behaviour. For example, when De Bondt & Thaler (1985) decided to see whether the stock market overreacts to new information—that is, whether prices tend to move too drastically in response to news—they found their benchmark against which to test their hypothesis in Kahneman and Tversky's study of violations of

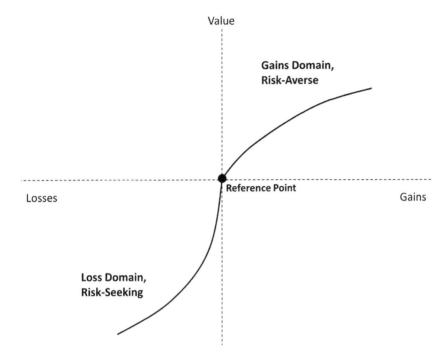

Value

Gains Domain,
Risk-Averse

Reference Point

Losses

Gains

Loss Domain,
Risk-Seeking

FIGURE 1.2 The famous (and much more exciting) S-shaped utility function

Bayes' rule and their rationale for doing so in Kahneman and Tversky's representativeness heuristic. By the turn of the century, behavioural economics was firmly established within economics. There was now a long list of results that could be used as building blocks for deeper narratives about human decision-making (Rabin 1998; Dellavigna 2009).

Applications to counter-terrorism

Economics is not just about money and markets. It is about decisions. And in this regard, economics is no longer a bastion of rationality, holding out against the odds. Rather, it has built and continues to build a set of explanations for human behaviour that draws on a blending of economics and psychology, behavioural economics. The orthodox models, however, continue to hold substantial value as benchmarks and prescriptions for optimal behaviour. There is also a good proportion of people whose behaviour is not far from those prescriptions. When the economics of crime was developed by Becker (1968), Stigler (1970) and Ehrlich (1973), they used expected utility theory and rational choice as their framework. This tradition was followed in criminology and in the economic analysis of terrorism. Modern work can draw on these traditional models and so many more tools that have been developed since. In this book, we present explanations for patterns of terrorist behaviour that we call 'pattern predictions'. We also present pattern predictions for law enforcement and counter-terrorism agencies. This is what we can say about behaviour in the counter-terrorism context:

1. *Terrorists don't fall for it lock, stock and barrel.* At times during the 1960s and 1970s in America, a plane was hijacked every six days (Hughes 2019). After metal detectors, air marshals and harsher prison sentences were put in place, the number of hijackings plummeted. But not because hijackers were caught but because they decided not to *try!* We can explain this pattern of behaviour, which is quite common among terrorists, including in their choices involving embassy attacks, using the basic economics of consumer theory.

2. *Terrorists are terrorists, bombers bomb.* Terrorists form a terrorist identity. This has been explored by terrorism researchers who try to explain why people become terrorists. We can explain why they don't want to stop, either terrorism or a particular type of attack methodology. Loss aversion combined with potential identity loss makes terrorists less responsive to changes in incentives. Even when the costs go way up, they will persist.

3. *Copycat terrorists take more risk chasing successful idols (or rivals).* We can use prospect theory and make the reference point the trigger for a copycat or emulation process. Here, the predecessor or rival's outcomes determine the reference point. Depending on how 'easy' it will be given the available attack methods to surpass the reference point, the terrorist finds himself either in the domain of gains or the domain of losses. If the idol or rival has set a 'difficult' benchmark, the terrorist is in the domain of losses and is compelled to take more risk.

4. *Terrorists are good, but potentially naïve, portfolio managers.* Terrorist groups and even some individuals combine attack methods in 'portfolios'. By doing so, even naïvely, they reap benefits in terms of increased expected payoffs and lower risks. Terrorist groups are already pushing beyond the boundaries of the risk-reward trade-offs that are apparent to law enforcement agencies who consider only one attack method at a time rather than combinations.

5. *Terrorist groups survive on relative shares, not absolutes.* Whatever 'payoffs' we consider, whether it's inflicted fatalities, media attention, grassroots support or political influence, a terrorist group's survival is dependent on how well it vies for absolute dominance. Does a plant have to grow to its maximum height to survive? No, it only needs to shade out its nearest competitors. The decision processes that terrorist groups apply to shade out their competition lead to patterns of behaviour that emerge from evolutionary game theory.

6. *Some terrorist groups are overconfident and this leads them to do too much terrorism.* Overconfidence has been found everywhere that researchers have looked. Overconfidence leads to more risk-taking. For terrorists, it leads to patterns of behaviour characterised by too much terrorism. Too much terrorism is terrorist activity, beyond some point, that actually reduces the terrorist's payoffs.

    (a) *Women terrorists are less overconfident than men are and this can make them deadlier.* In all contexts, even highly competitive ones, women are less overconfident than men. Whereas overconfidence leads men into too much risky activity, less overconfidence leads women to be more circumspect. Women terrorists engage in terrorism less frequently but this might help them to generate higher average fatalities per attack than men.

7. *Carlos the Jackal's preferences can be measured.* Decision theory, including economics and behavioural economics, are frameworks that can be used by law enforcement. Terrorists' preferences for different attack methods can be measured using either expected utility theory or prospect theory. By inputting different starting conditions, we can get a good idea about where different attack methods (and combinations) sit relative to each other in terms of terrorist preferences. This helps turn a chaotic decision context into a more structured decision context.

8. *Law enforcement agencies' reference points shape terrorism watch lists and suspect prioritisation.* Terrorists are not the only ones with reference points. Law enforcement agents and counter-terrorism agents also have reference points. In fact, they might have more than one reference point influencing their decisions at the same time. The influence of 'dual' reference points produces systematic errors in terrorism watch lists and suspect prioritisation. This pattern of behaviour can be overcome only by carefully unravelling its nature and causes.

9. *Heuristics and biases undermine the discovery and application of ideas.* At the elite level, in business and within the intelligence and law enforcement communities, people are tasked with keeping an eye on the flow of 'academic research'.[7] Or with finding solutions that might be in that research. This task is impacted by heuristics and biases, leading to patterns of search that might cause the best solution to be missed. Fortunately, these negative patterns can be avoided by using our knowledge of behavioural economics and decision theory to formulate better searches and better research engagement.

10. *Poor decisions from one law enforcement team or agency can precipitate an information cascade.* Information theory and economics have a close relationship. A cascade can start as soon as person number three enters in a decision series. If one investigator prioritises a suspect incorrectly based on some particular characteristic, this error can cascade through the team, the agency and across other agencies.

11. *Counter-terrorism decision-making is impacted by decision-making biases every second of every day.* Terrorism studies and economic analysis of terrorism might focus a little too much on rare events, such as hostage situations or hijackings, where reputations are publicly made and lost. For example, for tactical and negotiation teams, a terrorist hostage taking or barricade situation is not 'everyday'. Rather, it is a highly visible event, which handled well creates heroes and handled badly can end law enforcement careers (Vecchi 2002, p.2). This overlooks the everyday of policing and counter-terrorism. The daily grind, though usually mundane, is shaped continuously by decision-processing factors, including probability judgements. This extends to more innovative practices such as predictive policing.

On April 27, 1924, shortly after 2 o'clock in the afternoon, Alexander Alekhine walked into the Japanese room at the Hotel Almanac in New York City and proceeded to play 26 simultaneous games of chess across 12 hours without ever seeing a chessboard. The players were in rows behind him. He sat, smoking cigarettes, at the far end of the room looking out onto 71st Street (American Chess Bulletin 1924). On the basis of the announcements by the 'readers' about the other players' moves, Alekhine visualised the games and stated his own moves. While playing, Alekhine was creating images in his mind's eye based on the information he was receiving. These patterns and images are formed into chunks of information that elicit possible moves and sequences of moves (Campitelli & Gobet 2005, pp.27–28). Pattern recognition is something that all decision-makers use, not just chess players (Gobet & Simon 1996a, 1996b, 1998; Chabris & Hearst 2003; also see Kahneman & Klein 2009 and Dror & Cole 2010). Even though he could not see the boards or the pieces, Alekhine had more information in the Japanese room at the Hotel Almanac almost a century ago than any counter-terrorism unit has on a given day. In the terrorism context, there is no set playing surface and no set of rules and no finite set of moves.

Four dot points to end the chapter

- Together, over the past 30 years or more, economists and psychologists have documented quirky human decision-making patterns that appear systematically in various settings.
- Being patterns of human behaviour, these discoveries have implications for terrorism and law enforcement.
- Because formal mathematical modelling came to dominate economics, the sounder method of relying on verbal arguments, supported by theory, data and logic to explain patterns of behaviour has been overshadowed.
- Using orthodox and behavioural economics as complements allows us to develop deeper narratives about human behaviour, touching on humans' risk preferences, their tendency to follow others, copycat behaviour, their fears and hopes, their overconfidence and their ability to implement strategies consistent with their survival. All this and much more.

Notes

1 Coll (2018, p.24).
2 McCloskey (1985) and Summers (1991).
3 Probably the best known of the game theorists is John Nash, whose biography was dramatised in the film *A Beautiful Mind*. In game theory circles and in economics, Nash (1950a, 1950b, 1951, 1953) is known for his work on non-cooperative games and his Nash equilibrium concept.
4 Selten's work is too voluminous to list here. For example, see his early papers (in German), 'Bewertung strategischer Spiele' (1960) and 'Ein Oligopolexperiment' (1959) (with Heinz Sauermann).

5 A subject to which Reinhard Selten also made significant contributions (e.g. Selten 1998).
6 Also see Kahneman, Slovic and Tversky (1982).
7 We use 'academic research' as a catch-all for formal research. This could come from think tanks or from research divisions within the organisation itself.

References

American Chess Bulletin. 1924. Alekhine's New Blindfold Record. May–June. www. chesshistory.com/winter/extra/alekhineblindfold.html

Barberis, N. 2018. Richard Thaler and the Rise of Behavioural Economics. *Scandinavian Journal of Economics*, 120, 661–684.

Becker, G. 1968. Crime and Punishment: An Economic Approach. *Journal of Political Economy*, 76, 169–217.

Campitelli, G. & Gobet, F. 2005. The Mind's Eye in Blindfold Chess. *European Journal of Cognitive Psychology*, 17, 23–45.

Chabris, C.F. & Hearst, E.S. 2003. Visualisation, Pattern Recognition and Forward Search: Effects of Playing Speed and Sight of the Position on Grandmaster Chess Errors. *Cognitive Science*, 27, 637–648.

Coll, S. 2018. Directorate S: The C.I.A. and America's Secret Wars in Afghanistan and Pakistan 2001–2016. London: Allen Lane.

Dellavigna, S. 2009. Psychology and Economics: Evidence from the Field. *Journal of Economic Literature*, 47, 315–372.

De Bondt, W.F.M. & Thaler, R. 1985. Does the Stock Market Overreact? *Journal of Finance*, 40, 793–805.

De Groot, A. 1965. *Thought and Choice in Chess*. The Hague, the Netherlands: Mouton.

Dror, I.E. & Cole, S.A. 2010. The Vision in Blind Justice: Expert Perception, Judgement and Visual Cognition in Forensic Pattern Recognition. *Psychonomic Bulletin and Review*, 17, 161–167.

Ehrlich, I. 1973. Participation in Illegitimate Activities: A Theoretical and Empirical Investigation. *Journal of Political Economy*, 81, 521–565.

Friedman, M. & Savage, L.J. 1948. The Utility Analysis of Choices Involving Risk. *Journal of Political Economy*, 56, 279–304.

Gobet, F. & Simon, H.A. 1996a. The Roles of Recognition Processes and Look-Ahead Search in Time-Constrained Expert Problem Solving: Evidence from Grand-Master-Level Chess. *Psychological Science*, 7, 52–55.

Gobet, F. & Simon, H.A. 1996b. Templates in Chess Memory: A Mechanism for Recalling Several Boards. *Cognitive Psychology*, 31, 1–40.

Gobet, F. & Simon, H.A. 1998. Pattern Recognition Makes Search Possible. *Psychological Research*, 61, 204–208.

Hughes, R. 2019. TWA85: The World's Longest and Most Spectacular Hijacking. BBC News, October 26. www.bbc.com/news/world-us-canada-48069272

Kahneman, D. & Tversky, A. 1979. Prospect Theory: An Analysis of Decision under Risk. *Econometrica*, 47, 263–291.

Kahneman, D. & Klein, G. 2009. Conditions for Intuitive Expertise. *American Psychologist*, 64, 515–526.

Kahneman, D., Slovic, P. & Tversky, A. 1982. *Judgement under Uncertainty: Heuristics and Biases*. Cambridge, MA: Cambridge University Press.

Machina, M.J. 1987. Choice under Uncertainty: Problems Solved and Unsolved. *Journal of Economic Perspectives*, 1, 121–154.

Markowitz, H. 1952. The Utility of Wealth. *Journal of Political Economy*, 60, 151–58. McCloskey, D. 1985. *The Rhetoric of Economics*. University of Wisconsin Press, Madison, WI.

Nash, J. 1950a. The Bargaining Problem. *Econometrica*, 18, 155–162.

Nash, J. 1950b. Equilibrium Points in N-Person Games. *Proceedings of the National Academy of Sciences of the United States*, 36, 48–49.

Nash, J. 1951. Non-Cooperative Games. *Annals of Mathematics*, 54, 286–295.

Nash, J. 1953. Two Person Cooperative Games. *Econometrica*, 21, 128–140.

Rabin, M. 1998. Psychology and Economics. *Journal of Economic Literature*, 36, 11–46.

Robbins, L. 1932. *Essay on the Nature and Significance of Economic Science*. London: Macmillan.

Sauermann, H. & Selten, R. 1959. Ein Oligopolexperiment. *Zeitschrift für die gesamte Staatswissenschaft / Journal of Institutional and Theoretical Economics*, 115, 427–471.

Schoemaker, P.J.H. 1982. The Expected Utility Model: Its Variants, Purposes, Evidence and Limitations. *Journal of Economic Literature*, 20, 529–563.

Selten, R. 1960. Bewertung strategischer Spiele. *Zeitschrift für die gesamte Staatswissenschaft / Journal of Institutional and Theoretical Economics*, 116, 221–282.

Selten, R. 1998. Features of Experimentally Observed Bounded Rationality. *European Economic Review*, 42, 413–436.

Simon, H.A. 1947. *Administrative Behaviour: A Study of Decision-Making Processes in Administrative Organisation*. New York: Macmillan.

Stigler, G. 1970. The Optimum Enforcement of Laws. *Journal of Political Economy*, 78, 526–536.

Summers, L.H. 1991. The Scientific Illusion in Empirical Macroeconomics. *Scandinavian Journal of Economics*, 93, 129–148.

Thaler, R.H. 2016. *Misbehaving: The Making of Behavioural Economics*. New York: W.W. Norton.

Tversky, A. & Kahneman, D. 1974. Judgement under Uncertainty: Heuristics and Biases. *Science*, 185, 1124–1131.

Vecchi, G.M. 2002. Hostage/Barricade Management: A Hidden Conflict within Law Enforcement. *FBI Law Enforcement Bulletin*, 71, 1–13.

Von Neumann, J. & Morgenstern, O. 1944. *Theory of Games and Economic Behaviour*. Princeton, NJ: Princeton University Press.

Von Neumann, J. & Morgenstern, O. 1947. *Theory of Games and Economic Behaviour*, 2nd ed. Princeton, NJ: Princeton University Press.

2
PATTERNS OF REASON AND UNREASONABLENESS

> The description of the pattern that the theory provides is commonly regarded merely as a tool that will enable us to predict the particular manifestations of the pattern that will appear in specific circumstances [point predictions]. But the prediction that in certain general conditions a pattern of a certain kind will appear is also a significant (and falsifiable) prediction. If I tell somebody that if he goes to my study he will find there a rug with a pattern made up of diamonds and meanders, he will have no difficulty in deciding whether that prediction was verified or falsified by the result, even though I have said nothing about the arrangement, size, colour, etc., of the elements from which the pattern of the rug is formed [point predictions].[1]

What is the difference between a point prediction and a pattern prediction when it comes to terrorism and terrorist behaviour? If we know the history of terrorist activity, including the number and type of attacks in each previous year, and if we have data about other factors that are supposed to be relevant, how many terrorist attacks will there be next year? An answer to this question would be a 'point estimate' or 'point prediction'. That is, some particular number of attacks such as 42 or 106. Although this has become the standard in economic forecasting, we can make another, entirely different, type of prediction. If a terrorist group commits a very successful attack that attracts a lot of media attention, what type of attack method will a rival group choose? An answer to this question would be a 'pattern prediction'. Drawing on behavioural economics, psychology and decision theory, our answer is that if an attack by a rival creates a very high reference point relative to the outcomes that can normally be expected, a group will be prompted to choose an attack type with higher but more variable payoffs—a higher impact, higher risk attack method.

Our pattern predictions are drawn from well-established facts about human behaviour. Together, a set of pattern predictions does not tell us what every terrorist will do in every situation. A set of pattern predictions provides us with a framework that can be used to *think about* what a terrorist will do in certain situations. Much of counter-terrorism involves thinking about terrorist behaviour and trying to anticipate it and understand it. Pattern predictions developed from decision theory and the empirical results that support it, provides us with a valuable framework to guide our thinking. Not every terrorist will follow every pattern. That is, in fact, the point. We are better off with a *set* of pattern predictions that can be used to augment our thinking than we are with a single point prediction that could, and probably will, mislead us. And if we are going to see patterns in human behaviour, we are best advised to make sure that they are 'really there'. It is one of the quirks of human decision-making that makes us see patterns in random data (Gilovich, Vallone & Tversky 1985). Patterns of terrorist choice and law enforcement decision-making are 'really there' only if we can explain them in terms of what we know about the decision-making process.

Example #1: the Unabomber

It was 1969. Theodore John Kaczynski unexpectedly resigned his assistant professorship of mathematics at the University of California and, after a short period living with his parents, moved to a cabin he had built outside the town of Lincoln in Montana. Only in his early thirties at the time, Kaczynski lived a simple, self-sufficient lifestyle in the wilderness. Upset by the destruction of the forests and increasingly angered by the disruption caused by industrial developments, starting in about 1975 he began sabotaging equipment at construction sites. Just a few years later, he commenced a campaign of bombings targeting universities and airlines. His chosen targets earned him the name Unabomber (for universities and airlines bomber). In 1978, Kaczynski delivered his first bomb to his first victim, a university professor of materials engineering at Northwestern University in Illinois.

Northwestern seems like an obscure target for a terrorist living in Lincoln Montana, almost 1,500 miles away. However, Kaczynski had briefly moved back in with his parents, who lived in Lombard, Illinois, about 30 miles from Northwestern's campus. Kaczynski did not mail the bomb directly to the intended target. Rather, he left the parcel containing the bomb in a parking lot at a different university, the University of Illinois, about 20 miles from his parents' house. The target's name was given as the return address on the parcel. When the parcel was found in the parking lot, it was 'returned' to the materials engineering professor at Northwestern University where it injured the security guard who attempted to open it. The following year, Kaczynski mailed a bomb that exploded in the cargo hold of a commercial airliner. This federal crime initiated the FBI's involvement in a case that would become one of the biggest and longest manhunts in American history.

While he was at large and active between 1978 and 1995, Kaczynski puzzled authorities by disappearing for extended periods of time. No one would hear anything from him and there would be no attacks. This pattern of engagement and disengagement continued for almost 20 years, until he was finally apprehended in April 1996.[2] This is interesting because it is a common pattern among terrorists and terrorist groups that survive for any length of time. A part of the explanation will be found in mundane aspects of the terrorists' operations, including resource constraints. Another part might be found in the decision-making processes that shape the choices that terrorists make. Is there some aspect of human behaviour that might lead to pauses in violent behaviour after a run of success? The obvious answer is something that some economists (especially financial economists) don't actually believe in but which exists in economic models nonetheless. This thing is 'satiation'.

Satiation is not a complicated thing. It simply means that you are 'full', for the time being. Economists are wary of satiation for a few reasons. First, when they developed some of their theories during the Great Depression, satiation seemed impossible. Second, if it is 'utility' that a person seeks and that utility is linked to some set of payoffs, why wouldn't the person simply continue to always want more? If a terrorist's utility is linked to inflicted fatalities, supporters, recruits, media attention or some other relevant payoff, why wouldn't the terrorist always want more? Interestingly, this is one of those cases, common in science, where it might be best to trust the theory and the patterns of behaviour that it predicts rather than second-guess it. Psychologists have found very solid psychological and physiological foundations for satiation and the concept can be used to explain animal behaviour. Animals behave in bouts. Feeding bouts end in satiation. Satiation is the process that brings feeding bouts to an end (Collier & Johnson 2004).

Terrorism is not the only thing that terrorists do all day. Theodore Kaczynski did not constantly engage in terrorism. There must be time left over for other things. Satiation is a consequence of obtaining payoffs but it is also a tool for economising resources (Collier & Johnson 2004). Satiation, when understood in this way, is something that should be present in economic theories of rational behaviour. Theodore Kaczynski's actions, like all terrorist activity, were undertaken under conditions of risk. He expected some outcomes (injuries, fatalities, attention) and he sensed that the actual outcomes might differ from what he expected. In models of investor decision-making, economists (reluctantly) use a function that relates satisfaction to expected outcomes and risk. It is called the quadratic utility function:

$$U(W) = W - bW^2$$

As the accumulated payoffs, W, increase, there comes a point where the person no longer prefers more to less. The quadratic utility function is graphed in Figure 2.1. See how it slopes upwards as payoffs contribute to more utility but then it reaches a peak after which more payoffs actually decrease utility. Economists usually get around the 'problem' of satiation when using quadratic utility to represent choice. They do so by ruling parts of the function out of bounds. But if satiation is a logical and necessary part of human and animal behaviour, this seems unwise. If we used

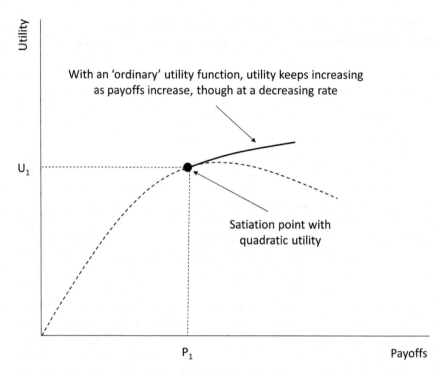

FIGURE 2.1 Quadratic expected utility function and satiation.

this popular representation of utility without any restrictions, we would be forced to conclude that once payoffs accumulate, there will be a point of satiation and the decision-maker will stop accumulating for the time being. Pauses in violent activity following periods of especially intense and successful action is a pattern of behaviour that is predicted from the narratives running beneath one of the most basic orthodox models of choice under conditions of risk. Once a decision-maker is temporarily satiated, he stops. Kaczynski's pauses in violent behaviour after periods of success is an orthodox economics pattern.

Example #2: the Red Army Faction

Around midnight on April 2, 1968, a world away from the Montana wilderness where Kaczynski would soon settle, firebombs exploded at two department stores in the German city of Frankfurt. Although no one was hurt, the fires caused DM1,900,000 damage (about $US500,000 in 1968 and more than $US3.7 million in 2020 dollars) (Peters 2007, p.40). This was the first act of terrorism attributed to the RAF. Over the next two decades, the group would be responsible for 34 fatalities inflicted in a series of assassinations, bombings and kidnappings. The group 'peaked' during the German Autumn of 1977, which began with the assassination of Siegfried Buback, the attorney general of West Germany, by four members of the RAF on April 7, 1977. This was followed by the kidnapping and murder of the chief of Dresdner Bank, Jürgen Ponto, on July 30, the kidnapping and subsequent murder of the president of the German employer's association in Cologne, Hanns Martin Schleyer, on September 5, and culminated with the ultimately unsuccessful Landshut hijacking on October 13. The events have been popularised in movies and books. Even today, one can see a range of books about the RAF in major German bookstores.

The ideology of the RAF was Marxist-Leninist. This ideology along with the group's primary purpose is probably best encapsulated in Ulrike Meinhof's *The Urban Guerrilla Concept*. In general, the group would target big business and government. It also viewed itself as anti-imperialist. Like other groups at other times, the RAF did not have the terrorism context to itself. The group had at least two major rivals, the most prominent being the 2nd of June Movement. Although the two groups shared a similar outlook, the 2nd of June Movement was primarily driven by an anarchist (vis-à-vis Marxist) ideology. Throughout the 1970s, both groups were well known in West Germany. These two groups, the RAF and the 2nd of June Movement, 'referenced' each other's actions as they attempted to gather more recognition for their respective campaigns. The 2nd of June Movement's successful kidnapping of Berlin mayoral candidate Peter Lorenz on February 27, 1975 served as a reference point for the kidnappings the RAF perpetrated during the German Autumn, two years later.

When a terrorist group observes the outcomes of an attack or action by another terrorist group, its thoughts may turn towards the possibility of achieving even more success. This might mean inflicting even more fatalities or, in the case of the West German groups that we have been discussing, achieving more press attention or extracting more concessions. The amount of attention or the scale and nature of the concessions received by the rival group becomes the reference point against which the terrorist group assesses its alternatives. In such a case, we can use the S-shaped utility function from prospect theory to generate a pattern prediction. If the reference point for the RAF was determined by the outcomes achieved by the 2nd of June Movement, this should affect the type of action that the RAF will choose. Let us say, hypothetically but not unrealistically, that the RAF was planning a bombing attack that could be expected to produce a few pages of media coverage for a few days. Then, the 2nd of June Movement's kidnapping of Peter Lorenz begins to dominate the newspapers (Pohl 2017). Now, the RAF finds itself in the domain of losses. This is depicted in Figure 2.2.

If a terrorist group is in the domain of losses, they will be risk seeking. If a terrorist group is in the domain of gains, they will be risk averse. Whether the terrorist group finds itself in the domain of gains or losses depends on how achievable the reference point is given its available (or planned) attack methods or targets. If this reference point is high but achievable relative to what may normally be expected from the available actions, the terrorist group will be compelled to take more risk. In this example, the RAF is planning a bombing but a bombing cannot reach the reference point set by the outcomes achieved by the 2nd of June Movement's

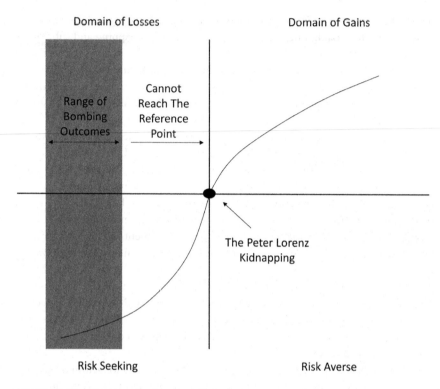

FIGURE 2.2 The RAF in the domain of losses.

kidnapping of Peter Lorenz. As such, the RAF might be forced to consider a higher risk approach such as copying the 2nd of June Movement's methods and switching from bombing to kidnapping or hostage taking. In fact, this is what members of the RAF later confirmed that they did.[3] We may expect successful terrorist actions to be followed by a choice of riskier attack methods by rival groups. This is a pattern of behaviour that emerges from applying behavioural economics to the analysis of terrorist behaviour. It is a logical inference from prospect theory once we make the outcomes achieved by predecessor or rival groups the reference point against which potential outcomes are assessed. It is a behavioural economics pattern.

Example #3: take me to the April sun in Cuba

It has been claimed that economics cannot provide the basis for understanding terrorism because the political, ideological and religious objectives that terrorist groups hold are so completely and obviously *irrational* that economic models based on rational choice theory cannot possibly apply. Victoroff (2005, p.15) says:

> Political scientist Martha Crenshaw (2000) has cautioned that the ostensible goal of terrorists often appears so unlikely to be achieved by the chosen

action that it is difficult to support an overarching rationalist theory of terrorism. Furthermore, the outrageous inhumanity of attacks on innocent civilians challenges the commonplace understanding of 'rational' behaviour. Given questions about incoherent motivations, ghastly means, and political inefficacy of terrorism, some scholars have proposed that the typical terrorist is not simply a 'rational actor' in the strict Weberian sense.

Brannan, Eslerm & Anders Strindberg 2001

If we use economic theory to guide our pattern predictions, won't we just end up with a series of unrealistic, perfectly rational, behavioural patterns? No, because behavioural economics is now such an established part of economics and its narratives are so much deeper than orthodox models that we shall have plenty of scope to develop pattern predictions that do not rely upon strict rationality. That being said, we cannot completely ignore orthodox economic theory. Even though its decision-makers are rational, which usually means 'purposeful' rather than 'perfect' and not necessarily 'cool and calculating', these models are more flexible than they appear. The tendencies of human behaviour are often in the direction predicted by orthodox economic theory even if the abstract depiction of the choice process leaves us doubting whether we have really described the decision-making process in any meaningful way. In fact, in laboratory experiments as well as in the field, expected utility theory and other decision rules based on maximisation hold up remarkably well and explain a good proportion of the choices that are observed.

On the behavioural economics side of the debate, Kahneman and Tversky (1979) have taken a fairly strong position against expected utility theory as a descriptive model. The person primarily responsible for the development of behavioural economics as a field of study, Richard Thaler, recognises the value of expected utility theory as a prescriptive model (he says he uses it himself when making decisions) but he writes in a mildly derisive tone about the theory's ability to explain human behaviour. He argues, in essence, that it only explains the behaviour of a separate species, *Homo Economicus* or *Econs* (Thaler 2016).[4] In contrast, the economist who shared the Nobel Prize with Kahneman in 2002, Vernon Smith, argues that expected utility performs well in the laboratory and explains quite a lot of human behaviour (Smith 1994, p.118):

> That economic agents can achieve efficient outcomes that are not part of their intention was the key principle articulated by Adam Smith, but few outside of the Austrian and Chicago traditions believed it, circa 1956. Certainly, I was not primed to believe it, having been raised by a socialist mother, and further handicapped (in this regard) by a Harvard education, but my experimental subjects revealed to me the error in my thinking. In many experimental markets, poorly informed, error-prone, and uncomprehending human agents interact through the trading rules to produce social algorithms which demonstrably approximate the wealth maximising outcomes traditionally thought to require complete information and a cognitively rational actor.

In fact, a day in an experimental economics lab is highly recommended to anyone who doubts that 'rational choice' can explain anything of human behaviour. It actually works reasonably well. For example, experimental asset markets can be set up where participants, usually students without any special knowledge about finance, can 'trade' stocks and bonds in a simulated market. Usually, the profits earned in the experiment are translated into some real money amount in order to provide an incentive to concentrate and try hard to make good decisions. Unlike a real-world stock market, the rational expectations equilibrium price (or efficient markets price) of the stocks and bonds is known to the experimenter. When the markets start, there is a period of volatility as the traders find their feet. Sure enough, though, the prices converge relatively quickly to the rational expectations price and stay there. It is like magic to watch the gravitational pull of rational expectations equilibrium. This is a useful reminder that if orthodox economics were so egregious, economists would have completely abandoned it either at the outset or soon after. They are not clinging stubbornly or ideologically to something that doesn't work at all, though their stubbornness may have stopped them seeking viable extensions and generalisations with more enthusiasm.

When it comes to models of rational choice of terrorist behaviour, some defence economists use consumer choice theory.[5] This theory was prominent in the 1930s and 1940s. When it is applied to terrorism, it depicts the terrorist group as a consumer of some abstract good such as political influence, which is 'purchased' by either terrorist activity or legitimate activity. The terrorist group allocates resources between these two activities in such a way as to maximise its utility (i.e. maximise its political influence) subject to the constraints that it faces. The group chooses to engage in some combination of legitimate activity and terrorism because it is optimal to do so given the relative costs and benefits. It is very unrealistic but the behavioural tendencies are plausible. If the costs of engaging in terrorism increase, we should expect less terrorist activity. Slightly deeper, the model implies that a terrorist group might be encouraged to switch from terrorism to legitimate political activity either by increasing the costs of terrorism through deterrence or by increasing the benefits of legitimate political engagement. As such, the analysis provided some hope that negotiating with terrorist groups and opening communication channels might be a potentially successful way of reducing terrorism.[6]

In the 1960s and 1970s, airplane hijackings were very common in the United States. In fact, there were 124 of them between 1968 and 1972. Usually, the hijackers demanded a ransom or passage to a particular location (often to Cuba). Landes (1978) used a basic theoretical model to analyse patterns of hijacking behaviour. The pattern he was most interested in explaining was the surge in incidences followed by an almost complete collapse in the number of hijackings. Once hijacking became such a prominent problem, various measures were taken to curtail it. Air marshals were introduced on airplanes along with metal detectors and better security checks at airports. The prison penalties for hijacking were greatly increased and different aircraft designs made it impossible to parachute out of the plane without serious injury or death. It seems obvious why hijackings declined after 1973. There were only 11 hijackings between 1973 and 1977. What could economic theory possibly add to an already obvious explanation?

Security measures and so forth would explain why more hijackers were apprehended or why more hijackers were unsuccessful. But this is not exactly what happened following the initiatives. What happened was that there were markedly fewer *attempts* at hijacking. Landes' (1978) economics explains why there were fewer attempts, not just fewer successful attempts. Hijackers were not led zombie-like into the new security apparatus. Nor did they lemming-like, one after the other, try to parachute out of planes with their ransom money only to meet a grisly end as a result of the redesigned aircraft. Rather, many of them figured out that the situation had changed dramatically to their disadvantage and decided that hijacking was no longer as feasible as it had been. The security innovations were not secret and potential offenders were alert to the new information. This is a subtle but important insight for which economic analysis can claim credit. It is based on the principle that antisocial behaviour can be reduced by disincentives such as harsher penalties and increased likelihood of apprehension and that pro-social behaviour can be encouraged by providing positive incentives. In general, people respond to incentives. This is a fundamental principle of orthodox economics and it works well as a general first-order predictor for behavioural patterns.

Decision theory and the 'criminological turn'

Terrorism studies might now be more receptive to these types of pattern predictions because there has been a 'criminological turn'.[7] One reason for this is the recognition that there are strong similarities between violent crime, especially crimes such as school shootings, and terrorism.[8] Another reason could be the more clearly defined theoretical roots of criminology, especially the logical structure provided by Becker's (1968) rational choice approach (Akers 1990; Nagin & Paternoster 1993). Also helping to move terrorism studies in this direction is weariness and general dissatisfaction with certain aspects of the terrorism studies literature, especially the endless search for a definition of terrorism.[9] The policy focus of defence economics also seems to be so far removed from the day-to-day activities of counter-terrorism that it gives the impression of having come from an earlier time, the time of spies meeting under the Weltzeituhr in Berlin, Harry Palmer and the rest. Indeed, the analytical frameworks that most economists have applied to the analysis of terrorism have Cold War written all over them and the economic analysis of terrorism is not exempt from the changes that are gradually reshaping terrorism studies.

In a dynamic and evolving terrorism context, new ideas are just as important as new information. The CIA's counter-terrorism centre, to name just one example, is based on the recognition that an understanding of the cutting edge in the 'world of ideas' is operationally indispensable. In most elite organisations and in nearly every field, there are people tasked with engaging with the research conversation, distilling it, synthesising it and identifying ways to use it to solve particular problems. Decision theories can supercharge the job of synthesising much of the research, encompassing much of what we know about decision processes in neat packages. In its four main features, for example, prospect theory encompasses more than a decade of prior investigation. In the next chapter, the consumer choice model that we present synthesises in just a few diagrams nearly 50 years of economic thought. These diagrams and the economic reasoning that they encapsulate tell us what patterns of behaviour to expect when terrorists' resource allocations shift and what patterns of behaviour to expect when the resource requirements of different attack methods change.

Four dot points to end the chapter

- If we were to use an econometric model to forecast the number of terrorist attacks to be expected next year, we would be making a point prediction.
- If we use theory, logic and argument to say that under certain conditions such and such behaviour is expected, we would be making a pattern prediction.
- Analytical tools that draw on economics and psychology can explain such observed behaviours as pauses in violence after success, risk taking in the presence of a rival's success and substitution away from certain activities if the incentives change.
- The main idea is 'ideas'. Ideas, conveyed as simply as possible but without understating their depth, placed in the right hands. Thinking about terrorist behaviour is an important part of counter-terrorism. Ideas from economics and psychology provide us with more things to think about.

Notes

1 Hayek (1967, pp.24–25). Friedrich von Hayek was awarded the Nobel prize for economics in 1974.
2 Kaczynski did not perpetrate an attack for three years from 1982 to 1985 and for six years between 1987 and 1993.
3 Discussed in more detail in Chapter 5.
4 Despite outside appearances, the meaning of 'economic man' has never been completely settled in economic theory. See Caldwell (1982, p.162).
5 This is discussed in more detail in Chapter 3.
6 It depends, of course, on the nature of the terrorist groups. We discuss this in more detail in Chapter 4.
7 Individual papers can be found that date back some way, such as LaFree and Dugan (2004) and Rausch and LaFree (2007) but the more visible shifts are evidenced by the growing amount of terrorism research published in criminology journals and the growing amount of criminology-type papers published in terrorism studies journals. Prominent terrorism studies journals such as *Terrorism and Political Violence* (see Freilich & LaFree 2015) have published special issues on the topic of criminology and terrorism while prominent criminology journals such as the *Journal of Criminological Research, Policy and Practice* (see Braddock 2017) have published special issues on terrorism.
8 For example, Phillips and Pohl (2014) and Azam and Ferrero (2017) draw strong parallels between school shooters and terrorists in developing an economic analysis of terrorism.

This parallel has been drawn by several criminologists and terrorism researchers including Lankford (2013), Böckler et al. (2018) and Liem et al. (2018).

9 There is a large literature devoted solely to the problem of defining terrorism. Examples that are characteristic of contributions to this literature are Weinberg et al. (2004), Herschinger (2013) and Ramsay (2015). Schmid and Jongman (1988) 'synthesised' 109 definitions of terrorism!

References

Akers, R.L. 1990. Rational Choice, Deterrence and Social Learning Theory in Criminology: The Path Not Taken. *Journal of Criminal Law and Criminology*, 81, 653–676.

Azam, Jean-Paul & Ferrero, M. 2017. Jihad against Palestinians? The Herostratos Syndrome and the Paradox of Targeting European Jews. *Defence and Peace Economics*, , 30, 687–705.

Becker, G. 1968. Crime and Punishment: An Economic Approach. *Journal of Political Economy*, 76, 169–217.

Böckler, N., Leuschner, V., Roth, V., Zick, A. & Scheithauer, H. 2018. Blurred Boundaries of Lone-Actor Targeted Violence: Similarities in the Genesis and Performance of Terrorist Attacks and School Shootings. *Violence and Gender*, 5, 70–80.

Braddock, K. 2017. Introduction to the Special Issue of the Journal of Criminological Research, Policy, and Practice: Terrorism and Political Violence. *Journal of Criminological Research, Policy and Practice*, 3, 153–157.

Brannan, D.W., Eslerm, P.F. & Anders Strindberg, N.T. 2001. Talking to 'Terrorists': Towards an Independent Analytic Framework for the Study of Violent Substate Activism. *Studies in Conflict and Terrorism*, 24, 3–24.

Caldwell, B.J. 1982. *Beyond Positivism: Economic Methodology in the Twentieth Century*. London: Routledge.

Collier, G. & Johnson, D.F. 2004. The Paradox of Satiation. *Physiology and Behaviour*, 82, 149–153.

Crenshaw, M. 2000. The Psychology of Terrorism: An Agenda for the 21st Century. *Political Psychology*, 21, 405–20.

Freilich, J.D. & LaFree, G. 2015. Criminology Theory and Terrorism: Introduction to the Special Issue, *Terrorism and Political Violence*, 27, 1–8, DOI: 10.1080/09546553.2014.959405

Gilovich, T., Vallone, R. & Tversky, A. 1985. The Hot Hand in Basketball: On the Misperception of Random Sequences. *Cognitive Psychology*, 17, 295–314.

Hayek, F.A. 1967. *Studies in Philosophy, Politics and Economics*. London: Routledge.

Herschinger, E. 2013. A Battlefield of Meanings: The Struggle for Identity in the UN Debates on a Definition of International Terrorism. *Terrorism and Political Violence*, 25, 183–201.

Kahneman, D. & Tversky, A. 1979. Prospect Theory: An Analysis of Decision under Risk. *Econometrica*, 47, 263–291.

LaFree, G. & Dugan, L. 2004. How Does Studying Terrorism Compare to Studying Crime? *Sociology of Crime, Law and Deviance*, 5, 53–74.

Landes, W.M. 1978. An Economic Study of U.S. Aircraft Hijacking: 1961 to 1976. *Journal of Law and Economics*, 21, 1–31.

Lankford, A. 2013. A Comparative Analysis of Suicide Terrorists and Rampage, Workplace and School Shooters in the United States from 1990 to 2010. *Homicide Studies*, 17, 255–274.

Liem, M.C.A., Buuren, G.M. & Schönberger, H.J.M. 2018. Cut from the Same Cloth? Lone Actor Terrorists versus Common Homicide Offenders. *ICCT Research Papers*, 9, 1–22.

Nagin, D.S. & Paternoster, R. 1993. Enduring Individual Differences and Rational Choice Theories of Crime. *Law & Society Review*, 27, 467–496.

Peters, B. 2007. *Tödlicher Irrtum: Die Geschichte der RAF*, 3rd ed. Frankfurt am Main: Fischer.

Phillips, P.J. & Pohl, G. 2014. Prospect Theory and Terrorist Choice. *Journal of Applied Economics*, 17, 139–160.

Pohl, G. 2017. Terrorist Choice and the Media. Unpublished PhD Thesis, University of Southern Queensland, Australia.

Ramsay, G. 2015. Why Terrorism Can, but Should Not Be Defined. *Critical Studies on Terrorism*, 8, 211–228.

Rausch, S. & LaFree, G. 2007. The Growing Importance of Criminology in the Study of Terrorism. *The Criminologist*, 32, 3–5.

Schmid, A.P. & Jongman, A.J. 1988. *Political Terrorism: A New Guide to Actors, Authors, Concepts, Data Bases, Theories, and Literature*. New Brunswick, NJ: Transaction Books.

Smith, V. 1994. Economics in the Laboratory. *Journal of Economic Perspectives*, 8, 113–131.

Thaler, R.H. 2016. *Misbehaving: The Making of Behavioural Economics*. New York: W.W. Norton.

Victoroff, J. 2005. The Mind of a Terrorist: A Review and Critique of Psychological Approaches. *Journal of Conflict Resolution*, 49, 3–42.

Weinberg, L., Pedahzur, A. & Hirsch-Hoefler, S. 2004. The Challenges of Conceptualizing Terrorism. *Terrorism and Political Violence*, 16, 777–794.

3

BOUNDED BY RATIONALITY

…Terrorism is often undertaken to achieve an indirect goal, which is usually political and can be at least partly associated with intrinsic motivation for the terrorist. It can be successful as a strategy, as can be observed in the case of the peace process in Northern Ireland, where power sharing has given seats in government to Sinn Féin that could not be won in regular elections. Terrorism and its close relative guerrilla warfare are often the weapons of minorities who feel excluded from regular power mechanisms in conventional politics. History is replete with terrorists who succeeded in their aims of driving off opponents and then became mainstream politicians, including Nelson Mandela (South Africa), Robert Mugabe (Rhodesia), Menachem Begin (Israel), and Martin McGuinness (Northern Ireland). Throughout history, terrorism has in fact often paid off for its participants.[1]

The Provisional Irish Republican Army (IRA) was the biggest of the Irish paramilitary groups. Between the late 1960s and late 1990s, the IRA was responsible for around 1,700 fatalities, about 500 of whom were civilians. The IRA itself suffered about 300 casualties and thousands of its members were imprisoned at one time or another. The IRA's political wing, Sinn Féin, did not participate in elections until 1982. Despite occasional good showings, support among voters gradually declined. Part of the reason for this was the IRA's Remembrance Day Bombing in 1987, which killed ten civilians, and the Warrington (England) bombing in 1993, which killed two schoolchildren. Following the ceasefire agreement in 1997, Sinn Féin has been able to accumulate enough support among voters to control one-third of the seats in the Northern Ireland Assembly. At least some part of the IRA began to substitute terrorism for legitimate political activity.[2] We can use a basic model of consumer choice from economics to explore the patterns of behaviour and basic decision processes involved in this type of substitution. This model is a good first step. It is rarely wrong but not very deep.

When terrorism is just one way to achieve an overarching goal and when a terrorist group is willing to trade off terrorism against other, legitimate options, there is an obvious model that economists can use. It is called the neoclassical model of consumer choice. This model was developed in the later 1930s.[3] It has become the standard way to talk about consumer choice. The logic and theory of the model is usually used in tandem with some simple diagrams to depict the main ideas. The model allows for a reasonable amount to be said about the effect of relative prices and incomes on demand for a particular good. The general idea is to explain how consumers will adjust to changes in their circumstances. If the price of a good increases, what will the consumer do? If the consumer's income changes, will he or she buy more of everything? How is income allocated among the available goods? Being a model of consumer choice, intended for use in situations where a person chooses how much of two or more goods to consume, the model does not take risk into account. Choices are made with as much certainty as a consumer would normally have at the local store.

Applied to an ordinary consumer choice situation, the theory explains how a person decides to allocate money to two[4] different but somewhat substitutable goods in an attempt to reach the 'best' outcome within the available budget. We can then introduce changes to prices and budgets to predict simple patterns of behaviour such as the prediction that the consumer will reduce demand for a good if its price rises relative to other goods or that the consumer will buy more of all goods if the budget is increased. Applied to terrorism, the same theoretical framework can be used to depict a terrorist decision-maker confronting an opportunity to allocate resources to two different things: (1) terrorism and (2) legitimate activity. In the same way that patterns of consumer behaviour can be predicted, patterns of terrorist behaviour can be predicted. For example, one prediction is that the terrorist group will reduce its engagement in terrorism if the relative 'price' of terrorism increases. This approach has been taken by Frey and Luechinger (2003) and Anderton and Carter (2005).

As a first step towards building the neoclassical consumer model, in Figure 3.1 we have drawn the indifference curve map that represents the terrorist group's preferences. The indifference curve was popularised by Hicks (1939). An indifference curve is just a series of points, joined together, representing various combinations of two different things that are equally satisfactory. A complete indifference curve 'map' represents the decision-maker's preferences for all different combinations of the available goods. 'Higher' indifference curves are better because they represent combinations of goods that are more satisfactory than other combinations. In Figure 3.1, the terrorist group is depicted as having a set of preferences for combinations of terrorism and legitimate activity. Higher indifference curves are associated with combinations of terrorism and legitimate activity that are more satisfactory.[5] The fundamental behavioural prediction is that the terrorist group will try to get onto the highest indifference curve. The slope of the indifference curves reflects what economists call 'the marginal rate of substitution' (MRS) between the two goods. The shape reflects the fact that, for most 'goods', the decision-maker's

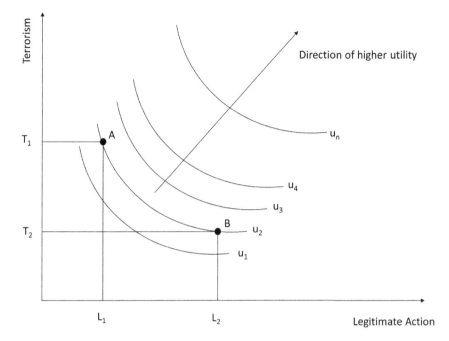

FIGURE 3.1 The terrorist group's indifference curve map.

MRS between the two goods is not constant. For a consumer whose choices involve either tea or coffee (two somewhat substitutable goods), the more coffee he gives up, the more tea he requires in compensation. Likewise, the terrorist group is willing to make trade-offs but towards the extremes of each indifference curve, the willingness to give up an additional unit of either legitimate activity or terrorist activity will necessitate compensation in the form of much more than proportional increase in the other type of activity.[6]

Limited resources: the budget constraint

The terrorist group, like the consumer trying to maximise consumption, faces a major hurdle. It does not have unlimited resources. As such, it will not be able to reach the highest indifference curve in some absolute sense. It will only be able to reach the highest indifference curve that is feasible given the amount of resources that the group has. This 'budget constraint' can be depicted as a frontier superimposed over the group's indifference map as shown in Figure 3.2. If the terrorist group allocates all of its resources to terrorism it could engage in T_A. If the group allocates all of its resources to legitimate activity it could engage in L_A. By allocating resources to both, the group may engage in some combination of terrorism and legitimate activity that lies somewhere along or within the budget constraint but not beyond it.

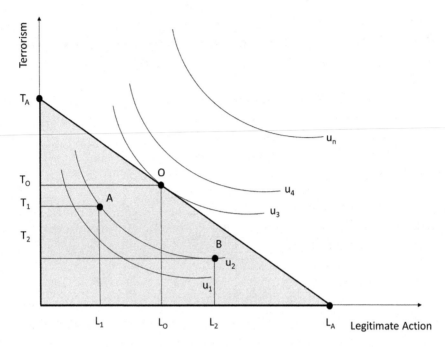

FIGURE 3.2 The terrorist group's budget constraint.

The budget constraint is used to represent the core constraint that terrorist groups face in attempting to maximise their political influence. It is because of limited resources that everyone, including terrorist groups, must make choices. Means that are scarce must be allocated to the most pressing ends. The budget constraint might be imagined to expand and contract as the terrorist group confronts different circumstances. For example, it might acquire a state sponsor, which will push its budget constraint outwards and permit it to engage in more of both types of activity. Conversely, the terrorist group may suffer losses in a conflict with a government or rival group, which will pull its budget constraint inwards. Using this model, we can make hypothetical changes in the budget constraint as well as changes to the terrorist group's preferences that allow us to generate predictions about the patterns of behaviour that will follow certain events.

Together, the indifference map and the budget constraint generate a prediction about the choices that the terrorist group will make. Given the available resources, indifference curves such as u_4 and u_n are not attainable. The group does not have the resources to allocate to the amount of terrorism and legitimate activity required to reach those indifference curves. The group could choose a bundle on u_1 or u_2, such as A or B. Although this is feasible given the group's resources, the group is not optimising. What we should observe, in theory, is that the terrorist group will seek out bundles that lie on ever higher indifference curves until it centres in on bundle O, the optimum bundle. At bundle O the group is on the highest indifference curve possible given its resources and is allocating its resources perfectly efficiently. This must be accomplished by some search process involving trial and error. Within this theoretical framework, however, this phase of the decision-making process is not explicitly represented.[7]

The rationality that is depicted here is simply the purposeful behaviour of trying to make the best use of scarce resources. The model explains why bundle O and not some other bundle is chosen. Bundle O is the utility maximising bundle given the available resources. Of course, the model does not predict the exact amount or quantity of terrorism and legitimate activity that we should observe.[8] Rather, it predicts that the terrorist group will exhibit the pattern of moving towards an optimal bundle and this 'moving towards' involves engaging in more and more terrorism and more and more legitimate activity. Because governments and law enforcement agencies can influence the context, it should be possible to affect the choices that the group makes. Most importantly, the terrorist group might be encouraged to reduce its engagement in terrorism if the relative prices can be changed such that terrorism becomes more expensive and legitimate activity becomes cheaper. Harsher penalties and stricter security measures may be put in place while, simultaneously, incentives may be directed towards encouraging more legitimate activity. In Figure 3.3, the budget constraint pivots and the group can now only afford to engage in T_{A1} terrorism. However, it can afford to engage in more legitimate activity L_{A1}. A new optimal bundle, O_N, is identified. The new optimum is characterised by less terrorism and more legitimate activity. Following such measures, therefore, the model predicts a pattern of adjustment away from terrorism. This is one of the main conclusions presented by Frey & Luechinger (2003). Such government policies change both the relative and absolute prices of terrorism and legitimate activity.

Unfortunately, there is no way to tell just how long this adjustment will take. The trial and error process that had to be worked through before the terrorist group was able to get to (or near or towards) O in the first place took some amount of time and the adjustment to O_N will also take time and will also be approached by a process of trial and error.[9] The neoclassical model, then, really only gives an indication of the nature and direction of any substitution that is expected to take place as a result of the change in the relative prices of terrorism and legitimate activity. It does not give us any further information about the duration of the adjustment process or any precise details about the process itself. The terrorist group might gradually reduce its terrorist activity in response to deterrence efforts. But if enough time passes, the terrorist group may be able to acquire new resources that allow it to expand its terrorist activity even in the face of higher resource requirements.

US embassy attacks and mass casualty bombings

US embassies have been a common target of terrorist attacks. The historical record of embassy attacks intertwines with some of the tactical changes that have characterised the methods that terrorist groups have deployed, especially the move

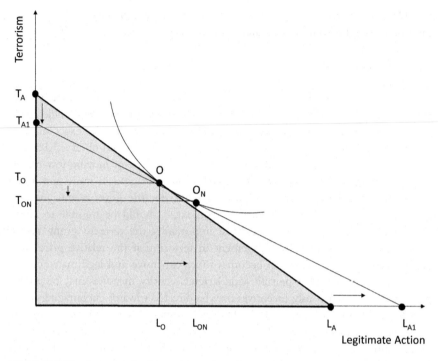

FIGURE 3.3 The impact of enhanced security measures.

towards 'mass casualty bombings' (Quillen 2002). On April 18, 1983, the US embassy in West Beirut, Lebanon, was the target of a suicide bombing perpetrated by a pro-Iranian group calling themselves the Islamic Jihad Organisation. The attack killed 63 people. The following year, on September 20, 1984, Hezbollah perpetrated a suicide bombing on the relocated US embassy in East Beirut. The attack killed 24 people. These attacks remained the deadliest to have been perpetrated against US embassies until Al-Qaeda's dual attacks in Kenya and Tanzania on August 7, 1998, which together killed 224 people.

In perpetrating embassy attacks, terrorists groups have displayed patterns of behaviour that can be captured by the neoclassical model of choice (with some adjustments). Bombing embassies was itself a relatively new activity. Although some of the earlier attacks on US embassies were bombings (such as the attack on the embassy in Saigon, Vietnam, in 1965), most attacks prior to the 1980s involved shootings and mob violence. At other embassies around the world, a common terrorist tactic was to storm an embassy and kidnap the diplomats and staff. Better security raised the relative price of this type of activity and made bombing a more attractive alternative (Jenkins 1983). This is a pattern of choice predicted by the neoclassical consumer theory applied to terrorism. In Figure 3.3, rather than 'terrorism' and 'legitimate activity' as the two choices, we could have 'kidnapping' and 'bombing'.[10] The efforts to reduce kidnapping could be said to have reduced the relative price of bombing, leading to a reallocation of resources by terrorist groups towards that type of attack. Substitution in response to deterrence initiatives could also be observed when embassies were increasingly fortified against bombings. At that time, terrorist groups switched course again to concentrate on assassinations and kidnappings of embassy staff outside of the fortified compounds (Enders & Sandler 2002).

Although embassies were among the early targets of mass casualty bombings, this was part of a general transition by terrorist groups of many diverse backgrounds towards this type of terrorist action. In between the two Beirut embassy bombings, the barracks of the peacekeeping forces in Lebanon were targeted in an October 23, 1983 bombing that killed more than 300 people. This is among the first on a long list of attacks, stretching from the Middle East to Sri Lanka to Oklahoma to Omagh (Northern Ireland). The Omagh bombing, carried out on August 15, 1998, killed 29 people, illustrating the stark departure that mass casualty bombing represented from existing attack methods for those terrorist groups who adopted it. The provisional IRA had perpetrated bombings across Western Europe for decades and had even carried out a bombing in the town of Omagh previously (in 1973). But the Omagh bombing of 1998 was different. Although the group responsible, the real IRA, denied it had targeted civilians, these denials appear to have been attempts to mitigate the damage caused by the backlash against the attack. The bomb had been planted in a car parked in a busy shopping district where, clearly, civilian casualties must have been expected.

The Beirut barracks attack and the Omagh bombing were just two examples of the more than 70 mass casualty bombings (where more than 25 people were killed) recorded between 1950 and 2000 and in which a total of more than 5,000 people were killed (Quillen 2002). In some ways, the transition to mass casualty bombings mirrors the transition towards bombing of civilians during military campaigns, especially during World War II. When particular targets, such as industrial facilities, became too difficult to destroy from the air at night, the British and US air forces lobbied for permission to strike much larger targets: cities (Ellsberg 2017). Analogously, specific traditional terrorist targets became far more difficult to attack and so terrorist groups shifted their resources towards much softer civilian targets. This is just another form of substitution, which is a standard pattern of behaviour that is predicted by the neoclassical model of choice. We would expect, based on the reasoning embedded in the model, that efforts to harden obvious civilian targets, such as airlines and public transport systems, will lead to a reduction in the number of attacks on those targets but that, unfortunately, the threat of terrorism will be shifted to different targets.

The willingness to exchange terrorism for legitimate activity

One limitation of reasoning within a neoclassical model where the two choices are 'terrorism' and 'legitimate activity' is that legitimate activity and terrorism might not even be vague substitutes from the perspective of committed terrorists. For the consumer choice model to work, it requires the decision-maker to be willing to make trade-offs between the two goods. If legitimate political activity is not something that a committed terrorist is willing to trade off against terrorism, then the indifference curve analysis collapses (though it could still be used quite effectively as a model of choice between two attack methods or two types of terrorism as we have just seen). Even if 'terrorism' and 'legitimate activity' are substitutes in the sense that either method could be used to obtain political influence, there is another, deeper reason why terrorists may be unwilling to move away from terrorism towards legitimate activity. A commitment to terrorism may very well be a core part of the 'terrorist identity'. As Rogers et al. (2007, p.258) explain:

> Pressure to commit acts of violence aids the process in which an individual socialized to one set of socially acceptable moral codes can progress into a situation where the group moral codes replace their individual moral codes, enabling them to commit acts of violence. In this case, terrorist groups must commit violent acts in order to reaffirm the group identity and justify the existence of the group. As Post (1998, p.36) put it, 'What are freedom fighters if they don't fight?'

Depending on how tenaciously a terrorist group clings to its identity as a *terrorist* group, the substitution effect in favour of legitimate activity when the price of terrorism increases may be undermined completely. While there may be some movement away from terrorism due to the change in terrorist group's opportunities resulting from the price increase, the movement may be much smaller than the neoclassical model predicts. The assumption that a terrorist group is willing to make trade-offs between terrorism and legitimate activity overlooks the importance of terrorism for a terrorist group's identity and minimises the role of identity in shaping the group's actions. A terrorist group that gives up terrorism, even in principle, and embarks upon a legitimate pathway of political engagement is not a terrorist group and loses its terrorist group identity. For many *terrorist* groups, the loss of their terrorist identity as such may be too high a price to pay. This provides a part of the explanation for why groups such as the Real IRA reject peace deals and continue to pursue terrorism.

Sometimes, the identity of the terrorist is intertwined with the 'celebrity of terrorism'. The story of Ilich Ramírez Sánchez illustrates this perfectly. Sánchez was a chubby kid from Venezuela who was teased at school and later became 'The Man Who Hijacked the World'. The chubby kid became Carlos the Jackal. The chubby kid became the man who attacked the Organization of the Petroleum Exporting Countries (OPEC) headquarters in Vienna. The man who attacked the French consulate in Berlin. The man who bombed Radio Free Europe in Munich. The man who bombed the Le Capitole train on the Paris-Toulouse express. Carlos was Sánchez's assumed name and 'The Jackal' was the name given to him by reporters because a copy of Frederick Forsythe's 'The Day of the Jackal' was found by a journalist in an apartment that Carlos shared with some other people (Thomas 2013).

Once such a powerful celebrity identity is established, it is not something that will be given up easily.

Unlike most other terrorists and terrorist groups, Carlos declared himself to be a terrorist for hire (Bowden 2007) and certainly did not disavow the title of 'terrorist'. When he appeared at his trial in France in 2011, against the backdrop of an emerging Islamic State, he seemed very much a relic of another age. His was an old-fashioned brand of terrorism, one that is neither perpetrated nor, perhaps, possible to perpetrate anymore. He is a 'dinosaur' (Sage 2011). Yet, he remained defiant. He claimed at the start of his trial that he had killed more people than anyone else associated with the Palestinian resistance (Anderson 2017). A search of Google's Ngram Viewer suggests that 'Carlos the Jackal' continued to receive a growing number of mentions in books published each year, well into the 2000s. This celebrity is part of the reason why terrorists who forge a terrorist identity are much less likely to give it up than our neoclassical model of choice would lead us to suspect. In the next chapter, we explore what happens to the patterns predicted by the neoclassical model of choice when the behavioural concept of loss aversion is introduced along with the possibility that a terrorist group can face losing its identity if it does not engage in acts of terrorism.

Four dot points to end the chapter

* A basic neoclassical consumer theory of choice can be applied to the terrorist's choice between 'terrorism' and 'legitimate activity'.
* The fundamental prediction is that the terrorist will engage in as much of both types of activity as possible in order to get the most satisfaction from the available resources.
* Because legitimate activity might not be a viable substitute for terrorism, the neoclassical model might be better used to explain choices between *attack* methods. This helps us to explain the patterns of behaviour observed around attacks on embassies.
* When terrorism becomes a part of the individual's or group's identity, the willingness to substitute away from terrorism may be far lower than the neoclassical model would lead us to expect.

Notes

1 Dnes and Brownlow (2017, p.702).
2 It should be noted, however, that splinter groups including Real IRA remain active.
3 Developed by Hicks and Allen (1934a & 1934b).
4 The model is depicted as a choice between two goods because it is easier to draw two-dimensional diagrams. We can easily explore the choices between coffee and tea, for example. If this sounds too restrictive, one good can be made a 'composite' good to stand in for everything else in the consumer's shopping basket. Then, if we want to analyse the consumer's choices regarding coffee and 'everything else' we can still do so with the help of two-dimensional diagrams.

5 Here satisfaction or utility is usually assumed to be some function of what the terrorist group wants. Frey and Luechinger (2003), among others, assume that this is political influence.

6 If terrorism and legitimate activity were perfect substitutes, the indifference curves would be straight lines. Regardless of how much or how little of either activity the group was currently involved in, they would always give up units of one activity in exchange for units of the other at a constant rate.

7 Pareto (1909) argued that this type of rational choice framework really represents the last step of a decision-making process characterised by much trial and error.

8 Economists can get themselves into difficulty here. If we observe a choice we might say that this must have been the optimal choice otherwise the group would have chosen differently. This is quite tenuous but it has not stopped a relatively intricate literature emerging that tries to show that chosen bundles result from utility maximising behaviour. This 'integrability' problem, as one might imagine, has not been resolved. Mirowski (1989) explores this matter in considerable depth. The technical economics literature upon which he sets his sights includes landmark theoretical papers by Samuelson (1948, 1950) and Houthakker (1950). Some of this work is also summarised by another major contributor to the debate, Hal Varian (see Varian 2006).

9 Time is not something that economists have overlooked and there is a large literature that deals with the problem. Much of economics is explicitly cast in a temporal setting. For an example of an attempt to address some of these issues in the particular setting that we have been discussing, neoclassical consumer theory, see DeSerpa (1971).

10 Another way in which this model can be used is as a framework for thinking about what the United States was trying to accomplish following the 9/11 attacks. Part of the rationale, beyond simple revenge, for pursuing Al-Qaeda was to disrupt any other attacks that the group might have been planning. This logic could be reflected in the neoclassical model by depicting Al-Qaeda as facing a trade-off between 'planning and perpetrating terrorism' and 'fighting the US Army in Afghanistan'. By attacking Al-Qaeda in Afghanistan, the group would be forced to reallocate some of their scarce resources away from terrorism and towards its own defence. The US attacks could be depicted as an attempt to pivot Al-Qaeda's budget constraint and preferences away from terrorism.

References

Anderson, G. 2017. Carlos the Jackal Jailed over 1974 Paris Grenade Attack. *Sky News*, March 28.

Anderton, C.H. & Carter, J.R. 2005. On Rational Choice Theory and the Study of Terrorism. *Defence and Peace Economics*, 16, 275–282.

Bowden, B. 2007. The Terror(s) of Our Time(s). *Social Identities*, 13, 541–554.

DeSerpa, A.C. 1971. A Theory of the Economics of Time. *Economic Journal*, 81, 828–846.

Dnes, A.W. & Brownlow, G. 2017. The Formation of Terrorist Groups: An Analysis of Irish Republican Organisations. *Journal of Institutional Economics*, 13, 699–723.

Ellsberg, D. 2017. *The Doomsday Machine: Confessions of a Nuclear Planner*. New York: Bloomsbury.

Enders, W. & Sandler, T. 2002. Patterns of Transnational Terrorism, 1970 to 1999: Alternative Time Series Estimates. *International Studies Quarterly*, 46, 145–165.

Frey, B.S. & Luechinger, S. 2003. How to Fight Terrorism: Alternatives to Deterrence. *Defence and Peace Economics*, 14, 237–249.

Hicks, J.R. 1939. *Value and Capital*. Oxford: Oxford University Press.

Hicks, J.R. & Allen, R.G.D. 1934a. A Reconsideration of the Theory of Value I. *Economica*, 1, 52–76.

Hicks, J.R. & Allen, R.G.D. 1934b. A Reconsideration of the Theory of Value II: A Mathematical Theory of Individual Demand Functions. *Economica*, 1, 196–219.

Houthakker, H.S. 1950. Revealed Preference and the Utility Function. *Economica*, 17, 159–174.

Jenkins, B.M. 1983. Some Reflections on Recent Trends in Terrorism. RAND Paper P-6897, RAND Corporation, Santa Monica, CA.

Mirowski, P. 1989. *More Heat Than Light: Economics as Social Physics, Physics as Nature's Economics*. New York: Cambridge University Press.

Pareto, V. 1909. *Manual of Political Economy*, English Trans. 1971. New York: Augustus M. Kelly.

Post, J.M. 1998. Terrorist Psycho-Logic: Terrorist Behaviour as a Product of Psychological Forces. In W. Reich (Ed.), *Origins of Terrorism: Psychologies, Ideologies, Theologies, States of Mind*. Baltimore, MD: Johns Hopkins University Press, pp.25–40.

Quillen, C. 2002. A Historical Analysis of Mass Casualty Bombers. *Studies in Conflict and Terrorism*, 25, 279–292.

Rogers, M.B., Loewenthal, K.M., Lewis, C.A., Amlot, Cinnirella, M. & Ansari, H. 2007. The Role of Religious Fundamentalism in Terrorist Violence: A Social Psychological Analysis. *International Review of Psychiatry*, 19, 253–262.

Sage, A. 2011. Carlos the Jackal Back in Court over 1980s Bombs. Reuters US, November 4. www.reuters.com/article/2011/11/04/us-france-trial-carlosidUSTRE7A321Y20111104

Samuelson, P.A. 1948. Consumption Theory in Terms of Revealed Preference. *Economica*, 15, 243–253.

Samuelson, P.A. 1950. The Problem of Integrability in Utility Theory. *Economica*, 17, 355–385.

Thomas, S. 2013. Yours in Revolution: Retrofitting Carlos the Jackal. *Culture Unbound: Journal of Current Cultural Research*, 5, 451–478.

Varian, H.R. 2006. Revealed Preference. In M. Szenberg, L. Ramrattan & A.A. Gottesman (Eds.), *Samuelsonian Economics and the 21st Century*. Oxford: Oxford University Press, pp. 99–115.

4

LOSS AVERSION AND THE TERRORIST IDENTITY

[T]errorists whose only sense of significance comes from being terrorists cannot be forced to give up terrorism, for to do so would be to lose their very reason for being.[1] pressures to conform to the group, combined with pressures to commit acts of violence, form a powerful psychological drive to carry on in the name of the cause, even when victory is logically impossible. These pressures become so prevalent that achieving victory becomes a consideration secondary to the unity of the group.[2]

The most basic orthodox model of choice, the neoclassical consumer theory, provides us with some plausible pattern predictions when we use it to talk about terrorist behaviour. These all involve the idea of the terrorist decision-maker trying to reach a more satisfactory state of affairs and substituting among different combinations of activities in order to get there. As one thing becomes more expensive, substitutes are found for it and the structure of choices evolves. Applied to terrorism, we might set up the model as a choice between terrorism and legitimate activities or, perhaps more soundly, as a choice between one type of attack method and another. Whatever the case may be, the group is just as happy to substitute in either direction as long as it can reach higher indifference curves or, at least, not slip backwards onto a lower indifference curve. In this chapter, we question this 'reversible' willingness to substitute one thing for another. If a terrorist group has formed its identity by doing one thing, will it really be as sensitive and responsive to changes in relative prices as the neoclassical consumer theory would lead us to expect?

Weatherman (the Weathermen or the Weather Underground) was a prominent terrorist group in the United States throughout the early 1970s. Between 1970 and 1975, the group was responsible for at least 46 terrorist actions, mostly bombings against government, police and military targets. It had forged an identity for itself, like many other groups of its era, as a social revolutionary (leftist) group (Post, Ruby & Shaw 2002). The attention that the Weather Underground attracted by being placed on the FBI's most wanted list was far beyond that which the group's actual activities could ever have mustered. By the later 1970s, however, the group was in steep decline as its members, under pressure from law enforcement, tumultuous internal dynamics and a changing cultural-historical context, gradually turned themselves in. There had never been much support for the group's methods and public support for most of the group's primary causes had long since faded away. Many of the group's members had been living as fugitives for years. Unable to engage in the types of activities that had defined its identity, the group declined and ultimately fell. When it ceased to engage in terrorist activity, its identity was lost.

What people have, including their identity, is not something that is considered within the basic neoclassical model of consumer choice. During the 1980s, evidence began to mount that 'starting positions' matter when it comes to the substitution of one good for another (Bishop & Heberlein 1979; Knetsch & Sinden 1984). A person's willingness to give something up in exchange for something else depends on what they start with. People are unwilling to give up what they have because they value it more than what they don't have. An explanation for this behaviour is 'loss aversion'. In their original paper on prospect theory, Kahneman & Tversky (1979) had relied upon a rather obscure study on sensation and measurement by Galanter & Pliner (1974) to support the concept of loss aversion.[3] That is, the aggravation experienced in losing something appears to be greater than the pleasure associated with gaining it (Kahneman & Tversky 1979, p.279). Thaler (1980) called this discrepancy the 'endowment effect' because people seem to value something more if they possess it (Tversky & Kahneman 1991). Within a decade or two, loss aversion (and the endowment effect) had assumed its place as the most robust finding in behavioural economics (Kahneman & Tversky 1979; 1984; Tversky & Kahneman 1991, 1992; Camerer 2005; Novemsky & Kahneman 2005; Tom et al. 2007). Loss aversion has become an explanation or a part of an explanation for a number of observed patterns in human decision-making across many different fields of study and in many different contexts.[4]

If loss aversion is a mainstay of behavioural economics, then the same could certainly be said for the concept of identity in psychology and sociology. Identity, though, has not attracted as much attention from economists. Akerlof & Kranton (2000) took some steps towards an economic analysis of identity by adding an identity term to a traditional utility function. This would allow gains and losses in identity to be treated as gains and losses in utility. Such an approach leaves out a lot of the substance of identity. For example, in the case of gender identity, which is a core theme in Akerlof & Kranton's (2000) article, feminist writers would argue that a utility function with an identity term added in does little to encompass the uniquely gendered lived experiences of women (Wesley 2006). Identity in Akerlof & Kranton's (2000) analysis is simply a payoff that attends certain decisions or actions. Although open to criticism, the treatment of identity as a payoff achieves at least one important thing. It highlights that identity can be lost as well as gained. If identity can be lost, people could experience identity loss aversion. If the choices that a terrorist group makes are intertwined with the group's identity, then identity loss aversion may obstruct the substitution of one activity for another, even in the face of changes in the relative prices.

Loss of a terrorist identity

Identity has become one of the most researched concepts in psychology (Schwartz 2001). Much of the work traces its origins to Erikson (1968, 1980), who defined identity as (1) an awareness of self-sameness and continuity and (2) an awareness that others recognise this style of one's individuality. Identity is spectrum-like, as Schwartz (2001, p.9) explains:

> For Erikson, identity is best represented by a single bipolar dimension, ranging from the ego syntonic pole of identity synthesis to the ego dystonic pole of identity confusion. Identity synthesis represents a reworking of childhood and contemporaneous identifications into a larger, self-determined set of self-identified ideals, whereas identity confusion represents an inability to develop a workable set of ideals on which to base an adult identity. Ego identity, then, represents a coherent picture that one shows both to oneself and to the outside world. Career, romantic preferences, religious ideology and political preferences, among other facets, come together to form the mosaic that represents who one is. The more complete and consistent that mosaic is, the closer to ego identity synthesis one is, whereas the more disjointed and incomplete the picture is, the more ego identity confusion one will manifest ….All individuals, at any time in their lives, can be placed at some point on Erikson's dimension between identity synthesis and identity confusion.

For our discussion, it is really important that there is such a thing as a terrorist identity, either individual or group, that exhibits more or less stability.[5] This is generally accepted. Indeed, it is a presupposition for much of the work that has been done by those[6] who have tried to develop an identity-based explanation for why people *become* terrorists (see Victoroff 2005, esp. pp.22–23; Phillips & Pohl 2011, esp. pp.105–106). Although there are many varieties of this type of work, one such identity-based explanation is that terrorism and other violent behaviour emerges via the construction of a negative (destructive or socially undesirable) identity in response to an identity crisis. This might be individual or it might involve group membership. The latter draws upon additional research into social identity and political identity and intergroup conflict (see Huddy 2001; Arena & Arrigo 2005; Konrad & Morath 2012 and, esp., Schwartz, Dunkel & Waterman 2009).

Identity can be lost, as well as formed. Weigert & Hastings (1977, p.1171) opened their paper with the following: 'The painful loss of an irreplaceable and personal identity is a common theme of human existence'. It is a small step to link the two concepts of identity and loss aversion. Once a terrorist identity has been formed, the individual or group is expected to be averse to losing it. Furthermore, identity might be formed by the act of engaging in terrorism or the act of engaging in particular terrorist actions (e.g. mass casualty bombings). If this were indeed the case, we would not expect the terrorist to switch seamlessly to legitimate activity or a different form of attack following a change in relative prices, at least not willingly or readily. Rather, we would expect some resistance. This expected resistance to substitution we might say is due to the possibility that the terrorist group is characterised by 'identity loss aversion'. The impact of loss aversion on the willingness of decision-makers to substitute one thing for another has been documented by Knetsch (1989; 1992) and Kahneman, Knetsch & Thaler (1991). The combination of having something (an endowment) and having an aversion to losing it makes the direction of substitution matter. People value what they have simply because they have it.

Identity and substitution

If the group has developed a terrorist identity and values it and does not want to lose it, there are far-reaching implications that diverge substantially from those that flow from a neoclassical consumer choice approach to the analysis of terrorist behaviour. According to the neoclassical model, if the terrorist group is indifferent between two states of affairs that can both be reached by some combination of 'terrorism' and some amount from 'legitimate activity', then the group will willingly substitute one type of activity for the other (and back again). That is, the indifference curves are 'reversible'. However, if either activity is essential to an identity that the terrorist group has and does not want to lose, conclusions such as those presented by Frey & Luechinger (2003) and that we presented in the first part of the previous chapter should not be expected to hold in all cases. Some terrorist groups will resist trading-off terrorism against any other good. If the terrorist group has defined its identity through a particular type of attack, it will resist trading-off opportunities to perpetrate this type of attack against opportunities to engage in some other attack type.

Irreversibility was first detected in the 1980s. The focus of the investigation at the time was on the so-called 'WP = WA' assumption. That is, the assumption that the maximum price a person is willing to pay (WP) for a good and the minimum price that a person who already had the good would be willing to accept (WA) are approximately equal (Hovenkamp 1991, p.225). Kahneman, Knetsch & Thaler (1991, p.196) explain further:

> if an individual owns x and is indifferent between keeping it and trading it for y, then when owning y the individual should be indifferent about trading it for x.

As Hovenkamp (1991, p.226) explains,

> the assumption that WP = WA is critical to the creation and use of indifference curves … If WP and WA are substantially different from one another, the 'exchange rates' of the two goods could be different in one direction than the other, and the curve would be 'non-reversible'.

In economics and psychology experiments, people have been observed to exhibit this type of behaviour consistently. Knetsch & Sinden (1984) and Knetsch (1989, 1992) are the two most prominent early studies of this phenomenon but Kahneman, Knetsch & Thaler's (1990) experiments became the most iconic, introducing a generation of behavioural economists to the so-called 'Cornell University mug' experiment. In this experiment, the experimenters first calibrated a market for 'tokens' that represented a certain amount of value. The tokens' values were different for different subjects and some subjects were issued with tokens while others were not. Across three trials, this ownership was varied. Trading among the subjects created supply and demand curves for the tokens and at the end of the series of trials, three buyers and three sellers were selected at random and paid off in real dollars according to the preferences that had emerged during the experiments and the market-clearing price. The markets worked perfectly well.

Once this was established and the participants in the markets were experienced, the experimenters introduced the Cornell coffee mugs, which were distributed alternately to the subjects. The subjects were also told that the mugs sell for $6.00 at the university bookstore. Using the established market structure and value tokens, the subjects were then permitted to trade the mugs. There were 22 subjects and 11 mugs. As Kahneman, Knetsch & Thaler (1991, p.196) explain, economic theory predicts that the mugs will be owned by those who value them most once the trading stops. If the mugs are distributed randomly among 'mug lovers' and 'mug haters', the prediction is that half of the mugs will change hands. However, the observed number of trades of mugs was 4, 1, 2, and 2 in repeated trials. The average owner was unwilling to sell for less than $5.25 and the average buyer was unwilling to buy for more than $2.25–$2.75. The market price was in the range $4.25–$4.75. This pattern repeated itself even as ownership of the mugs varied. The same individual has an indifference curve for 'money' and 'mugs' that has a different slope depending on whether he or she possesses one or the other of the two goods. Regardless of who owned the mugs, they always valued them more than potential buyers (WA > WP). This is called the endowment effect. It is a consequence of loss aversion.

The result of the endowment effect is that WA is much larger than WP and the indifference curves are not reversible. Rather than moving up and down an indifference curve, the individual who possesses one of the goods is reluctant to give it up in exchange for the other good. If the individual possesses the other good instead, then he would now be reluctant to part with that good. We cannot orchestrate an exchange that leaves the individual on the same indifference curve because he is unlikely to accept the terms of the exchange. Although this does not lead to a complete collapse in exchange, it certainly curtails the scope of the neoclassical model. Knetsch (1989, p.1283) explains:

> The widespread irreversibility of indifference curves would not imply that people will not make any trades, or that consumers will not change future consumption patterns in response to changing relative prices. However, the

presence of irreversibilities would imply that fewer trades will be made than predicted by standard assumptions, and they offer little assurance that the shifts in future consumption will be as complete or as prompt as would be expected if indifference curves were reversible.

We can extend the reasoning to terrorism, identity and the trade-off between terrorist activity and legitimate activity. In Figure 4.1, we have drawn a picture of indifference curves that emerge when (1) identity is important to the terrorist group and (2) when it has formed that identity based on one type of action or the other. The indifference curves for each 'type' of decision-maker are completely different shapes and rule out any possibility that either type of group will substitute terrorism and legitimate activity at the same rate. One group has formed its identity mainly by terrorist action. The second group has formed its identity mainly by legitimate activity. The rates of substitution implied by the two types of indifference curves are so extreme as to effectively rule out exchange. Certainly, the rates of exchange will be nowhere near those implied by neoclassical consumer theory. Once the terrorist group has established its identity, incentives designed to prompt it to substitute legitimate activity in place of terrorism are less likely to succeed. The neoclassical model of consumer choice has no feature to represent the psychology of loss aversion and the endowment effect. This does not cause many problems in pure market exchange where, for example, a person expects to part with a good in

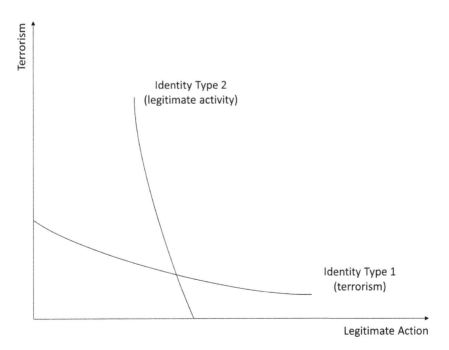

FIGURE 4.1 Indifference curves, identity and loss aversion.

exchange for money and, indeed, has acquired the good for that purpose. Once a person *feels* the possession of the article or good or identity, especially if time and trouble were involved in acquiring it, loss aversion and the endowment effect begin to act on the choice process.

Identity, loss aversion and patterns of terrorist choice

In a neoclassical treatment, the terrorist group wants to get to the highest indifference curve regardless of what type or combination of actions is required. It would just as soon get to a better state of affairs by terrorist activity as it would by legitimate activity and if it had to substitute one activity for the other, it would do so at the same rate regardless of which activity had defined its actions up to that point. Once identity and loss aversion become factors in the terrorist group's choices, this reversibility is no longer to be expected. This gives us some reason to expect a pattern of persistent involvement in terrorism, even when the price of doing so has increased substantially relative to alternative activities. In the previous chapter, we noted that it is more plausible to use the neoclassical model to explain choices between two (or more) attack methods rather than between terrorism and legitimate activities. We found that even the basic neoclassical model explains at least one pattern that can be observed in practice. That is, the tendency to substitute one type of attack for another when relative prices change. Once we introduce loss aversion, we become aware that we should not expect this substitution effect to operate smoothly and in all cases. There may be groups with distinct identities that have been formed by engaging in particular types of attacks and those groups will not willingly substitute one attack method for another at the same rate of substitution.

Consider a situation in which two different terrorist groups, A and B, form their identities by the types of attacks they engage in. Let us say that A forms its identity by bombing and B forms its identity by hostage taking. Neither group is much interested in substituting away from its identity defining attack method. In Figure 4.2, therefore, we must draw two different indifference curve maps, one for each terrorist group. For each group, the indifference curves must be very steep or very flat depending on which attack method is identity defining. This reflects an unwillingness to substitute one type of attack for the other. Group A values 'bombing' so much more than 'hostage taking' that it would only substitute if it could undertake a lot more hostage taking actions. Group B, conversely, values 'hostage taking' so much more than 'bombing' that it too is unwilling to substitute unless it was able to undertake a lot more bombings. The main point, of course, is that if we were to confuse the identities of two different groups and expect both groups to substitute at the same rate in either direction we would be wrong.

When the terrorist group's identity is reflected in its attack method choice, an increase in the relative price of its preferred attack method may not result in a seamless transition of resources to alternatives. Some groups may be expected

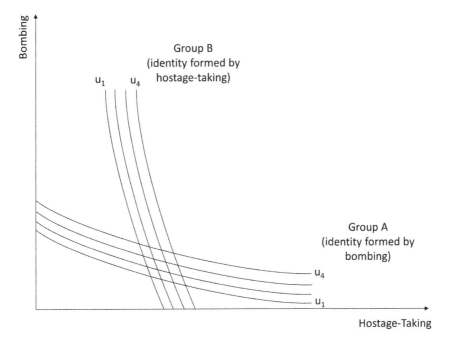

FIGURE 4.2 Two attack methods, two groups, two identities.

to cling to their 'signature attack method' despite enhancements in security or changes in resource requirements that make it relatively costlier. Simply, when identity is bound up in attack method choice we can expect a pattern of behaviour characterised by the continuation of a structure of preferences in spite of factors that would normally lead us to expect the terrorist group to substitute away from one attack method or another. The decision by Al-Qaida, for example, to continue to attempt what are usually called 'spectacular' attacks despite the steps that have been taken to circumvent them is not only coherent behaviour consistent with the group's identity but is a pattern of behaviour that economic analysis leads us to expect once that economic analysis has been re-worked to reflect the implications of identity, the endowment effect and loss aversion.

Bargaining with a loss averse decision-maker

Beyond attack method choice, loss aversion can also affect bargaining and negotiation whenever the parties involved view concessions as losses. This can lead to bargaining impasses. Tversky & Kahneman (1986, p.262) give an example:

> In negotiating over missiles, for example, the subjective loss of security associated with dismantling a missile may loom larger than the increment of security produced by a similar action on the adversary's part. If the two

> parties both assign a two-to-one ratio to the values of the concessions they make and of those they obtain, the resulting four-to-one gap may be difficult to bridge. Agreement will be much easier to achieve by negotiators who trade in 'bargaining chips' that are valued equally, regardless of whose hand they are in. In this mode of trading, which may be common in routine purchases, loss aversion tends to disappear.
>
> *Kahneman and Tversky (1984)*

Not surprisingly, as research into the effects of loss aversion on decision-making accumulated, steps were taken to incorporate it into game theory-based models of bargaining (Bazerman et al. 1985; Neale & Bazerman 1985; Neale et al. 1987; Kahneman 1992; Shalev 2002). The key implication of loss aversion is that negotiators will experience *concession aversion*. Levy (1996, p.187) explains:

> Bargaining involves making concessions on some issues in return for compensation on others. Loss aversion and the endowment effect imply that actors have a tendency to treat the concessions they give up as losses and the compensation they receive from the other actor as gains and to overvalue what they give relative to what they get. As a result, there is a shrinkage in the size of the bargaining space of mutually beneficial exchanges, a greater tendency to risk the consequences of a non-agreement or deadlock in an attempt to minimize one's concessions, and a lower probability of a negotiated agreement than utility-based bargaining theory might predict.

Loss aversion has important implications for negotiating with terrorists. Imagine a very classical situation where a terrorist group captures hostages and makes demands while trying to preserve their own lives. In such a situation, the hostages are the bargaining chip. In this case, the hostages have been deliberately acquired in order to serve this purpose and loss aversion might not be as strong as it would be if the hostages had some other intrinsic value to the terrorists (Levy 1996, p.187). However, the longer the hostages are held and the more time, trouble and cost the terrorists went to in order to acquire them, the greater their perceived value (Levy 1996, p.187). The possibility that terrorists experience concession aversion has never been an explicit part of traditional game theoretical models of hostage negotiations.

Loss aversion may not only affect the decisions of the terrorists who have taken the hostages. It can also affect the decisions of hostage negotiators. What is more interesting still is that loss aversion may even influence the policymakers with overarching authority over a particular situation. For example, on November 4, 1979, 52 American hostages were seized at the US embassy in Tehran. The siege eventually ended in January 1981. However, in April 1980 there was a dramatic and ultimately unsuccessful rescue attempt orchestrated by the American military and ordered by President Carter. The operation was to involve eight helicopters but when, for various reasons, only five were operational at the first staging post the mission was aborted. Upon attempting to return to their naval vessel, one of the helicopters crashed killing eight servicemen. The embarrassing failure has been analysed repeatedly by military experts. McDermott (1992) argues that President Carter's decision to order the military to rescue the hostages can be explained as the result of his facing heavy losses in prestige at home and abroad. McDermott (1992) suggests that loss aversion prompted more risk taking than normal as the President attempted to recoup his lost standing in the lead up to the 1980 presidential election.

While narratives based on concepts such as loss aversion can be used to provide new perspectives on historical situations, loss aversion also holds very important implications for more contemporary hostage taking situations. Imagine a situation where the terrorist group seizes hostages but has no intention to negotiate, as appears to have been the case for the Bataclan Theatre attack in Paris in 2015.[7] Loss aversion in these types of situations obviously has no relationship to strength or weakness in bargaining because no bargaining is going to take place. It also has no relationship to concession aversion, since the terrorists are not intending to make any. Rather, as the situation unfolds and the terrorists assess their gains or losses dynamically against their reference points,[8] loss aversion shapes the steps that the terrorists take to either protect the gains or recover the losses they have experienced so far. If some hostages escape or if a lower number of potential victims than expected are corralled at the location, for example, the terrorists will seek ways to recover from these losses. This may produce increasingly undesirable outcomes as the terrorists try with increasing desperation to reverse the situation. This tendency for loss aversion to cause risk seeking behaviour in the domain of losses is discussed in more detail in our next chapter.

Identity loss aversion and unwillingness to disengage

The quotes with which we opened the chapter are just two from a long list that express similar sentiments. That is, terrorism researchers know that there are terrorists who will not willingly trade off terrorist activity against an alternative. Indeed, some terrorists will not willingly trade off one type of terrorist action (say, armed assault) against another type (say, arson). Loss aversion and behavioural models of decision-making provide a theoretical foundation for this practical knowledge and, indeed, predict it as a pattern of behaviour. A terrorist group's identity is hard fought. It is not an easy thing to build and develop. This only adds to the aversion that the group will associate with its possible loss. With loss aversion comes a pattern of behaviour that will be quite different from that predicted by the neoclassical model of consumer choice. That is, there will not be a set of perfectly reversible indifference curves but, more realistically, the terrorist group will be characterised by a set of very steep or very flat indifference curves depending on the nature of the activities that have defined its identity.

The pattern predictions that can be drawn from the neoclassical theory of consumer choice are unobjectionable but will not always hold. This is not because decision-makers are less rational than the neoclassical model depicts. It is because human decision-makers value what they have more than what they do not have. This is the endowment effect. The best explanation that we have for this 'endowment effect' is that people are loss averse. Loss aversion and the endowment effect undermine the seamless substitution of one good for the other that is at the centre of neoclassical consumer theory. When it comes to applying the model to terrorist choice, we must recognise that there is such a thing as a terrorist identity that the terrorist has and does not want to lose. We can still expect the basic patterns of the neoclassical model to hold but we must not expect them to hold in all cases. We have a new pattern with which to complement the old. When a terrorist has an identity and does not want to lose it, the terrorist may be far more committed to terrorism than the neoclassical model suggests.

The impact of loss aversion on choice is substantial. It disrupts the MRS, potentially ruling out substitution altogether. When risk is introduced, loss aversion also prompts the human decision-maker to be more risk seeking when confronting the possibility of losses. But loss aversion is just one of several important behavioural characteristics embedded within Kahneman and Tversky's (1979) descriptive model of the decision-making process. Prospect theory draws together a lot of research in economics and psychology in a logically consistent theoretical framework that describes the decision-making process under conditions of risk and uncertainty. Up until now, apart from brief glimpses here and there, we have considered choice in the absence of risk. In reality, none of the outcomes of terrorist activities is certain and there is always a chance that the actual outcome will diverge from what was expected. Terrorist actions are risky prospects. Prospect theory is the most prominent descriptive model of the process that decision-makers undertake when deciding whether to choose one risky prospect over another. It is to a discussion of prospect theory and its implications for terrorist choice that we now turn.

Four dot points to end the chapter

- Identity is a fundamental concept of modern psychology but it hasn't received as much attention from economists.
- The neoclassical model of consumer choice that we discussed in the previous chapter says that the decision-maker will substitute A for B or B for A at the same rate.
- Behavioural economists have found that it matters whether the person possesses A or B. If he or she possesses A or B, it is valued more and the person is less willing to accept something in exchange for it. This is the endowment effect.
- The endowment effect, which might be explained by loss aversion, applies to identity. The more a terrorist has worked to develop the terrorist identity, the less willingly it will be given up. This diminishes the effectiveness of incentives and deterrence and makes the terrorist more difficult to bargain with than orthodox economics would lead us to expect.

Notes

1 Post (1998, p.38).
2 Martin (2003, p.72).
3 In fact, 'loss aversion' is not the term used in Kahneman and Tversky's (1979) original paper. They speak only of aversion to losses and then only once or twice. They preferred the more general statement of the concept: losses loom larger than gains. This became the definition of loss aversion in the economic literature.
4 One of the most cited attempts at explaining an aspect of observed behaviour by appealing to the concept of loss aversion is Benartzi and Thaler's (1995) study of the equity premium: the difference between the returns on company stocks and the returns on treasury securities on the financial markets.
5 Identity is fluid to some degree and recognition that identity exhibits some (variable) degree of stability is evident in the very early literature (e.g. Marcia 1966; Markus & Kunda 1986).
6 As an example, consider this statement by Crenshaw (2000, p.408): 'Profound narcissistic disappointment ... led to a terrorist identity ... Radical political action provided powerful psychological rewards, such as the acquisition of a new positive identity'. Many similar statements abound in this part of the literature.
7 It seems that the terrorists were planning to execute the hostages, possibly on video stream or on television (BBC News 2015).
8 In this case, perhaps against the benchmark of what they had imagined to be a successful attack.

References

Akerlof, G.A. & Kranton, R.E. 2000. Economics and Identity. *Quarterly Journal of Economics*, 115, 715–753.

Arena, M.P. & Arrigo, B.A. 2005. Social Psychology, Terrorism and Identity: A Preliminary Re-examination of Theory, Culture, Self and Society. *Behavioural Sciences and the Law*, 23, 485–506.

Bazerman, M.H., Magliozzi, T. & Neale, M.A. 1985. Integrative Bargaining in a Competitive Market. *Organizational Behavior and Human Decision Processes*, 35, 294–313.

BBC News 2015. What Happened at the Bataclan? December 9, 2015. www.bbc.com/news/world-europe-34827497

Benartzi, S. & Thaler, R.H. 1995. Myopic Loss Aversion and the Equity Premium Puzzle. *Quarterly Journal of Economics*, 110, 73–92.

Bishop, R.C. & Heberlein, T.A. 1979. Measuring Values of Extra-Market Goods: Are Indirect Measures Biased? *American Journal of Agricultural Economics*, 61, 926–930.

Camerer, C. 2005. Three Cheers—Psychological, Theoretical, Empirical—for Loss Aversion. *Journal of Marketing Research*, 42, 129–134.

Crenshaw, M. 2000. The Psychology of Terrorism: An Agenda for the 21st Century. *Political Psychology*, 21, 405–420.

Erikson, E.H. 1968. *Identity: Youth and Crisis.* New York: W.W. Norton.

Erikson, E.H. 1980. *Identity and the Life Cycle: A Reissue.* New York: W.W. Norton.

Frey, B.S. & Luechinger, S. 2003. How to Fight Terrorism: Alternatives to Deterrence. *Defence and Peace Economics*, 14, 237–249.

Galanter, E. & Pliner, P. 1974. Cross-Modality Matching of Money against Other Continua. In H.R. Moskowitz, B. Scharf & J.C. Stevens (Eds.), *Sensation and Measurement*. Dordrecht, Holland: D. Reidel, pp.65–76.

Hovenkamp, H. 1991. Legal Policy and the Endowment Effect. *Journal of Legal Studies*, 20, 225–247.

Huddy, L. 2001. From Social to Political Identity: A Critical Examination of Social Identity Theory. *Political Psychology*, 22, 127–156.

Kahneman, D. 1992. Reference Points, Anchors, Norms, and Mixed Feelings, Organisational Behaviour and Human Decision Processes, 51, 296–312.

Kahneman, D. & Tversky, A. 1979. Prospect Theory: An Analysis of Decision under Risk. *Econometrica*, 47, 263–291.

Kahneman, D. & Tversky, A. 1984. Choices, Values, and Frames. *American Psychologist*, 39, 341–350.

Kahneman, D., Knetsch, J.L. & Thaler, R.H. 1990. Experimental Tests of the Endowment Effect and the Coase Theorem. *Journal of Political Economy*, 98, 1325–1348.

Kahneman, D., Knetsch, J.L. & Thaler, R.H. 1991. The Endowment Effect, Loss Aversion and Status Quo Bias. *Journal of Economic Perspectives*, 5, 193–206.

Knetsch, J.L. 1989. The Endowment Effect and Evidence of Nonreversible Indifference Curves. *American Economic Review*, 79, 1277–1284.

Knetsch, J.L. 1992. Preference and Nonreversibility of Indifference Curves. *Journal of Economic Behaviour and Organisation*, 17, 131–139.

Knetsch, J.L. & Sinden, J.A. 1984. Willingness to Pay and Compensation Demanded: Experimental Evidence of an Unexpected Disparity in Measures of Value. *Quarterly Journal of Economics*, 99, 507–521.

Konrad, K.A. & Morath, F. 2012. Evolutionarily Stable In-Group Favouritism and Out-Group Spite in Inter-Group Conflict. *Journal of Theoretical Biology*, 306, 61–67.

Levy, J.S. 1996. Loss Aversion, Framing and Bargaining: The Implications of Prospect Theory for International Conflict. *International Political Science Review*, 17, 179–195.

Marcia, J.E. 1966. Development and Validation of Ego-Identity Status. *Journal of Personality and Social Psychology*, 3, 551–558.

Markus, H. & Kunda, Z. 1986. Stability and Malleability of the Self Concept. *Journal of Personality and Social Psychology*, 51, 858–866.

Martin, G. 2003. *Understanding Terrorism: Challenges, Perspectives and Issues*. Thousand Oaks, CA: Sage.

McDermott, R. 1992. Prospect Theory in International Relations: The Iranian Hostage Rescue Mission. *Political Psychology*, 13, 237–263.

Neale, M.A. & Bazerman, M.H. 1985. The Effects of Framing and Negotiator Confidence on Bargaining Behaviours and Outcomes. *Academy of Management Journal*, 28, 34–39.

Neale, M.A., Huber, V.L. & Northcraft, G.B. 1987. The Framing of Negotiations: Contextual versus Task Frames. *Organisational Behaviour and Human Decision Processes*, 39, 228–241.

Novemsky, N. & Kahneman, D. 2005. The Boundaries of Loss Aversion. *Journal of Marketing Research*, 42, 119–128.

Phillips, P.J. & Pohl, G. 2011. Terrorism, Identity, Psychology & Defence Economics. *International Research Journal of Finance and Economics*, 77, 102–113.

Post, J.M. 1998. Terrorist Psycho-Logic: Terrorist Behaviour as a Product of Psychological Forces. In W. Reich (Ed.), *Origins of Terrorism: Psychologies, Ideologies, Theologies, States of Mind*. Washington, DC: Woodrow Wilson Centre Press, pp. 25–40.

Post, J.M., Ruby, K.G. & Shaw, E.D. 2002. The Radical Group in Context: 2. Identification of Critical Elements in the Analysis of Risk for Terrorism by Radical Group Type. *Studies in Conflict and Terrorism*, 25, 101–126.

Schwartz, S.J. 2001. The Evolution of Eriksonian and Neo-Eriksonian Identity Theory and Research: A Review and Integration. *Identity*, 1, 7–58.

Schwartz, S.J., Dunkel, C.S. & Waterman, A.S. 2009. Terrorism: An Identity Theory Perspective. *Studies in Conflict and Terrorism*, 32, 537–559.

Shalev, J. 2002. Loss Aversion and Bargaining. *Theory and Decision*, 52, 201–232.

Thaler, R. 1980. Toward a Positive Theory of Consumer Choice. *Journal of Economic Behaviour and Organisation*, 1, 39–60.

Tom, S.M., Fox, C.R., Trepel, C. & Poldrack, R.A. 2007. The Neural Basis of Loss Aversion in Decision-Making under Risk. *Science*, 315, 515–518.

Tversky, A. & Kahneman, D. 1986. Rational Choice and the Framing of Decisions. *Journal of Business*, 59, 251–278.

Tversky, A. & Kahneman, D. 1991. Loss Aversion in Riskless Choice. *Quarterly Journal of Economics*, 106, 1039–1061.

Tversky, A. & Kahneman, D. 1992. Advances in Prospect Theory: Cumulative Representation of Uncertainty. *Journal of Risk and Uncertainty*, 5, 297–323.

Victoroff, J. 2005. The Mind of a Terrorist: A Review and Critique of Psychological Approaches. *Journal of Conflict Resolution*, 49, 3–42.

Weigert, A.J. & Hastings, R. 1977. Identity Loss, Family and Social Change. *American Journal of Sociology*, 82, 1171–1185.

Wesley, J.K. 2006. Considering the Context of Women's Violence: Gender Lived Experiences and Cumulative Victimisation. *Feminist Criminology*, 1, 303–328.

5

PROSPECT THEORY AS A DESCRIPTIVE
THEORY OF TERRORIST CHOICE

On April 19th, 1995, Timothy McVeigh ignited a homemade truck bomb that destroyed the Alfred P. Murrah Federal Building in downtown Oklahoma City, killing 168 persons, injuring close to 700 more, and triggering massive news coverage at home and abroad. Five days later, the director of the California Forest Association, Gilbert Murray, was killed instantly when he opened a small package that had been mailed to his office. The enclosed message revealed that the sender was the mysterious person dubbed 'Unabomber' by the FBI; he had killed already 2 other people and injured 23 via mail bombs since 1978. That same day, The New York Times received a letter from the Unabomber threatening another deadly parcel bomb mailing unless the newspaper published a 35,000 words manifesto he had written to explain his motives. It is difficult to imagine that there was no link between the non-stop coverage of the terrorist spectacular in Oklahoma City and the timing of the simultaneous mailings to Murray's office and the Times. My guess was then and is now that the Unabomber, Theodore Kaczynski, was miffed because of the relatively modest news coverage his mail bombs had received over the years compared to the tremendous attention the mass media paid to the Oklahoma City bombing.[1]

Each terrorist action is characterised by a range of possible outcomes. This is the essence of risk. We need a way to represent risky decision-making if we are to find patterns in choices made under these conditions. There are a number of different but related models of decision-making under risk that we can use to work out preference orderings over risky prospects. The orthodox model is called expected utility theory. It was developed by von Neumann & Morgenstern (1947). It is a mathematical model that *prescribes* the best ranking. In some parts of economics, this prescription has become synonymous with the rational choice. How decision-makers *should* choose has become blended with a prediction about how decision-makers *will* choose (i.e. in such a way as to maximise their expected utility). Prospect theory was developed in the late 1970s as a generalisation of expected utility theory that incorporates not a prescription for rational behaviour but a *description* of actual behaviour. Once we begin to view terrorist behaviour through the prospect theory lens, a whole set of new pattern predictions and possible explanations for observed behaviour opens up before us. This includes a natural trigger for copycat behaviour.

One of the most famous hijacking cases in US history is the so-called D.B. Cooper case. On November 24, 1971, a man who the press dubbed 'D.B. Cooper' hijacked a Boeing 727 over the Pacific Northwest. He was paid a ransom of $200,000[2] in cash before parachuting out of the plane, never to be heard from again. The case remains unsolved. It is just one of the many hijackings to take place in the late 1960s and early 1970s,[3] but the D.B. Cooper case is interesting not just because of its details and the fact that the identity and fate of the hijacker remains a mystery. The D.B. Cooper hijacking, which was covered widely by the press, appears to have initiated a series of copycat hijackings. In 1972, there were 15 hijackings of commercial aircraft that bore remarkable similarities to the D.B. Cooper case. For example, on April 7, 1972, Richard McCoy Jr also hijacked a Boeing 727. He was paid a $500,000[4] ransom before parachuting from the plane. He was identified and apprehended a few days later. Each of the other 14 hijackings were similar in nature. Although most of the hijackers escaped with ransom money, they were invariably arrested a short time later.

Copycat acts of violence are usually studied as emulation processes triggered by some action and amplified by some medium, usually news, television or film (Coleman 2007; Nacos 2009; Dahl & DellaVigna 2009). Although it has been recognised that many offenders seek to outdo a predecessor, this motivation is simply encompassed within—perhaps even submerged beneath—an emulation process that is driven primarily by *contagion* (Midlarsky, Crenshaw & Yoshida 1980; Fagan, Wilkinson & Davies 2007). Prospect theory, however, has a natural application to copycat behaviour with real decision-maker agency that we first operationalised in our 2014 paper, *Prospect Theory and Terrorist Choice* (Phillips & Pohl 2014). That is, the outcomes achieved by a predecessor or rival become the reference point for the copycat. This produces a set of inferences and pattern predictions about copycat violence and copycat terrorism. For example, that a copycat terrorist will choose a more risky attack method than his predecessor if the reference point that has been set by that predecessor's achievements is very high relative to the expected outcomes of the available attack methods. This approach has the added advantage of predicting that a copycat might be driven to depart from the precise details of his predecessor's actions depending on whether he finds himself in the domain of gains or losses. There are other pattern predictions besides. In order to get at them, let us explore some of the basics of prospect theory.

The basics of prospect theory

Kahneman & Tversky (1979) had been documenting 'biases' in decision-making for many years.[5] Over time, their research program came to be known as the 'heuristics and biases' research program. It is essentially summarised by Kahneman (2011) in his book, *Thinking: Fast and Slow*. The central theme is that people use heuristics or shortcuts when making decisions and this leads to biases or systematic errors in decision-making. For example, people use the availability heuristic, or the number of instances of something that they can easily recall, in judging the likelihood that something will occur in the future. This leads to systematic underestimation or overestimation of probabilities. Kahneman and Tversky's research method was to pose hypothetical but realistic choice problems for subjects in laboratory settings. Most of these problems are of the following form:

> **A:** 50% chance to win $1,000   **B:** $450 for sure
>   50% chance of $0

By cleverly introducing subjects in their experiments to a series of carefully constructed problems of this type, Kahneman and Tversky were able to demonstrate systematic patterns of results. The results, documented in their 1979 article, reveal several systematic characteristics of decision-making. The results were the same across quite different samples, including participants in experiments undertaken in Israel, students *and* faculty in Sweden and students at Stanford University. With approximately 70 participants in each experiment, 'systematic' patterns refer to a frequency of about 55 participants choosing in a particular way with the remainder choosing differently.[6] Patterns of preferences for risky prospects were observed to exhibit the following characteristics:

1. People overweight outcomes that are considered certain, relative to outcomes that are merely probable. This is the certainty effect.
2. People are risk averse in the domain of gains and risk seeking in the domain of losses. This is the reflection effect.[7]
3. In contrast to expected utility theory, most people dislike probabilistic insurance. That is, insurance where there is a small probability that the purchaser of the insurance will not be reimbursed. This is another manifestation of the certainty effect because a small move away from certainty dramatically reduces the attractiveness of the prospect (insurance in this case).[8]
4. People simplify the problems that they are confronted with by eliminating aspects that are shared by alternatives and focusing on what is different between them. This process of simplification may lead to more than one representation of the alternatives and choices can depend on the precise ways in which simplification takes place and which elements of the alternatives are deemed similar enough to cancel each other out. This is the isolation effect.

In the main part of their paper, Kahneman & Tversky (1979) set out to develop prospect theory as a descriptive model of decision-making under risk that would include these characteristics. The resulting theory partitions the decision-making process into two parts or phases: (1) editing[9] and (2) evaluation. Kahneman & Tversky (1979, p.274) explain, 'The editing phase consists of a preliminary analysis of the offered prospects, which often yields a simpler representation of these prospects. In the second phase, the edited prospects are evaluated and the prospect of the highest value is chosen'. If a terrorist or terrorist group must choose from among alternative actions under conditions of risk, what patterns of behaviour should characterise this choice if prospect theory describes the terrorist group's decision-making process? The first thing that we should expect and plan for if we are in the business of counter-terrorism is that the terrorist's view of the alternatives that are open to him and the terrorist's view of the context generally is distorted by the way in which he edits or frames the risky prospects from which he can choose. The distortions are systematic.

Editing (or framing) risky prospects

If we say that a terrorist action like bombing or armed assault is a risky prospect, by this we mean that the action will result in an outcome, x_i, that occurs with some probability, p_i. On the basis of the possible outcomes and their probabilities the decision-maker can form an expectation of what might happen but there is always a chance that the actual outcome will be different. The higher this chance of divergence between expected and actual outcomes, the riskier the prospect. For example, a bombing might be expected to attract some amount of attention in the print media, say 100 column inches.[10] The actual amount, however, might be anywhere from 85 to 115 column inches. This makes bombing a risky prospect. Consider another attack method. Armed assault might be expected to attract 150 column inches of coverage. However, this attack method might be riskier. The actual amount of coverage could be anywhere between 50 and 250 column inches. The terrorist group would have to decide whether it wants to take a chance on the riskier attack method that has a higher expected outcome or whether it wants to play it safer, with narrower limits on both the up and downsides.

The terrorist group's editing process will have certain implications for the way the group comes to view the alternatives and, ultimately, implications for the particular action or attack method that will be chosen. Kahneman & Tversky (1979, p.274) break the editing phase into four distinct operations:

1. Coding outcomes as gains or losses. Imagine that the terrorist group is interested, among other things, in the publicity that its action will receive and that a particular action is expected to attract 100 column inches of coverage. In orthodox economic theory, this would automatically be treated as a 'gain'. But what if a rival group had recently been accorded far more coverage? If this has become the terrorist group's reference point in assessing its possible

future actions, 100 column inches may actually be perceived as a 'loss'. Whether outcomes are coded as gains or losses depends on the terrorist group's reference point. Prospect theory allows for positively valued outcomes to be treated as losses if they are less than the reference point.

2. Simplification by combination. Suppose that the terrorist group is aware of a correlation between fatalities inflicted and media attention such that 10 fatalities is associated with 100 column inches of coverage. Now suppose that bombing has a 20 percent chance of inflicting 10 fatalities and a 20 percent chance of generating 100 column inches of coverage from fatality counts *other* than 10. The terrorist group will perceive this as a 40 percent chance of receiving 100 column inches of coverage.

3. Separating the risky and risk-free parts of the prospect. Kahneman and Tversky call this segregation. For example, armed assault may be expected to inflict 20 fatalities with a likelihood of 0.40 and 5 fatalities with a likelihood of 0.60. This can be broken into two parts: (1) 5 fatalities for sure and (2) 15 fatalities with a likelihood of 0.40.

4. Cancelling out common elements. When two different prospects share common features, the decision-maker cancels them out. For example, if there is a multi-stage process involved in each prospect and the first stage is common to both, it is ignored. If an additional payoff of the same magnitude is added to both prospects, it is also ignored. The terrorist group might see the initial stages of a campaign as being shared similarly by each of the possible attack methods that are available to it. This common feature of each attack method will therefore be ignored when the terrorist group is assessing and ranking the alternative attack methods. In a period of deteriorating security, for example, each terrorist attack method may inflict 10 more fatalities than before. This will be ignored in assessing the alternative attack methods because it is common to all of them.

Usually, editing results in a simpler representation of the choice problem. In fact, this is one of the key features of human decision-making. People tend to turn difficult problems into simpler representations. Recognising that there might be such a thing as an editing phase helps us to avoid the conclusion that a terrorist group does not have the capacity to think about and weigh up payoffs and probabilities for all of its potential actions before choosing what it determines to be the best one. In fact, it is the very complexity of the problem that makes editing necessary and editing is the very thing that introduces certain systematic errors into the decision-making process. We cannot simply sweep away concepts such as expected payoffs and probabilities because we think that terrorist groups do not or could not 'think like that' because it's too 'hard'. On the contrary, prospect theory leads us to expect that they will think in a certain way because the decision-making task is 'hard'.

The important question is, how simple can simple get? Research into framing or editing has led to the exploration of alternative frameworks, one of which is called *fuzzy trace theory* (Reyna & Brainerd 1991, 1995). According to fuzzy trace theory, simple can get very simple. In this theory, it is only the 'gist' of the situation that matters. Consider a terrorist group editing the possible outcomes of three alternative attack methods. The editing might be as simple as the terrorist group concluding that two attack methods have some chance of 'some fatalities' while the third attack method has some chance of 'zero fatalities'. The 'some' will be favoured over the 'none' (Kühberger & Tanner 2010, pp.317–318) and the third attack method will be edited out of further consideration. While more research is required, the answer to our question is that editing might boil down different prospects to very simple terms. Having so simplified the range of alternatives that will be considered, the decision-maker then moves on to evaluate the remaining options.

The evaluation phase

Quirks of the human decision-making process shape the way the terrorist group frames its options but we have not yet described how the group will actually make a choice from the options that confront it. In orthodox models of decision-making under risk, the utility of an outcome is weighted by the probability that the outcome occurs. Summing over all outcomes gives the expected utility of a risky prospect. A risky prospect with a higher expected utility is preferred.[11] The evaluation phase of prospect theory is not dissimilar in principle but outcomes that would be viewed as gains in an orthodox model can be viewed as losses in prospect theory if they are below the reference point. Also, probabilities that would serve as weights in an orthodox decision-making process now enter into the process in a transformed or distorted way. People tend to overweight less likely outcomes and underweight more likely outcomes. Furthermore, whether the decision-maker is trying to avoid further losses or consolidate prior gains determines the appetite that he or she has for risk.

A number of these features are reflected in Kahneman and Tversky's (1979) S-shaped utility function, which we have drawn in Figure 5.1. The reference point is the inflection (or reflection) point that divides the domain of losses and the domain of gains. Because of loss aversion, losses loom larger than gains. In the loss domain, the utility function is steep and convex. This indicates that the individual is loss averse and that his or her loss aversion prompts risk seeking in order to avoid losses or to recover from losses experienced. In the domain of gains, the utility function is concave to indicate that the individual has a desire to protect gains and is prompted thereby towards exhibiting risk averse behaviour whenever gains have been experienced or whenever an available prospect almost certainly results in a gain. As we explained before, the reference point can be the outcomes achieved by a predecessor or rival that the terrorist seeks to emulate or surpass. Whenever the terrorist group perceives itself to be below the reference point because an attack has turned out worse than expected and has not surpassed the predecessor's benchmark or when the terrorist group feels itself in danger of producing an outcome that is below that which was achieved by the predecessor or rival, it will be compelled to choose a riskier method of attack. The terrorist group can even feel compelled to take a riskier course of action as an attack unfolds if it is not turning out as well as they had hoped.

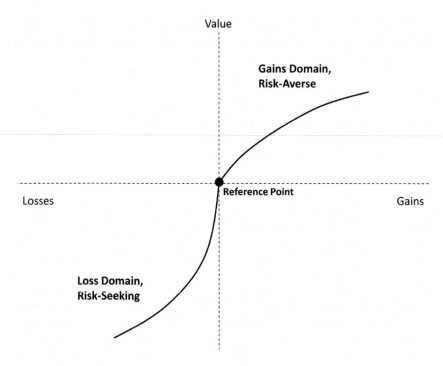

FIGURE 5.1 The S-shaped utility function of prospect theory.

Risk is the possibility that the actual outcome will diverge from the expected outcome. Since this possibility is greater when the variability of the outcomes is greater, risk can be measured by the variance or standard deviation of the outcomes. The relevant outcomes might be any number of things considered individually (media attention, social media followers, grassroots supporters, ransoms, fatalities inflicted) or as an index where several of these relevant payoffs are combined in a weighted average. In Table 5.1, the average fatalities inflicted by each attack method (globally) in 2016 along with the standard deviation (variability) of the outcomes is reported. We have chosen the year 2016 because it is the first year where the category 'unarmed' assaults emerged with any significance. The Global Terrorism Database (GTD) has always had such a category but only when the vehicle attacks that became prominent in the mid-2010s are added to the record of unarmed assaults does the category begin to carry more significance.

The terrorist seeking to inflict fatalities or obtain the payoffs that are correlated with fatalities, such as media attention, will favour different attack methods from Table 5.1 depending on how the group views the world and where it perceives its current or future position to be relative to its reference point. There are three main pattern predictions:

TABLE 5.1 Attack methods 2016, least risky to most risky[a]

Attack method	Number of incidents	Average fatalities per attack	Standard deviation of outcomes
Hijacking	41	1.14	1.79
Assassination	779	2.32	6.11
Hostage taking	1,086	2.38	6.64
Armed assault	2,579	2.68	9.51
Bombing	6,655	2.69	9.54
Facility/infrastructure	654	3.60	15.70
Unarmed assault	64	5.96	20.23

[a] There were 915 attacks where the attack method is listed as 'unknown'. These have not been included. Unarmed assault is the category under which the Global Terrorism Database records 'vehicle' attacks.

1. If the terrorist group's reference point is high relative to the average payoffs expected from the available attack methods, the terrorist group will perceive itself to be in domain of losses. It will take more risk in an attempt to generate an outcome above the reference point. That is, the higher the reference point, the more the terrorist group favours attack methods further and further down the list in Table 5.1. If the terrorist group can use more than one attack method, it will consider riskier combinations of attack methods.[12]

2. If the terrorist group's reference point is low relative to the average payoffs expected from the available attack methods, the terrorist group perceives itself to be in the domain of gains. It will take less risk in an attempt to protect and consolidate those gains. It will choose attack methods or combinations of attack methods with less variable outcomes.

3. If the group has undertaken attacks that have generated outcomes above (below) its reference point, it will take less (more) risk in its future attacks. Successful groups might be emboldened but they do not automatically become more risk seeking. In fact, quite the contrary.

As an example, consider a rival group has recently used one of the attack methods listed in Table 5.1 to perpetrate an attack in which there were 20 fatalities inflicted. Given the average outcomes listed in Table 5.1, it is clear that exceeding this number in a future attack will not be a straightforward matter. To have any chance of achieving such a goal, the terrorist group must take more risk. When the reference point is high relative to the expected outcomes of the available options, the terrorist group confronts the very real possibility of failing to exceed the reference point. In this case, the group's loss aversion prompts risk seeking. The terrorist group will tend to favour attack methods with more variable outcomes. The opposite holds true as well. If a rival or predecessor has inflicted just two fatalities, this sits much more readily within the range of likely outcomes even for the less risky attack methods listed in Table 5.1. A terrorist group with this reference point will see little need to take undue risk. This is prospect theory in action.

Patterns of terrorist choice and copycats

In the economics literature, including in Kahneman and Tversky's papers, the nature of the reference point is somewhat mysterious. Sometimes it is treated as the status quo or 'zero'. Sometimes there are allusions to how it might derive from an experience of some sort. In our work, we treat the reference point as emerging from two primary sources: (1) either an outcome achieved by the terrorist or terrorist group previously or (2) an outcome achieved by a predecessor terrorist or terrorist group where predecessor might be a rival or it might be an individual or group that others seek to copy, emulate or out-do (Phillips & Pohl 2014, 2017). When the reference point is identified like this, some of the primary conclusions that follow directly from prospect theory are:

1. The action with the highest expected outcome is not necessarily the one that the decision-maker favours. If the reference point is low, the terrorist can exceed it without bearing the risks that attend the highest-yielding attack method. Indeed, under these circumstances the terrorist will be very averse to risk.
2. By contrast, if the reference point is very high, the terrorist must take more and more risk to exceed it. When almost every attack method is unlikely to produce an outcome above the reference point, the terrorist faces a higher probability of losses (outcomes below the reference point). Under these circumstances, the terrorist becomes more risk seeking.
3. Attempting to emulate or surpass a predecessor or rival does not necessarily involve copying the precise method or attack type that the predecessor used. Another attack method might represent the best way to exceed the reference point. The reference point is outcome-centric, not action-centric.

In several papers Enders, Parise and Sandler (1992) and Enders and Sandler (1999, 2000) argue that copycat behaviour underlies observed cycles in terrorist activity. When a successful attack occurs, others follow and a cluster of actions is observed. Law enforcement then introduces a counter-measure and the cycle ebbs before another innovation in terrorism is observed (Enders & Sandler 2000, p.156). While this is a plausible argument, there is a missing piece of the puzzle. Beyond an attack method being successful, there is no other rationale for copying it. This problem stems from confusing the action with the outcomes. The outcomes are the basis for the reference point, not the attack type. An innovative and successful attack method might establish a reference point in terms of outcomes but even if it does so, copying the attack method itself may not be the only way to surpass its outcomes. The choice to use the new attack method, an old attack method or a combination is a choice that is shaped by the various factors that are embedded within prospect theory.

There is also the matter of rivalries that go beyond simply learning which attack methods are better. Terrorist groups try to outdo each other. The RAF and the 2nd of June Movement engaged in a series of attacks designed to attract attention to their respective causes. We would say that the outcomes of each group's actions created a reference point for the other group in a tit-for-tat contest for prominence. An interview conducted with Stefan Wisniewski, an active member of the RAF, suggests that rivalries and reference points shaped the choices of the RAF. In 1978, Stefan Wisniewski was charged and sentenced to life in prison for participation in the RAF kidnapping and murder of Hanns-Martin Schleyer, president of the German Employers' Association, in 1977. In an interview conducted in an Aachen prison in 1997, Wisniewski commented that the 2nd of June Movement's kidnapping of Lorenz in 1975 indicated a scale or proportion of action of which the RAF took note:

> *Am Augenmaß der Bewegung 2. Juni (im Bezug auf die Lorenz-Entführung) hätten wir uns ruhig ein Beispiel nehmen können.* [We could have learned a lesson from the sense of proportion displayed by the 2nd of June Movement (in the Lorenz-kidnapping).]
>
> *Wisniewski (1997, p.36, translation by the authors)*[13]

The RAF later kidnapped Hanns-Martin Schleyer, an action that also involved the RAF trying to 'force the government's hand' during negotiations over Schleyer by hijacking a German plane with 80 passengers on board with the assistance of members of the Popular Front for the Liberation of Palestine (PFLP). The hijacking was also conceived with reference to the actions of other groups, especially the Japanese RAF. As Wisniewski says:

> *Wir dachten dabei auch an die fast gleichzeitig erfolgreich durchgeführte Entführung eines japanischen Flugzeugs durch die japanische Rote Armee.* [We also thought of the almost simultaneously successful execution of the hijacking of a Japanese plane by the Japanese Red Army.[14]]
>
> *Wisniewski (1997, p.50, translation by the authors)*

In their study of terrorism and the media, Weimann & Winn (1994, p.217) conclude, '… Several biographical studies of terrorists show that many were motivated by a desire to emulate the publicity achievements of precursors'. Prospect theory can be applied whenever this desire surfaces for payoffs of any kind, including media attention, concessions, inflicted financial damage or inflicted fatalities.[15] Not only does exceeding a reference point become a key motivation for engaging in a particular type of action, it also becomes a motivation for *communication*. It is not surprising to learn that terrorist groups are more likely to claim responsibility in contexts where there are many active terrorist groups (Hoffman 2010). More troubling, Caruso & Schneider (2013) found evidence that Jihadist groups engage in brutality contests where the brutality escalates as each group tries to supersede the others in terms of inflicted violence. In all cases, we must keep in mind that the most recent or newest attack method is not the only one that a terrorist group can choose as its reference point. Many years of attacks may pass before a terrorist or terrorist group emerges with a desire to emulate or surpass a predecessor. This predecessor's actions might have disappeared from public memory but not from terrorists with a particular cause, motivation or objective. The case of Sam Melville highlights this perfectly.

Sam Melville and the mad bomber

Samuel Joseph Grossman took the name Melville from the Moby Dick author. In his mid-thirties, Sam Melville became increasingly angry. Sam Melville became actively opposed to apartheid and the Vietnam War. Sam Melville developed links with radical leftist groups. He also became interested in George Metesky, the Mad Bomber, who had been responsible for a series of bombings in New York City during the 1940s and 1950s. Metesky's bombing campaign was sparked by his grievance with his old employer, Consolidated Edison. Metesky had an accident at work and later lost his job. His application for compensation was not successful. Over the course of 17 years, Metesky placed 30 bombs in various places around New York. He would target public places. Although the targets usually had no connection to Consolidated Edison, often the bombs would contain notes critical of the company. Metesky also wrote to various newspapers, informing journalists that the bombings would continue until Consolidated Edison was held accountable for what they had done to him. The bombing campaign created real fear in the city because of the targets that Metesky chose. For example, Metesky would hide his bombs inside the upholstery of movie theatre seats. His devices injured 15 people, some seriously. He was arrested in 1957. He was found unfit to stand trial and spent more than a decade in a psychiatric institution.

In the mid-1960s, when Sam Melville became interested in Metesky's history, Metesky was still in that psychiatric institution. Melville formed a small group of accomplices, including Jane Alpert, and together they began a bombing campaign of their own. The little band of accomplices, some of whom have never been identified, had loose ties with the Weather Underground and Black Panther Party. The first bombing took place on July 27, 1969. Seven bombings followed until Melville was arrested on November 12, 1969. Most of the bombings took place late at night. The targets were mainly corporate buildings, such as the Chase Manhattan Bank headquarters, which Melville targeted on November 11. In some ways, we could link Melville with Metesky through the reference point concept. Metesky injured people but he did not kill anyone. There is no doubt that Melville tried in some way to emulate Metesky's 'one man' assault on corporate America (Pickering 2007, p.8) and there is evidence to suggest that Melville's reference point, taken from

Metesky, was 'zero fatalities'. For a while, Melville would scrawl graffiti on walls across New York City that read 'George Metesky Was Here'.

We might be inclined to think that Kahneman & Tversky's (1979) editing process is a more or less ordered sorting through of the alternative prospects. Indeed, sometimes Melville and Alpert devoted a great deal of time assessing the probability of success. For example, during 1969, Melville helped to hide two members of a Canadian terrorist group, Front de libération du Québec (FLQ). He was as fascinated by their activities as he was with George Metesky. In determining whether it would be possible to help the two fugitives escape by hijacking a plane to Cuba, Alpert spent hours in the library figuring out the success rate of similar hijackings that, as we saw earlier, were occurring regularly at the time (Pickering 2007, p.10). At other times, Melville seemed to make his decisions on the move. In what is his most infamous bombing, the bombing of the Marine Midland Bank building on August 20, 1969, Melville set the timer on some dynamite *before* knowing where he would actually place the bomb! According to Alpert, Melville told her that he just walked around Wall Street until he found a likely target. A corporate building. A glass tower. A building with a 'phony sculpture' in front (Pickering 2007, p.19). The editing (and evaluation) of the alternative prospects was done with deliberation but not the sort of deliberation that we might usually associate with bombings.

Not surprisingly, Melville's haste on this occasion led to a miscalculation. Melville's bombings, as mentioned, were carried out at night. Apart from the possibility that the bomb would not detonate or that more or less damage would be caused, the range of possible outcomes was fairly narrow. That is, the risk was relatively low. Or at least it seemed to be. What Melville overlooked when he hastily chose the Marine Midland Bank building was the presence of staff working nightshift for the bank's bookkeeping division. When the bomb exploded at 10.30 pm, around 20 people were injured. The news of the injuries was, according to Alpert, upsetting to Melville, who had not intended to hurt anyone (Pickering 2007, p.22). In this case, we might say that Melville attributed a negative value to injuries and fatalities, placing the value of injuries and fatalities below his reference point (zero). As such, the infliction of injuries was viewed by Melville as a loss. Prospect theory can help us see the decisions made by Melville and his group of accomplices in a new way. The role of predecessors to provide reference points and inspiration. The research of possible outcomes. The sometimes hasty editing and evaluation of alternatives. The divergence of actual outcomes from expected outcomes that is the very nature of the risk that makes risky prospects risky. The feelings of loss that loom larger than feelings of gain.

From single attack methods to combinations

Earlier we said that attempting to emulate or surpass a predecessor or rival does not necessarily involve copying the precise method or attack type that the predecessor used. An obvious innovation that is available to the copycat (and any other terrorist or terrorist group) is the combination of attack methods. We can illustrate the importance of this by two cases: (1) Brenton Tarrant's March 2019 mosque attack in New Zealand and (2) the copycat or emulation attempt perpetrated by Stephan Balliet on a synagogue in Halle, Germany, in October 2019.

In March 2019, Brenton Tarrant perpetrated New Zealand's most deadly mass shooting when he attacked mosques in Christchurch. There were 51 people killed and a further 50 injured. At one mosque, he killed 42 people at the scene. At a second mosque, he killed seven people. Two other victims died later in hospital. Around 20 minutes of the attack was 'live streamed' on Facebook Live. The attack was an armed assault, using up to five different firearms. He discarded weapons along the way, at times retrieving new weapons from his car when he ran out of ammunition. There were some improvised explosive devices (IEDs) attached to Tarrant's car. These appear to have been booby-traps and were defused without incident. The attack was motivated by extreme ideologies, which Tarrant outlined in a 74-page manifesto (banned from distribution in New Zealand). In it, he apparently claims not to be a Nazi but rather to be an ethno-nationalist and eco-fascist. In a sense, Tarrant might also be viewed as something of a copycat. He claims inspiration from Anders Bering Breivik, the Norwegian lone wolf terrorist who killed 77 people in a combined bomb and spree-shooting attack in Norway in 2011.

Just over 6 months later, 27-year-old Stephan Balliet attempted a similar attack in Germany. This time the target was a synagogue. The suspect was heavily armed with guns when he drove to the synagogue and attempted to enter. There were around 60 worshippers inside. The synagogue's heavy doors were locked and Balliet was unable to enter. After shooting at the doors, he shot dead a woman on the street and then shot dead a man at a kebab shop around the corner (which was possibly symbolic given the idea of kebabs as a symbol of ethnicity is prominent in the type of literature referred to by Brenton Tarrant in his manifesto). Two other people were wounded before the gunman was arrested. Part of the attack was also live streamed, this time on the gaming platform Twitch. The prosecutors will argue that Balliet aimed to create a worldwide effect by deliberately copying the actions of Brenton Tarrant (BBC News 2019). The copycat element is obvious. How does it illustrate some of our pattern predictions?

The first thing that we notice about Tarrant's armed assault is that the outcomes are high. In Table 5.1, the average inflicted fatalities for armed assaults worldwide in 2016 were 2.68. The standard deviation, though, is relatively high at 9.51, indicating that outcomes well above average are not out of the question, especially if a log normal distribution is assumed. Even so, the number of people killed (42) at the first mosque that Tarrant attacked is an unlikely number for an armed assault. The seven people killed at the second mosque, where Tarrant was initially unable to find the entrance, is much closer to the expected outcome. Because the reference point set for prospective copycats by Tarrant is so high, we would expect one of two different choices to characterise a copycat. We would expect a similarly motivated individual either to choose an entirely different attack method such as a vehicle attack or, more likely, a combination of attack methods. The second approach is the pathway chosen by Balliet. While Balliet was armed with guns and attempted to enter the synagogue with the same intent that possessed Tarrant when he entered the mosques in New Zealand, Balliet had four kilograms of explosives in his car. He tried to detonate the explosives at the synagogue. Balliet attempted a combined armed assault and bombing attack, closely matching the type of actions chosen by Breivik and deviating in this regard from Tarrant. Breivik, of course, inflicted 77 fatalities to Tarrant's 51. Balliet may have seen in Breivik's choices a method for exceeding the reference point set by Tarrant.

A key feature of the attacks that we have been discussing as well as the entire history of terrorist attack method choice is that terrorists do not always choose single attack methods. In fact, choosing combinations of attack methods is the most common characteristic of terrorist choice. It is also the most commonly overlooked characteristic of terrorist choice. This oversight is a significant problem because combinations of attack methods have quite a distinct nature, with features that affect the outcomes that we can expect from terrorist attacks. We must understand not only the nature of attack method combinations but also why terrorists choose to combine attack methods. One of the absolutely fundamental risk management strategies that people follow is diversification. They try not to put all their eggs in a single basket. This results in combinations of things in portfolios. Modern portfolio theory (MPT) was created in the 1950s (Markowitz 1952). We can use portfolio theory to explore how terrorist groups combine attack methods in order to achieve desired payoffs (Phillips 2009). Advances in behavioural economics have provided us with behavioural portfolio theory (BPT). BPT provides us with another, deeper, level of narrative to describe how these combinations are chosen and formed. We turn now to a discussion of MPT and BPT in a context where terrorist groups choose not one but a combination of attack methods. The result is that terrorists face less risk than we might think.

Four dot points to end the chapter

- Prospect theory is a descriptive model of the decision-making process that people follow when making decisions under conditions of risk and uncertainty.
- The reference point is a key concept in prospect theory. Among other things, it is a natural trigger for copycat behaviour.
- Terrorists seeking to emulate or surpass the achievements of an idol or prede-cessor choose attack methods and targets from the perspective of the reference point set by the outcomes the predecessor achieved.
- Various positions relative to the reference point are possible. If the terrorist confronts a strong possibility of failing to surpass the reference point, the terrorist will be more risk seeking and might even be prompted to innovate, especially by combining attack methods.

Notes

1 Nacos (2009, p.3).
2 More than $1,280,000 in 2020 dollars.

3 See Chapter 1.
4 Approximately $3,100,000 in 2020 dollars.
5 For example, Tversky and Kahneman (1974).
6 In most cases, the minority number is reflective of the number of participants who chose in a manner consistent with the axioms of expected utility. This is an interesting result on its own because it shows that expected utility theory, despite not being a descriptive model of choice, may still describe the decision-making process of about 20 percent of the subjects! In other studies, the figure is roughly 40 percent.
7 See Hershey and Schoemaker (1980).
8 See Wakker et al. 1997.
9 Tversky and Kahneman (1992) revised the terminology and now call it the 'framing phase'.
10 We use 'column inches' as a catch-all unit of measurement for media attention. One could just as easily use 'hits', 'downloads' and so on.
11 This process is discussed in more detail and compared with prospect theory in Chapter 8.
12 Terrorists and terrorist groups commonly combine attack methods. Combinations are discussed in the next chapter.
13 Proportion here refers to the 'magnitude' or 'scale' of the effect of the terrorist action. RAF members decided that their next action had to be 'bigger' than the kidnapping of Lorenz (Winkler 2007, p.252).
14 Another terror group on friendly terms with the Palestinians, that is, the Japanese Red Army, successfully hijacks a Japanese aircraft on September 28 1977. On the first day of the event the Japanese government gives in to the demands of the hijackers: 9 Japanese Red Army group members are released from prison and 6 million dollars paid in ransom. Algeria, one of the possible 'countries of choice' for RAF prisoners to be exchanged for Schleyer, agrees to accept all released Japanese Red Army prisoners (Winkler 2007, p.330).
15 The correlation between inflicted fatalities and media attention is probably quite obvious but if 'proof' were needed that more fatalities equates to more media attention, one need look no further than Australian journalist James Glenday's (2019) comments:

> When a mass shooting takes place in the United States, a morbid question is immediately asked in cash-strapped newsrooms across the country and around the world. Is the death toll high enough to justify sending reporters to the scene? Between travel costs and manpower, coverage is expensive. For many media organisations, the threshold for sending a team to the site is a death toll with double figures. The bloody yardstick is not the only consideration, though it is a common one. In my former ABC bureau in London, 10 or more dead in an Islamic State-inspired terrorist attack in mainland Europe meant we would usually hit the road.

References

BBC News 2019. German Synagogue Shooting Was Far Right Terror, Justice Minister Says. October 11. www.bbc.com/news/world-europe-50003759

Caruso, R. & Schneider, F. 2013. Brutality of Jihadist Terrorism: A Contest Theory Perspective and Empirical Evidence for the Period 2002 to 2010. *Journal of Policy Modeling*, 35, 685–696.

Coleman, Loren. 2007. The Copycat Effect. blogspot.com, April 19.

Dahl, G. & DellaVigna, S. 2009. Does Movie Violence Increase Violent Crime? *Quarterly Journal of Economics*, 124, 677–734.

Enders, W. & Sandler, T. 1999. Transnational Terrorism in the Post-Cold War Era. *International Studies Quarterly*, 43, 145–167.

Enders, W. & Sandler, T. 2000. Is Transnational Terrorism Becoming More Threatening? A Time-Series Investigation. *Journal of Conflict Resolution*, 44, 307–322.

Enders, W., Parise, G.F. & Sandler, T. 1992. A Time-Series Analysis of Transnational Terrorism: Trends and Cycles. *Defence and Peace Economics*, 3, 305–320.

Fagan, J., Wilkinson, D.L. & Davies, G. 2007. Social Contagion of Violence. In D. Flannery, A. Vazsonyi & I. Waldman (Eds.), *The Cambridge Handbook of Violent Behaviour and Aggression*. Cambridge: Cambridge University Press, pp. 688–723. Columbia Public Law Research Paper No. 06-126. Available at SSRN: https://ssrn.com/abstract=935104

Glenday, J. 2019. US Shootings Force Journalists to Make Tough Decisions about Covering Gun Violence. ABC News (Australia), September 1. www.abc.net.au/news/2019-09-01/mass-shootings-the-celebrities-of-american-gun-violence/11444830

Hershey, J.C. & Schoemaker, P.J.H. 1980. Prospect Theory's Reflection Hypothesis: A Critical Examination. *Organisational Behaviour and Human Performance*, 25, 395–418.

Hoffman, A.M. 2010. Why Groups Take Credit for Acts of Terror. *Journal of Peace Research*, 47, 615–626.

Kahneman, D. 2011. *Thinking, Fast and Slow*. New York: Farrar, Straus, Giroux.

Kahneman, D. & Tversky, A. 1979. Prospect Theory: An Analysis of Decision under Risk. *Econometrica*, 47, 263–291.

Kühberger, A. & Tanner, C. 2010. Risky Choice Framing: Task Versions and a Comparison of Prospect Theory and Fuzzy Trace Theory. *Journal of Behavioural Decision-Making*, 23, 314–329.

Markowitz, H.M. 1952. Portfolio Selection. *Journal of Finance*, 7, 77–91.

Midlarsky, M.I., Crenshaw, M. & Yoshida, F. 1980. Why Violence Spreads: The Contagion of International Terrorism. *International Studies Quarterly*, 24, 262–298.

Nacos, B.L. 2009. Revisiting the Contagion Hypothesis: Terrorism, News Coverage and Copycat Attacks. *Perspectives on Terrorism*, 3, 3–13.

Phillips, P.J. 2009. Applying Portfolio Theory to the Analysis of Terrorism: Computing the Set of Attack Method Combinations From Which the Rational Terrorist Group Will Choose in Order to Maximise Injuries and Fatalities. *Defence and Peace Economics*, 20, 193–213.

Phillips, P.J. & Pohl, G. 2014. Prospect Theory and Terrorist Choice. *Journal of Applied Economics*, 17, 139–160.

Phillips, P.J. & Pohl, G. 2017. Terrorist Choice: A Stochastic Dominance and Prospect Theory Analysis. *Defence and Peace Economics*, 28, 150–164.

Pickering, L.J. 2007. *Mad Bomber Melville*. Portland, Oregon: Arissa Media Group.

Reyna, V.F. & Brainerd, C.J. 1991. Fuzzy Trace Theory and Framing Effects in Choice: Gist Extraction, Truncation and Conversion. *Journal of Behavioural Decision-Making*, 4, 249–262.

Reyna, V.F. & Brainerd, C.J. 1995. Fuzzy Trace Theory: An Interim Synthesis. *Learning and Individual Differences*, 7, 1–75.

Tversky, A. & Kahneman, D. 1974. Judgement under Uncertainty: Heuristics and Biases. *Science*, 185, 1124–1131.

Tversky, A. & Kahneman, D. 1992. Advances in Prospect Theory: Cumulative Representation of Uncertainty. *Journal of Risk and Uncertainty*, 5, 297–323.

Wakker, P.P., Thaler, R.H. & Tversky, A. 1997. Probabilistic Insurance. *Journal of Risk and Uncertainty*, 15, 7–28.

Weimann, G. & Winn, C. 1994. *The Theater of Terror: Mass Media and International Terrorism*. New York: Longman.

Winkler, W. 2007. *Die Geschichte der RAF*. Reinbek bei Hamburg: Rowohlt Taschenbuch Verlag.

Wisniewski, S. 1997. *Wir waren to unheimlich konsequent …*. Berlin: ID-Verlag.

6

THE HIDDEN SIDE OF ATTACK METHOD COMBINATIONS AND INTERNATIONAL TERRORISM

We recognised that sport is the modern religion of the Western world. We knew that the people in England and America would switch their television sets from any program about the plight of the Palestinians if there was a sporting event on another channel. So, we decided to use their Olympics, the most sacred ceremony of this religion, to make the world pay attention to us. We offered up human sacrifices to your gods of sport and television. And they answered our prayers. From Munich onwards, nobody could ignore the Palestinians or their cause.[1]

Most terrorist groups are diversifiers. But why? Why don't terrorist groups always choose the single attack method with the highest expected payoff attached to it? In 1973, for example, the IRA perpetrated 108 attacks. These were a mixture of bombings, facility/infrastructure attacks, hostage taking, armed assaults, assassinations and hijackings. That is, nearly all of the attack method categories identified by the GTD were used by the IRA in a single year of operation. Why didn't the IRA simply choose the attack method with the single highest payoff, whether that was fatalities, grassroots support, potential concessions from the government or media attention? Why didn't they do that? Is there some logic to it or is it just happenstance? To answer these questions, we need a theory of *portfolio* choice that deals in *combinations*.

In looking for an answer, we also uncover something interesting about international terrorism. Apart from the obvious fact that terrorist groups have targets in different countries, what is there to be gained by terrorist groups (and some individual terrorists, like Carlos the Jackal) from operating internationally? Is there some aspect of the payoffs that such international groups attain or some aspect of the risk that they bear that we are missing? The epigraph to this chapter is from a member of the Black September Organisation (BSO) and refers to the Munich

Olympic Games attack on the September 5, 1972. It was this single terrorist action that generated a vast amount of attention for the group. But from 1971 to 1973, BSO was responsible for more than 30 attacks using a variety of attack methods, including armed assault, hijacking, bombing, assassination and hostage taking.[2] In just three years, the group used a combination of five different attack methods and, what is more, they used them across more than a dozen different countries. Why didn't Black September just choose one attack type and what are the implications of choosing a combination of attack types? And what else might they have gained from attacking targets in Austria, West Germany, the United Kingdom, Jordan, Egypt, Switzerland, the Netherlands, Italy, Canada, the United States and elsewhere that we might have been overlooking up until now?

The key to the hidden logic of attack method combinations and international terrorism lies in the basic, even mundane, concept of *diversification*. Diversification or not putting all the eggs in a single basket is, according to Markowitz (1952, p.77), both observed and sensible. Since diversification is something that is not done accidentally, though it might be done naïvely, we can look for the underlying logic or rules of behaviour that imply it. Because, as Markowitz says, diversification is observed, we can also use the concept to *rule out* certain theories that might be candidates for explaining attack method choice. Any theory that does not imply diversification must be ruled out (Markowitz 1952, p.77). For example, in parts of the 'qualitative' terrorism studies literature, researchers argue that terrorists seek the maximum expected value of whatever payoffs they are interested in (e.g. Surette, Hansen & Noble 2009). This, of course, implies that the terrorist will always choose the single attack method with the highest expected value of payoffs. Since this rules out diversification and since diversification is both observed and sensible (for reasons to be explained in a moment), this 'basic expected value' hypothesis must be ruled out.

Why would we make a fuss about diversification? If terrorist groups purposely or naïvely avoid putting all their eggs in one basket isn't that just a basic fact? Interesting perhaps but surely not important in any deep and meaningful way. On the contrary. The importance of diversification runs very deep indeed. Diversification reshapes the entire risk–reward trade-off for terrorism. The implications of terrorists' observed diversification, even if it is a product of naivety, are important because a combination of terrorist attack methods can have a higher expected payoff and less risk than any attack method deployed individually. Furthermore, international diversification expands the terrorists' opportunities to generate higher payoffs with *less* risk. If we look at Table 5.1, we can see the average fatalities and standard deviations for each attack method category. We might think that the upper limit of expected fatalities is the average outcome of the highest risk attack method. It isn't. A combination of two or more of these attack methods can produce a higher average outcome with more certainty (less standard deviation) than any attack method considered on its own! And this applies to *every* type of payoff the terrorist group might seek.

It is entirely likely that, by failing to consider terrorists' combinations of attack methods, terrorism analysts have underestimated the payoffs accruing to terrorist groups while simultaneously overestimating the risks that those groups have to bear. In this chapter, our primary task is to show how diversification changes the terrorists' opportunities. It does not just provide more opportunities in some banal sense. The fact that a terrorist group that attacks two European countries instead of one has twice the number of opportunities is not the sort of increase in opportunities that we are talking about. Rather, what we will show is that diversification of both attack methods and target locations increases the terrorists' expected payoffs (whatever they may be) and decreases the risk that must be borne to obtain them. There is a decision rule that implies diversification. This is the mean-variance rule. We sketch the outlines of what this rule says about decision-making in a risk-reward context with diversification and extend it with some insights from behavioural finance. On the orthodox side, we have MPT. It is complemented on the behavioural side by BPT.

How diversification creates higher rewards with lower risk

Let us start with a basic idea. The more risk you take, the more return you can expect. There is a positive trade-off between risk and reward. This will be found to be the case for any of terrorism's possible payoffs: recruits, online support, grassroots support, media attention and fatalities. In the simplest representation of risk and reward that we can develop, the expected payoff is the mean (average) payoff. The risk is the possibility that the actual outcome will be different. The risk can be measured by variance or standard deviation. If, for simplicity, we use fatalities as the direct payoff to terrorism, the positive risk-reward (mean-variance) trade off that characterised the attack method categories (for all attacks, globally) of the GTD during 2016 is depicted in Figure 6.1. We have deliberately chosen 2016 because

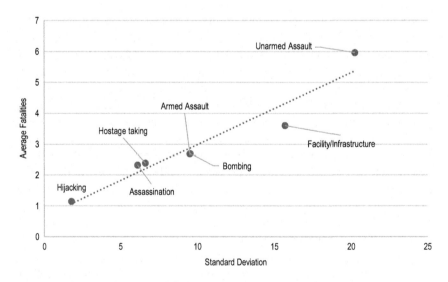

FIGURE 6.1 Risk-reward trade-off (fatalities), GTD attack methods, 2016.

the vehicle attacks, recorded as 'unarmed assaults', prominent during that year are clearly reported. Before the mid-2010s, unarmed assaults rarely registered any significant number of injuries or fatalities.

We can imagine that this static picture oscillates up and down, in and out. As terrorist groups innovate, choosing new attack methods or making old ones more effective, and as law enforcement agencies respond, the risk-reward trade-off moves. From a law enforcement perspective, the objective is to push the trade-off downwards. From a terrorist group perspective, in the first instance, the objective is to choose an attack method that provides a reward commensurate with the risk while in the second instance the objective is to develop innovations that move the risk-reward trade-off upwards. This constant interplay results in oscillating risks and rewards. If we wanted to, we could draw trade-offs for each year to see the oscillation in the whole trade-off over time. Or we could draw a trade-off that encompassed decades of data, presumably to get the best estimate of fatality numbers for certain types of attacks.

In Figure 6.1 we can observe that the terrorist group that could choose any of the individual attack methods would choose the one that best matched its preferences for risk and reward (more on this later). If the group's appetite for risk increased, it would move upwards along the trade-off line until it was satisfied with its choice. If the group became more averse to risk, it would move downwards along the line. How does this set of opportunities change if we allow the terrorist group to combine attack methods? Interestingly, when the terrorist group can combine attack methods into a portfolio, the risk-reward trade-off is stretched towards the North-West and becomes *concave*. And by becoming concave in the direction of North-West, the terrorist group's opportunities now yield higher expected outcomes for every level of risk. The terrorist group can place, say, one-third of its resources in armed assault, bombing and hostage taking respectively. Any other combination too is possible. As such, the terrorist group can locate itself at any point on the concave set of opportunities (Figure 6.2).

By what mechanism does this concavity occur? How do combinations of attack methods increase the expected rewards for terrorist groups at all levels of risk? The answer has to do with the way that the payoffs to different attack methods move relative to each other over time. If all the payoffs moved perfectly positively in lock-step with each other, there would be no benefit to combining attack methods and the risk-reward trade-off would be linear. If when the average payoffs to bombing increased by 10 percent, the average payoffs to all other attack methods increased by 10 percent and vice versa, no gains would be had from combining attack methods. A simple example can demonstrate this. Assume that there are two attack methods, bombing and armed assault. Bombing has an average payoff (measured in whatever units we like) of 5 and a standard deviation of 7. Armed assault is riskier and has an average payoff of 9 and a standard deviation of 12. Assume that the correlation is a perfect +1. Now, with perfectly positive correlation, look at what happens in Table 6.1 to the portfolio standard deviation if we start with 100 percent of

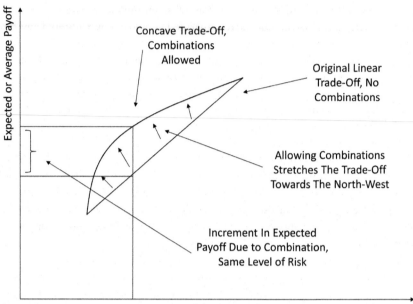

FIGURE 6.2 The concavity brought about by allowing combinations.

TABLE 6.1 Linear changes in risk and reward with perfectly positive correlation

Proportion of resources allocated to armed assault	Proportion of resources allocated to bombing	Portfolio standard deviation	Expected payoffs
1	0	12	9
0.9	0.1	11.5	8.6
0.8	0.2	11	8.2
0.7	0.3	10.5	7.8
0.6	0.4	10	7.4
0.5	0.5	9.5	7
0.4	0.6	9	6.6

resources allocated to the riskier attack method and gradually diversify towards the less risky attack method:

As the proportion of resources allocated to either attack method changes, the portfolio risk decreases (increases) linearly while the expected payoffs follow the same pattern. If, however, average payoffs to different attack methods move imperfectly relative to each other rather than one-for-one, this imperfect correlation introduces gains from diversification. With imperfectly correlated payoffs to attack methods, the

TABLE 6.2 Non-linear changes in risk and reward with imperfectly negative correlation

Proportion of resources allocated to armed assault	Proportion of resources allocated to bombing	Portfolio standard deviation	Expected payoffs
1	0	12	9
0.9	0.1	10.68	8.6
0.8	0.2	9.42	8.2
0.7	0.3	8.24	7.8
0.6	0.4	7.18	7.4
0.5	0.5	6.31	7
0.4	0.6	5.71	6.6

terrorist group can offset the decreases in the payoffs to one type of attack with increases in the payoffs to another type of attack. Assuming that the correlation is slightly negative, say −0.20, such that increases (decreases) in the average payoffs to armed assault are accompanied by slight decreases (increases) in the payoffs to bombing, we can see the difference that this makes to the portfolio standard deviation. The results are included in Table 6.2. With the same changes to resource allocation, portfolio risk decreases (increases) non-linearly. Importantly, the same payoff can now be earned with less risk. For example, a payoff of 7 can be earned by bearing almost 30 percent less risk if the payoffs are slightly negatively correlated (a standard deviation of 6.31 versus 9.5). The outcome of diversification is higher payoffs with less risk.

When more than two attack methods are available, the gains from diversification are even more pronounced. What is perhaps most surprising is that combinations of attack methods can have higher payoffs with less risk than any of the attack methods considered on their own. Tables 6.1 and 6.2 reflect the opportunities from just two attack methods. Terrorist groups can combine at least seven different attack methods (by the GTD's classification). As more and more attack methods, each with different correlations with each other, are combined, the risk-reward trade-off is gradually re-shaped from linear to concave and the terrorists' opportunities correspondingly expand. These are the gains from diversification. This is the underlying logic of attack method combination. How was this worked out originally? What are the preliminary steps? Formalising these statistical relationships was at the core of Markowitz's (1952) development of MPT. Probably the most interesting thing about this process of development is the gradual uncovering of structure in apparently random or haphazard phenomena.

MPT: a decision rule consistent with diversification

In the early 1950s, Harry Markowitz (1952) developed the MPT that would eventually win him the Nobel Prize in 1990. He starts his 1952 paper by pointing out that expected values do not provide a satisfactory foundation for a decision rule covering individual risky prospects or combinations of risky prospects. Simply, if decision-makers were solely interested in the expected value of risky prospects, they would choose the risky prospect with the highest expected value. This behaviour is not observed. In financial markets, for example, people do not always choose the single stock with the highest expected value because it likely comes with high risk. Also, most people are observed to combine stocks in a portfolio. Likewise, for terrorism. Terrorist groups are not observed to allocate all of their resources to a single attack method. In place of the expected value criterion, Markowitz (1952) introduced, instead, the mean-variance or expected-value-variance (EV) criterion. Now, the decision-maker would consider each risky prospect as a 'pairing' of expected reward (E) and risk (V). Portfolios, too, are risk-reward pairings and so the decision-maker's set of opportunities is the whole set of risk-reward pairs.

For attack method combinations, the expected payoff for a portfolio of attack methods is simply the weighted average of the payoffs of each of the attack methods in the portfolio. The weights are the proportion of resources allocated to each attack method. Formally,

$$E(R_P) = \sum_{i=1}^{n} w_i E(R_i)$$

Where $E(R_P)$ is the expected reward or payoff to the portfolio, w_i is the percentage of total resources allocated to attack method i and $E(R_i)$ is the expected reward on attack method i. For example, in Tables 6.1 and 6.2, a 50–50 combination of armed assault and bombing has an expected payoff equal to:

$$E(R_P) = \sum_{i=1}^{n} w_i E(R_i) = (0.50 \times 9) + (0.50 \times 5) = 7$$

Working out the risk for a portfolio is more complicated. Portfolio risk is not a simple weighted average of the standard deviation of each attack method. That is, we *cannot* simply workout the portfolio risk for a 50–50 combination of armed assault and bombing as:

$$\sigma_p = (0.50 \times 12) + (0.50 \times 7) = 9.50$$

That only works if the payoffs are perfectly positively correlated (Table 6.1). Any divergence from this, such as in Table 6.2, and we get the wrong answer. And the payoffs to different attack methods are not perfectly positively correlated (Phillips 2009; Pohl 2017). Calculating portfolio risk requires us to consider the imperfect correlations. The ones that are responsible for gains from diversification and a concave opportunity set. Formally,

$$\sigma_p = \sqrt{\sum_{i=1}^{n}\sum_{j=1}^{n} w_i w_j \rho_{ij} \sigma_i \sigma_j}$$

Where σ_p is the portfolio standard deviation, ρ_{ij} is the correlation coefficient that expresses the degree of correlation between each pair of attack methods i and j. The double summation sign in the formula simply implies that all possible pairs of risky prospects must be accounted for in the calculation. To calculate portfolio risk, we must include the proportion of resources allocated to each attack method, the variance of each attack method's payoffs and the correlation of the payoffs for every possible pair of attack methods.

To see a rather amazing result, we start calculating using both formulas and plot the results on a graph. We work meticulously for every combination. For seven attack methods, a practically infinite number of different portfolios can be formed. There is 100 percent allocated to one method, zero to all the rest. There is 10 percent allocated to one, 25 percent each to three others and 5 percent to each of the remaining three. And so on. If we run the calculations and plot the results, the structured shape that we expect emerges from the data. That is, if we repeatedly calculated the mean and standard deviation of the payoffs of all of the possible combinations of attack methods and plotted the results in *EV*-space, we would find the shape depicted in Figure 6.3. It is important to note that this will be the case for *any*

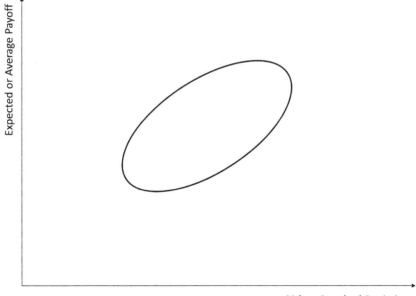

FIGURE 6.3 Structure! All possible combinations of attack methods.

type of risky prospects with payoffs that have a reasonably dense historical record of data. If data points are too scarce, there will be flat segments in the opportunity set. Concavity will gradually increase and the opportunity set will gradually come to resemble the stylised shape once more information is added. Regardless how messy a context might appear, Markowitz's structure underlies it. In this case, the apparently random ups and downs of the various payoffs that terrorists groups seek are held together in a tight oblong-shaped disc with a concave upper edge.

Markowitz realised that decision-makers would not be interested in the whole opportunity set. They would be most interested in those opportunities or combinations that have the highest expected payoff for a given level of risk. He realised that they would be most interested in the upper edge of the opportunity set. He called this upper edge the 'efficient set'. It is efficient in the sense that combinations on the upper edge of the opportunity set yield the maximum expected reward for the level of variance. Is there a way to compute the 'upper edge' without computing and graphing every single combination? Yes, and Markowitz (1952) provided it.

Although the efficient set can be calculated relatively easily using modern computing power, at the time the task of running what is essentially a quadratic optimisation problem was practically insurmountable without some sort of algorithm. Markowitz's precise technique for solving this problem and computing the efficient set is called the 'critical line algorithm'. Just as the S-shaped utility function is synonymous with Kahneman & Tversky's (1979) prospect theory, Markowitz's portfolio theory is synonymous with the concave or bullet-shaped 'efficient frontier'. This is the upper edge of the complete set of opportunities depicted in Figure 6.3. If we followed his 'algorithm' for the different attack method combinations and the payoffs they generate for terrorists who have used them, we would find that the structure of risk and reward that characterises the efficient frontier of attack methods is a concave, positively sloped set. This has been worked out for fatalities and injuries by Phillips (2009) and for media attention by Pohl (2015, 2017).[3] Pohl's (2017) efficient frontier for West German terrorism and media attention for the period 1970–1980 is depicted in Figure 6.4.

Pohl (2017) computed the efficient set, depicted in Figure 6.4, for media attention (newspapers, measured in column inches [c'']). That is, each attack method generated some amount of media attention. In aggregate for the period, the average and standard deviation of media attention as a payoff for each attack method can be computed. Attack methods can be combined and each combination is similarly characterised by an average amount of media attention and standard deviation. The optimisation problem can be solved by applying Markowitz's method and the set of combinations that yields maximum expected media attention for each level of risk can be determined. As Figure 6.4 shows, the classical concave shape emerges from the calculations due to the imperfect correlation of media attention accorded to different attack methods over time. Also plotted in Figure 6.4 are the combinations or portfolios chosen by active groups. The efficient set represents, at any given time, the upper boundary of expected outcomes for each level of risk. The next question that we must ask is how a model of choice fits into this statistical structure of attack method risk and reward. How did the terrorist groups depicted in Figure 6.4 come to choose those particular combinations?

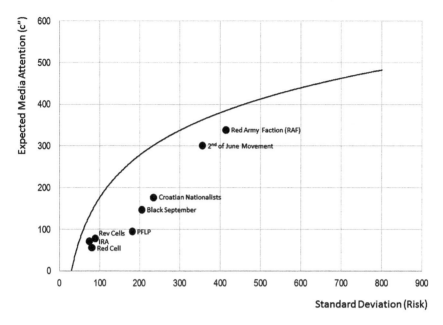

FIGURE 6.4 Markowitz's efficient frontier for West German terrorism and media attention, 1970–1980.

Mean-variance utility: patterns of choice

Markowitz's next question, to which his fellow Nobel Laureate James Tobin (1958) also provided a part of the answer, was what would happen if all decision-makers made their choices based solely on mean and variance (EV). The result was a model of decision-making that we might call a 'computable' method of preference ordering since all that is required is a series of payoffs and the two other things: (1) the mean (μ) and (2) variance (σ^2). If we have the data, we can estimate the order in which a decision-maker will rank alternative risky prospects, in this case combinations of attack methods. This is an alternative to what might be called a 'full' expected utility analysis where the expected utility would be calculated for each possible risky prospect by first converting the outcomes to a utility number then weighting those utility numbers by the probability that the outcome occurs and then, finally, summing over all the outcomes. This requires not only quite a bit of additional calculation time but also additional assumptions about the nature of a decision-maker's utility and assumptions about the probability distribution governing the outcomes of the risky prospects. Mean-variance utility analysis is a pragmatic short cut that nonetheless approximates the preference orderings that would be arrived at by a full utility analysis.[4]

The primary factor shaping the terrorist group's choice in this EV or mean-variance framework is risk aversion. Very risk averse groups will choose an attack method or combination with lower risk. Groups that are not so risk averse will choose an attack method or combination with higher risk. An optimal choice in either case will be located somewhere on the efficient frontier. As terrorist groups learn more about the risk-reward structure of the terrorism context, we would expect a pattern to be observed. That is, there should be a general tendency (for groups that survive for long enough) to converge towards the efficient frontier, remembering that the frontier dynamically changes position. The preferences of different types of terrorist groups along with this general pattern of convergence towards the efficient frontier is depicted in Figure 6.5. The logic complements the real-world data from Figure 6.4 where the terrorist groups can be seen to cluster in different regions. We would explain this clustering by risk aversion. It is also interesting to see just how close most groups managed to get to the efficient frontier. This gives us a strong indication that law enforcement and counter-terrorism agencies need to be aware of the location of the efficient set at any given time.

Preferences for risk and reward are reflected in the decision-maker's indifference curves. In the same manner that an indifference curve map could be superimposed over a budget constraint in neoclassical consumer theory,[5] an indifference curve map can be superimposed over the efficient frontier. This is shown in Figure 6.6. The indifference curves are positively sloped to reflect the fact that higher mean payoffs are required if more risk must be borne. The indifference curves can be steeper or flatter depending on the nature of the decision-maker's risk aversion. Flatter indifference curves mean less risk aversion. The decision-maker is willing to bear more risk for a small increase in the expected payoff.

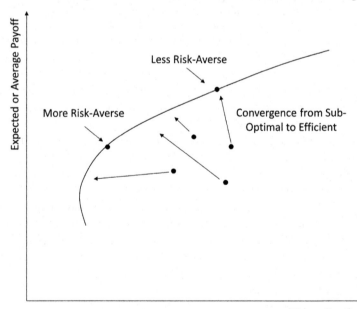

FIGURE 6.5 Terrorist risk aversion and convergence towards the efficient frontier.

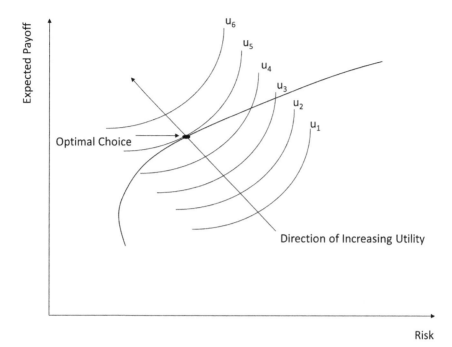

FIGURE 6.6 Indifference curves for mean-variance decisions.

Steeper indifference curves mean greater risk aversion. To entice such a decision-maker to bear more risk, a much greater increment in the expected payoff must be provided. A practical implication for law enforcement, discussed at length by Phillips (2013), is that risk preferences can be revealed by terrorist group choice. If a particular choice is repeatedly observed, the group's risk aversion can be inferred. This may yield additional inferences, including the group's expected future choices and actions.

In making an optimal choice, a risk averse decision-maker need not shun the riskiest attack methods (Phillips 2009; Pohl 2015, 2017). An optimal combination formed by even the most risk averse terrorist group can contain some allocation of resources to the riskiest of the attack methods. Such behaviour is not inconsistent and, in fact, is quite rational. Imperfectly correlated payoffs accruing to different attack methods make it beneficial in terms of risk management to diversify across the spectrum of risk and reward. The choice to do so may not be completely conscious or calculated. It may simply be based on an implicit understanding that it is better not to place all of one's eggs in a single basket combined with a basic understanding that certain attack types appear to yield a certain number of fatalities or a certain amount of media attention. Whatever the case may be, terrorist groups do combine attack methods from up and down the risk-reward trade-off. We have in mean-variance portfolio theory a rationale and explanation for such behaviour.

International terrorism, international diversification

International terrorism was once a new thing. And its 'spread' was a major concern. For example, Brian Jenkins (1974) called international terrorism 'a new kind of warfare'. Midlarsky, Crenshaw & Yoshida (1980) devoted their attention to the factors driving the 'contagion' of international terrorism. In an approach that we have encountered in other places (copycat behaviour), Midlarsky, Crenshaw & Yoshida (1980) and other terrorism researchers following them disregard the agency of the terrorists and the decision-making processes. The terrorism researchers want to depict the decision to operate across borders as the outcome of a pure contagion process. Although there is something elegant about diffusion processes, they are external to the decision-maker. Using them to explain aspects of human action that are the outcome of human decisions leads us to overlook the rationale for those decisions. Carlos the Jackal, Black September and many of the groups that were active in West Germany (Figure 6.4) operated internationally. Apart from the obvious (e.g. that there were targets in different locations), what did they have to gain by doing international terrorism rather than focusing on a particular geographic location?

A simple, yet powerful answer presents itself. What they had to gain was all of the gains from diversification that we have been discussing. It is the same rationale that prompts international diversification among investors. If we were to calculate the efficient set for any payoffs (fatalities, media attention, recruits, supporters, financing etc.), it would be located somewhere in risk-reward space, just like the diagrams we have presented previously. What extra dimension does international diversification add to this picture? It pushes the entire efficient set further to the North-West, allowing higher expected payoffs with less risk. International diversification *works* because the payoffs across different locations are not perfectly positively correlated. An armed assault in Berlin might receive some amount of media attention while an armed assault in Paris receives a different amount. If a group or individual terrorist operates simultaneously or over time across different locations, the overall expected payoffs to such an 'international attack method combination' will be higher for each level of risk than for 'homebound' terrorists. There is no need for a contagion process in our explanation when there are incremental payoffs available even to naïve decision-makers.

Behavioural portfolio theory

The paper[6] that introduced financial economists to BPT is a strange one. After some considerable reflection, the source of the strangeness becomes apparent. At first, when you pick up the paper, you are expecting a method or a tool comparable to MPT but incorporating behavioural insights. You are expecting something that you can use to compute a behavioural portfolio efficient frontier analogous to Markowitz's bullet-shaped set. The ample discussion and formal analysis presented by Shefrin & Statman (2000) never actually gets to the point of providing such a tool and one could be forgiven for setting BPT aside for now to await its further development. This would be a mistake because while the paper does not provide a BPT replacement for MPT, it provides ample insights into how we can use advances in decision theory to understand more fully the decision-making process involving combinations of risky prospects and how that decision-making process may lead to systematic departures from the optimal benchmark provided by MPT. Shefrin & Statman (2000) have provided a pathway for adding deeper behavioural narratives to the MPT framework that we presented earlier.

One thing that usually bothers people about MPT is the idea that decision-makers develop some understanding of the degree to which the payoffs to different risky prospects move up and down together over time (Levy & Markowitz 1979; Tversky & Kahneman 1986; Kroll et al. 1988). That is, that they are aware of and use the correlation structure. If we doubt this, a natural conclusion might be that the correlation structure can be ignored in analysis of decision-making because decision-makers are unaware of it. BPT highlights the folly of this position. The correlation structure is critically important to the risk-reward trade-off and the outcomes that decision-makers will achieve whenever combinations of risky prospects are possible, notwithstanding the fact that they might neglect it. The key point is that even if we think that terrorist groups which form combinations of attack methods neglect the correlation structure, it does not follow that the correlation structure is irrelevant to the outcomes of those combinations of attack methods and can be ignored.[7]

BPT-SA

Shefrin & Statman (2000) explain how the types of decision-maker characteristics encompassed within behavioural models of choice such as Lopes' (1987) SP/A theory[8] and Kahneman & Tversky's (1979) prospect theory lead decision-makers away from the efficient set (though there is a twist to the story that we shall come to in a moment). In their first iteration of BPT, which they call BPT-SA, Shefrin & Statman (2000) develop a picture of the decision-making process in which combinations of risky prospects are formed into a single account (SA) in a manner that is somewhat similar to the mean-variance decision-maker's approach. The correlations *are* considered and the decision-maker prefers a higher mean (E) payoff and lower variance (V). The only psychological variable governing choice in MPT is risk aversion. Following Lopes (1987), Shefrin & Statman (2000) build a BPT where the decision-maker's expectations are distorted by their fears, hopes and aspirations in addition to their risk aversion. The interplay of these factors distorts the decision-maker's view of the opportunities and makes them very concerned about obtaining an outcome above some aspiration level. Once these emotional factors are added to MPT, the model is transformed into BPT-SA. Now a multitude of emotional and psychological variables shape the choices that are made.

Perhaps the most important difference in the choices that might be made by a BPT-SA decision-maker vis-à-vis an MPT-(EV) decision-maker is that it might very well be 'efficient' under some particular circumstances for the BPT-SA decision-maker to choose a risky prospect that has a *low* expected payoff and a very *high* level of risk or variance. While the outcome will probably be a loss, the high level of variance means that there is great upside potential. Choosing such a risky prospect is something that an MPT decision-maker would never knowingly do because such a risky prospect will usually lie on the underneath edge of the opportunity set and will be dominated by many other alternatives. The BPT-SA decision-maker will do so, however, if the high variance is necessary to improve the chances that the aspiration level will be met and there is no equally volatile risky prospect with a higher expected outcome.[9] Only when a situation arises that is analogous to being locked in a casino with just one night to make enough money to meet a high aspiration level should we expect these choices to be made. It is conceivable that an analogous situation could arise for a terrorist group. Allowing decision-makers to have an aspiration level is how BPT-SA can extend the application of MPT.

BPT-MA

BPT-SA is one version of BPT. Shefrin & Statman (2000) also develop BPT-MA, where the decision-maker forms multiple mental accounts (MA). In BPT-MA, decision-makers completely overlook the correlation structure and compartmentalise their choices from among risky prospects, forming one combination in one compartment and another combination in another, never considering the overall combination of risky prospects that has been selected by this process. That people do tend to compartmentalise rather than work in terms of an overall portfolio was an early result from behavioural economics (Thaler 1980, 1985, 1999).

In a classic experiment, Tversky & Kahneman (1981) asked people to imagine a scenario in which they were on their way to see a movie with a ticket in their pocket that cost $20. Upon arriving at the cinema, you find that you have lost your ticket. Do you buy another? Most people say that they would not. Next, Tversky & Kahneman asked their subjects to consider a situation in which they are on their way to the cinema with the cash that they need to buy a ticket in their pocket. Upon arriving at the cinema, you find that you have lost a $20 bill. Do you still buy a ticket? Most people now answer yes. In both cases, the decision-maker has lost $20. So why do people say that they will not buy a ticket in one case and yet say that they will buy it in the other case? Rather than view their overall wealth position as a portfolio, it seems that people compartmentalise their funds into mental accounts. In this example, there is a 'movie account' and a 'cash account'. Losing the ticket and having to buy another is recorded in the movie account. This makes the cost of a ticket $40 instead of $20. Most people seem to think that this is too much to pay to see the movie. Losing the cash, however, is recorded in the cash account as a $20 cash loss while the purchase of the ticket remains a separate $20 expenditure.

BPT-MA draws on this observed behaviour to depict decision-makers as forming combinations of risky prospects in separate distinct mental accounts, each with potentially very different risk-reward characteristics. For example, there might be some state of affairs that is absolutely essential for the decision-maker to achieve (call the mental account 'subsistence'). The combination for this mental account might be very conservative. Next, there might be a desirable but not essential state of affairs that the decision-maker would like to achieve (call the mental account 'comfortable'). The combination designed to achieve this state of affairs might be moderately conservative. Finally, consider some state of affairs that the decision-maker would like to achieve but which he views as a bonus if it were to happen (call the mental account 'bonus'). The combination of risky prospects contained within this mental account might be quite risky by comparison with the other two mental accounts. Hence, what might appear to be a single combination to the outsider looking in is actually three distinct combinations in the mind of the decision-maker.

In thinking about terrorist attack method choice in this way, we are led to consider the possibility that terrorist groups may divide or partition their total set of activities into sub-groupings that have very distinct objectives. Whereas risk aversion and thinking 'holistically' guide behaviour in the Markowitz MPT mean-variance framework, distinct objectives and the perceived likelihood of achieving those distinct objectives guide behaviour in a BPT-MA framework. This provides us with some deeper narratives around the terrorist group's choice to form combinations. For example, terrorist groups might very well be serving different masters with different sets of actions and certainly trying to achieve different objectives. Rather than viewing each action or combination of actions as directed towards a single overarching objective, BPT-MA leads us to consider the nuances of terrorist group decision-making.

Consider the structure of Al-Qaeda's objectives as described by Keeney & von Winterfeldt (2010, pp.1806–1808). Here, the group's objectives are depicted as a hierarchy that develops from shorter-term, more basic objectives to higher-level military objectives. We might use BPT-MA to explain Al-Qaeda's decisions to achieve one set of objectives more basic on the hierarchy through a combination of attacks directed towards American targets in Iraq while simultaneously attempting to achieve a higher-order objective through a combination of attacks directed towards targets inside the United States. Each portfolio is a segment of a layered pyramid each with a particular aspiration level. The decision-maker overlooks the correlation between the layers (Shefrin & Statman 2000, p.149). This is depicted in Figure 6.7.

While ignoring the correlation structure, the BPT-MA decision-maker might or might not make choices that are mean-variance (EV) efficient. That is, the decision-maker's choices might still be on or near the efficient set. One of the most interesting results in this field makes a strong case for why we should expect BPT-MA combinations to be found on the efficient set. By dividing the overall set of activities into compartments with distinct goals, the decision-maker

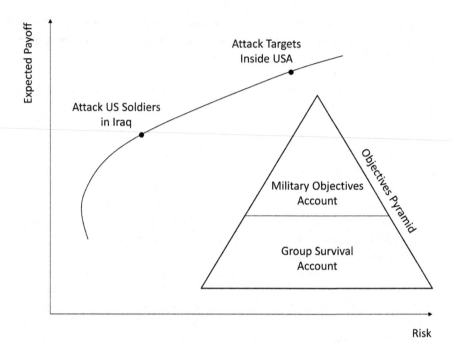

FIGURE 6.7 Al-Qaeda's objectives and choices: a BPT-MA perspective.

Note that there is an element of 'international mental accounting' here. That is, terrorist groups can view different locations as different mental accounts.

confronts a narrower, easier choice problem where he has more time to develop an understanding of the risks and rewards that characterise the available risky prospects as well as the risks that he is willing to bear within a particular compartment. The overall combination, even though the decision-maker never explicitly considers it, may be more efficient than it would be if he tried to form one all-encompassing portfolio (Das et al. 2010). A BPT type of combination may be more efficient than a Markowitz mean-variance combination! This is a behavioural rationale for an orthodox model.[10]

Using BPT and MPT together

That terrorists and terrorist group combine different attack methods is a fact. Unfortunately, the implications of this fact are rarely explored. And the implications are stark. When terrorists combine attack methods, their expected payoffs increase at every level of risk. Remember, too, that this applies to all of the payoffs (fatalities inflicted, media attention, supporters, online recruitment etc.). It is even possible through combination to generate higher payoffs with the same or less risk than before. Law enforcement and counter-terrorism agencies need to take this into account when assessing terrorists' opportunities because these 'benefits of diversification' can be reaped naïvely, without any conscious assessment of the correlation structure. In this chapter, we were at pains to point out these hidden aspects of the structure of the payoffs to different attack methods. The patterns of behaviour that we should expect and that we can now explain are as follows:

1. Terrorists should be expected to combine attack methods. They do so. The gains from diversification due to imperfectly correlated payoffs to attack methods yield higher expected payoffs for every level of risk. These gains can be had naïvely.
2. Terrorists should be expected to diversify internationally when they have the means to do so. They are observed to do so. The 'spread' of international terrorism is not something that must rely on agency-less contagion processes. International diversification expands the terrorists' opportunities, increasing payoffs and decreasing risk.
3. Terrorists' combinations of attack methods should be located along the efficient set. This will be determined by (and give insights into) the terrorists' level of risk aversion.
4. By balancing risk and reward and learning from experience, terrorist groups should converge towards the efficient set. As Pohl's (2015, 2017) work shows, terrorist groups can get remarkably close. Importantly, terrorist groups who are close to the efficient set are likely already above the linear risk-reward trade-off that characterises individual attack methods. Terrorists groups already generate expected payoffs that are higher for each level of risk than terrorism analysts overlooking correlations would anticipate.
5. Mental accounts simplify the decision-making context. While people who use mental accounts formally overlook the correlation structure, the simplification of the context actually improves the efficiency of their decisions. Terrorist groups may partition their objectives (or target locations) into different mental accounts. The end result, though, is likely to be a combination of attack methods that is located near the efficient set.

BPT leads us to expect compartmentalisation of decision-making into distinct mental accounts. Within those mental accounts, quite different levels of risk may be borne by the terrorist group. More than this, the behavioural model opens up new possibilities for describing terrorist choice. In particular, it is not only because decision-makers compartmentalise that we can account for the different levels of risk being borne simultaneously by a single decision-maker. Rather, it is because each compartment or mental account is characterised by a distinct goal that we observe this behaviour. The terrorist group may operate two mental accounts in which one is very conservative and low risk while the other is very aspirational and high risk. The goals that the terrorist group holds can be separated and do not have to be viewed holistically. It wants to succeed but it does not want to risk everything. The result is at least two distinct types of choice characterised by low risk conservative actions on the one hand and higher risk aspirational actions on the other.

This discussion of portfolios highlights for us a broader implication regarding the use of ideas in counter-terrorism and counter-intelligence. One of our themes has been the benefits of diversification in economic analysis. Orthodox and behavioural models as well as the different methodologies that have been used to generate them (e.g. field experiments, pure deduction, reasoning by analogy, laboratory experiments etc.) provide us with a set of frameworks that can be used to guide our decisions and to think about how we are making decisions. We can see from the discussion in this chapter how different things can be learned from different approaches without necessarily declaring that one approach or the other is mistaken or that one approach or the other is better. If we take a position that no single framework or methodology is perfect and that each is characterised by pros and cons, then we must conclude that each single framework or methodology is susceptible to particular errors while holding particular advantages. The errors, of course, can be mitigated by methodological diversification. This type of argument has been put forward by Berg (2003). Using both MPT and BPT provides us with a more diversified narrative with which to describe and better understand portfolio decisions. Either approach taken individually might yield higher rewards but, as we know, this comes with greater risk.

Four dot points to end the chapter

- Terrorist groups diversify. Even if they do this naïvely, it shapes the group's risks and rewards.
- Terrorist groups diversify their attack methods and targets. International terrorism allows further diversification, increasing the payoffs that can be obtained at each level of risk.
- Modern portfolio theory (MPT) is a complete framework for analysing the risks and rewards that terrorist groups confront and the choices that they make.
- Behavioural portfolio theory (BPT) expands on MPT by allowing such things as aspirations and mental accounts to shape decisions.

Notes

1 Dobson and Paine (1977, p.15).
2 The GTD classifies the Munich attack as an 'assassination'.
3 Also see Phillips and Pohl (2012).
4 This has been a hotly contested and much researched sub-field in financial economics. To name just a selection of important papers, see Baron (1977), Bessler, Opfer and Wolff (2017), Borch (1969), Feldstein (1969), Friedman and Savage (1948), Grinblatt and Han (2005), Hakansson (1971), Johnstone and Lindley (2013), Pulley (1983) and Tobin (1969).
5 See Chapter 3.
6 Shefrin and Statman (2000).
7 We should also note that a complete opportunity set computed using the Markowitz MPT approach (depicted in a stylised fashion in Figure 6.2) is *the* opportunity set. A BPT

decision-maker cannot craft anything different from the basic underlying statistical structure of the context.

8 For a discussion of the application of SP/A theory to terrorist choice see Phillips and Pohl (2018).

9 Shefrin and Statman (2000, p.141) create such a situation.

10 Shefrin and Statman (2000) also explore the evolutionary implications. BPT/MA decision-making will not generally be 'growth optimal'. Like mean-variance decision-making, it depends on how closely the type of decision-making that is applied approximates the choices of the logarithmic utility maximiser.

References

Baron, D.P. 1977. On the Utility Theoretic Foundations of Mean-Variance Analysis. *Journal of Finance*, 32, 1683–1697.

Berg, N. 2003. Normative Behavioural Economics. *Journal of Socio-Economics*, 32, 411–427.

Bessler, W., Opfer, H. & Wolff, D. 2017. Multi-Asset Portfolio Optimisation and Out-of-Sample Performance: An Evaluation of Black-Litterman, Mean-Variance and Naïve Diversification Approaches. *European Journal of Finance*, 23, 1–30.

Borch, K. 1969. A Note on Uncertainty and Indifference Curves. *Review of Economic Studies*, 36, 1–4.

Das, S., Markowitz, H., Scheid, J. & Statman, M. 2010. Portfolio Optimisation with Mental Accounts. *Journal of Financial and Quantitative Analysis*, 45, 311–334.

Dobson, C., & Paine, R. (1977). *The Carlos Complex: A Pattern of Violence*. London: Hodder and Stoughton.

Feldstein, M.S. 1969. Mean-Variance Analysis in the Theory of Liquidity Preference and Portfolio Selection. *Review of Economic Studies*, 36, 5–12.

Friedman, M. & Savage, L.J. 1948. The Utility Analysis of Choices Involving Risk. *Journal of Political Economy*, 56, 279–304.

Grinblatt, M. & Han, B. 2005. Prospect Theory, Mental Accounting and Momentum. *Journal of Financial Economics*, 78, 311–339.

Hakansson, N.H. 1971. Multi-Period Mean-Variance Analysis: Towards a General Theory of Portfolio Choice. *Journal of Finance*, 26, 857–884.

Jenkins, B. International Terrorism: A New Kind of Warfare. Santa Monica, CA: RAND, P-5261, 1974.

Johnstone, D. & Lindley, D. 2013. Mean-Variance and Expected Utility: The Borch Paradox. *Statistical Science*, 28, 223–237.

Kahneman, D. & Tversky, A. 1979. Prospect Theory: An Analysis of Decision under Risk. *Econometrica*, 47, 263–291.

Keeney, G.L. & von Winterfeldt, D. 2010. Identifying and Structuring the Objectives of Terrorists. *Risk Analysis*, 30, 1803–1816.

Kroll, Y., Levy, H. & Rapoport, A. 1988. Experimental Tests of the Separation Theorem and the Capital Asset Pricing Model. *American Economic Review*, 78, 500–518.

Levy, H. & Markowitz, H.M. 1979. Approximating Expected Utility by a Function of Mean and Variance. *American Economic Review*, 69, 308–317.

Lopes, L.L. 1987. Between Hope and Fear: The Psychology of Risk. *Advances in Experimental Social Psychology*, 20, 255–295.

Markowitz, H.M. 1952. Portfolio Selection. *Journal of Finance*, 7, 77–91.

Midlarsky, M.I., Crenshaw, M. & Yoshida, F. 1980. Why Violence Spreads: The Contagion of International Terrorism. *International Studies Quarterly*, 24, 262–298.

Phillips, P.J. 2009. Applying Portfolio Theory to the Analysis of Terrorism: Computing the Set of Attack Method Combinations From Which the Rational Terrorist Group Will Choose in Order to Maximise Injuries and Fatalities. *Defence and Peace Economics*, 20, 193–213.

Phillips, P.J. 2013. *In Pursuit of the Lone Wolf Terrorist*. New York: Nova.

Phillips, P.J. & Pohl, G. 2018. The Deferral of Attacks: SP/A Theory as a Model of Terrorist Choice When Losses Are Inevitable. *Open Economics*, 1, 71–85.

Pohl, G. 2015. Media and Terrorist Choice: A Risk-Reward Analysis. *Journal of Applied Security Research*, 10, 60–76.

Pohl, G. 2017. Terrorist Choice and the Media. PhD Thesis, University of Southern Queensland, Australia.

Pulley, L.B. 1983. Mean-Variance Approximations to Expected Logarithmic Utility. *Operations Research*, 31, 685–696.

Shefrin, H. & Statman, M. 2000. Behavioural Portfolio Theory. *Journal of Financial and Quantitative Analysis*, 35, 127–151.

Surette, R., Hansen, K. & Noble, G. 2009. Measuring Media Oriented Terrorism. *Journal of Criminal Justice*, 37, 360–370.

Thaler, R.H. 1980. Toward a Positive Theory of Consumer Choice. *Journal of Economic Behaviour and Organisation*, 1, 39–60.

Thaler, R.H. 1985. Mental Accounting and Consumer Choice. *Marketing Science*, 4, 199–214.

Thaler, R.H. 1999. Mental Accounting Matters. *Journal of Behavioural Decision-Making*, 12, 183–206.

Tobin, J. 1958. Liquidity Preference as Behaviour towards Risk. *Review of Economic Studies*, 25, 65–86.

Tobin, J. 1969. Comment on Borch and Feldstein. *Review of Economic Studies*, 36, 13–14.

Tversky, A. & Kahneman, D. 1981. The Framing of Decisions and the Psychology of Choice. *Science*, 211, 453–458.

Tversky, A. & Kahneman, 1986. Rational Choice and the Framing of Decisions. *Journal of Business*, 59, S251–S278.

7

CYCLES IN TERRORISM AND EVOLUTIONARY STABILITY

In the wake of 11 September 2001, Americans can be forgiven for thinking that terrorist threats come from abroad and have a distinctly Islamic character. In fact, home grown terrorists of all kinds continue to flourish in the US. Case in point: The Earth Liberation Front (ELF). ELF has become the most active and the most destructive environmental terrorist group in the United States. According to the Federal Bureau of Investigation (FBI), the Earth Liberation Front, together with its sister organization, the Animal Liberation Front (ALF), in the past 6 years has committed more than 600 criminal acts that have resulted in more than $43 million in damages. Moreover, attacks have been perpetrated in virtually every region of the US against a wide variety of targets.[1]

In March 2001, the FBI ranked the ELF as the top domestic terror threat. The group, which emerged in the United Kingdom as *Earth First!* less than ten years before, had quickly swept through Europe and arrived in the United States in 1996. Practicing a form of 'leaderless resistance' based on disconnected cells, not dissimilar in nature to that used by the Revolutionary Cells in West Germany during the 1970s, the ELF had initiated a wave of criminal actions. The list includes 49 actions between 1999 and 2004 but, interestingly, only 18 actions since. The ELF's terrorist actions exhibited an initial surge followed by a marked subsidence. This pattern, not uncommon for terrorist groups,[2] is a part of a broader cycle of terrorist activity that we can observe. The actions of individual groups, including their emergence, their choices of operations and their eventual subsidence, generates an oscillating periodicity in the total record of terrorist incidences.

Many explanations have been given for 'cycles' in terrorism.[3] First, following a successful attack, contagion and copycat effects might stimulate further attacks until law enforcement introduces countermeasures that lead to a downturn and so on periodically. Second, attack and counterattack processes may drive cycles. A group plans an attack, which turns into an offensive, which turns into a campaign, which might encourage other groups, which provokes a reaction from the government, which eventually subsides, which leads to an opportunity for another offensive. Third, terrorism might be characterised by economies of scale. This leads to 'bunching' of attacks, which means that we will see periodic bursts of activity followed by steep declines. Fourth, upswings in terrorism may be due to precipitating events, which if they occur periodically, will cause cycles in terrorism. Fifth, technological advances on both the terrorism and counterterrorism sides may lead to upswings and eventual downswings as countermeasures are developed. None of these explanations is a theory of cycles in terrorism and most of them are secondary to a more fundamental driving force that can be found within the interplay between the decision-making processes of terrorist groups and the struggle for survival governed by the external environment in which a terrorist group operates.

Cycles in terrorism, just like cycles or patterns in other datasets, remain a constant source of fascination. Consider the 'cyclical' behaviour that characterises terrorism in just two periods: 1970–1980 and 2010–2017. The emergence and proliferation of left-wing terrorist groups during the 1970s produced a surge in terrorist activity. Figure 7.1 shows how Western Europe experienced terrorism during the 1970s. Oscillations within this period of time are interesting enough but these are merely a part of a bigger cycle where a period of intense activity was followed by a great lull. We know that terrorism of a different kind emerged in the later 1990s and continues to the present day. It too appears to exhibit its own cycles and these cycles also are merely a part of a bigger cyclical oscillation in terrorist activity. Figure 7.2 shows how Western Europe has experienced terrorism more recently. Despite its considerable brutality, the peaks of violence reached in the 1970s have not been surpassed.

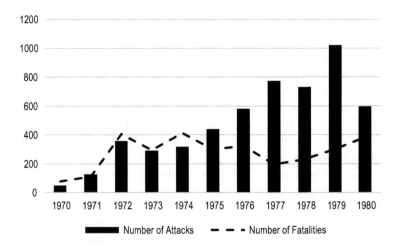

FIGURE 7.1 Terrorist activity Western Europe, 1970–1980.

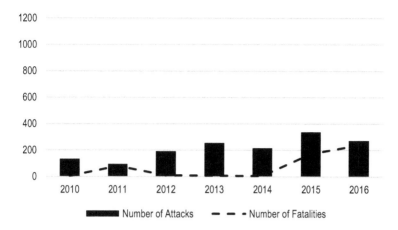

FIGURE 7.2 Terrorist activity Western Europe, 2010–2017.

Does this cyclical behaviour possess any structure that would enable us to predict what is going to happen next? In all likelihood, the terrorism context is a chaotic and complex system in the sense of Lorenz (1964). If so, it has an order but the order itself produces irregular and unstable fluctuations that do not allow for point prediction. Nevertheless, if there is an order it will have to have something to do with the structure of the choices that terrorists make. The explanations for cycles that we listed above are not theories of cycles because they have no fully worked out connections with the decision processes that govern terrorist choice.

How can we develop a theory of the order that underlies the overlapping cycles of terrorist activity? We can start by asking a preliminary question that is at once very basic and very penetrating. Is the ebb and flow in the brutality that characterises the terrorism over time a pattern that is consistent with any of the models of the decision-making process? The answer to this question lies in the relationship between decision-making under risk and uncertainty and the fitness or survival of the decision-makers. Evolutionary concepts have been woven into the very fabric of von Neumann and Morgenstern's (1947) game theory, so much so that evolutionary game theory is now a major research program in mathematics, economics and theoretical biology. Wild and Taylor (2004, p.2345) summarise:

> The theory of games is now standard fare in evolutionary biology. Game theoretic models of evolution describe the fitness of a mutant who competes in a social group, composed mainly of normal (wild-type) individuals. From the description of fitness, certain strategies are identified as being 'evolutionarily stable'. Such strategies are typically regarded as the end result of evolution.

Using game theory structures as analogues for natural contexts, evolutionary game theorists try to identify those strategies that are 'fit' within those game theory structures and, by analogy, the real-world contexts to which the games map. Falster & Westoby (2003, p.338) elaborate:

> Evolutionary game theory provides a formal, logical framework for investigating traits whose success is frequency dependent, that is, where the success of a strategy depends on which other strategies are present ... The characteristic thought experiment is to introduce a novel strategy, at low density, into the mixture of strategies already present. The question is whether novel strategies can increase from rarity.

A strategy consistent with fitness or survival is called an evolutionarily stable strategy (ESS). The ESS, if it exists in a particular context, provides, as Falster & Westoby (2003, p.337) explain,

> a prediction about what we might expect to observe in communities in which both natural selection and colonisation from elsewhere can potentially introduce a wide range of alternative strategies. The prediction depends on the traits and processes that the model represents as being decisive in competition and co-existence.

And Taylor & Jonker (1978) elaborate:

> The basic idea is this: the more fit a strategy is at any moment, the more likely it is to be employed in the future. The mechanism behind this is either that individuals tend to switch to strategies that are doing well, or that individuals bear offspring who tend to use the same strategies as their parents, and the fitter the individual, the more numerous his offspring. In any case, as time goes on, the strategy mix may change. A dynamic game theory will look at how the [set of strategies] moves with time, and will look for equilibrium states and examine their stability.

John Maynard Smith's (1982) work provided the foundations. In economics, the idea of using evolutionary game theory followed quickly on the heels of Smith's work. The scene had already been set by Hirshleifer (1977), who, with his long article titled 'Economics from a Biological Viewpoint' had argued that economic analysis could benefit greatly by applying evolutionary games to a variety of contexts.[4] It is somewhat surprising that evolutionary game theory has not been applied as widely as one might expect in defence economics, especially given Hirshleifer's prominence in the field[5] and Smith's early work on animal conflict.[6] It took the better part of a decade before the smattering of articles in the economics literature accumulated enough critical mass to attract the interest of a wider audience of economists. Despite the similarities in technique and mathematics there are a number of differences between what biologists find interesting and what economists find interesting. This made direct importation of the ideas somewhat clunky. Friedman (1991, p.638), in his article promoting the use of evolutionary game theory in economics, explained:

> Economists and other social scientists can, I believe, usefully employ many of the ideas introduced by the biologists, but the biologists' formal structure needs to be adapted and extended. A fundamental point is that biologists almost always deal with the genetic mechanism of natural selection .... For economists the social mechanisms of learning and imitation are usually more important than the genetic mechanism.

By the early 1990s, in addition to Friedman's (1991) article, Blume & Easley (1992) published one of the more far-reaching applications of the principles of evolutionary game theory to economics, especially market behaviour. They presented a number of important conclusions, including the more surprising one, that rational behaviour (expected utility maximising behaviour) is not necessarily evolutionarily fit behaviour and evolutionarily fit behaviour is not necessarily expected utility maximising behaviour. It depends on what sort of utility function the decision-maker is attempting to maximise. In arriving at this conclusion Blume & Easley (1992) identified a number of 'fitness' rules and highlighted the importance of the 'growth optimal' rule for agents competing on the basis of the share of payoffs they can accumulate in a given context. This is significant because it draws our attention towards the relevance of share of payoffs and away from absolute magnitude of payoffs.

Different strategies and different ESS result in different observable dynamics. We are interested in one particular aspect of the observable dynamics: the ebb and flow of brutality and the attention that it receives. Is there a fitness rule that terrorist groups might be following that is consistent with this ebb and flow? If so, what is the relationship of this rule to orthodox and behavioural models of decision-making under risk and uncertainty? The answer to the first question is yes. A fitness rule that is consistent with the ebb and flow of inflicted brutality that characterises the terrorism context is the 'growth optimal' rule applied to the *share* that each terrorist group can claim—and receive credit and attention for—from the total number of fatalities inflicted by the aggregate of terrorist activity. The answer to the second question is that the growth optimal rule is analogous to the maximisation of logarithmic expected utility.[7] As such, we can indeed find a basis within economics and decision theory for the observable dynamics that characterise the brutality of global terrorism.

'Share' and survival

Not the terrorist group's absolute amount of accumulated successes (attacks, fatalities inflicted, and media attention garnered etc.) but its share of aggregate successes is the key to its survival. To keep things simple, let us assume that the terrorist group's primary operational expectation revolves around the number of fatalities that its actions will inflict and the amount of attention the action will receive. The neoclassical model implies that more is always better for the terrorist group and we have previously seen that satiation is viewed suspiciously by some economists. However, it is not completely accurate to equate fitness or survival with a terrorist group strategy that is always focused on striving to increase the *absolute* impact of its actions or its absolute level of accumulated payoffs. Rather, a fitness rule or ESS is more likely to be characterised by a strategy to maximise the growth of a terrorist group's *share* of inflicted fatalities and attention. We can reasonably expect terrorist groups to be focused on their 'share'. Shares of payoffs rather than absolute payoffs have been found to capture the attention of decision-makers in other settings.[8]

That an ESS might emerge from relative rather than absolute payoffs is not surprising for reasons that are even more fundamental. Analogous situations can be found in ecology. Falster & Westoby (2003, p.337) highlight the importance of relative vis-à-vis absolute advantages in the struggle for survival. Height for plants is extremely important because it will usually determine the plant's access to light. The competition for light is critical in densely forested and canopied environments. A maximum canopy height for different species may range from just a few centimetres to more than 50 metres but this maximum is not driven ever higher by competition and natural selection. Height leads to benefits but also involves costs and there is no need for plants to achieve the tallest possible height. A plant that can extend its height just marginally above the others will hold an advantage. When the plants that are already present are short, a new species gains an advantage by being short too, but marginally taller than the others. When the plants that are already present are tall, once more it is not the absolute maximum height to which a new species may be able to grow that will determine its competitive advantage. It can stop once it has exceeded the others by some degree even if its structure would permit greater height. When the average height of existing plants falls,[9] new plants can establish themselves at lower heights and vice versa.[10]

Competition focused on the share of payoffs rather than absolute payoffs will shape and be shaped by the overall structure of activity that characterises the terrorism context during a given period. It will also be shaped by the ways in which terrorist activities are covered and presented by the media. A pattern prediction emerges from a consideration of each individual terrorist group's attempts to secure its share of inflicted fatalities and recognition for its actions. This pattern is the cyclical ebb and flow of violence or, more accurately, spirals upwards and downwards in aggregate brutality. In economics, the analysis of the cyclicality of terrorism—the number of attacks, not necessarily the number of fatalities inflicted or the amount of publicity received—has been a longstanding research program (Cauley & Im 1988; Enders, Parise & Sandler 1992; Enders & Sandler 1999, 2002). The fatalities inflicted by terrorism is a series characterised by even more pronounced spirals. Figure 7.3 charts the annual global percentage change (year to year) in fatalities inflicted by acts of terrorism (from GTD).

In some times and places, it will be perfectly rational and evolutionarily stable for a terrorist group to decrease the intensity of its brutality. The key point is that

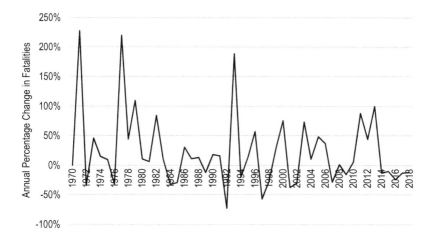

FIGURE 7.3 Annual percentage change, total global terrorism fatalities, 1970–2019.

if brutality is spiralling in one direction or the other, there will be a rational and evolutionarily stable way to respond. When brutality and the media attention that it receives increases overall, and no one can deny that this happens from time to time, each individual terrorist group must choose how to respond. Reducing or maintaining its current level of activity during a period in which brutality is increasing will see a diminution in the terrorist group's share of inflicted brutality and recognition. If the terrorist group tries to maintain or enhance its relative share of brutality and recognition, it can do so only by attempting to increase the brutality of its actions or its number of actions or both and we should observe such attempts. When the brutality cycle turns downwards, the terrorist group can maintain or even grow its share of inflicted brutality with *less* brutal actions or *less* activity.

The initial upward movement in aggregate inflicted brutality to which individual terrorist groups respond may have any number of different causes. It could be as straightforward as an attack with an accidentally high number of fatalities. It does not necessarily result from a deliberate attempt by one group to escalate its brutality though, of course, it may.[11] The initial decline could also have many causes. Most straightforwardly, a government's targeting of the resources of a particularly violent terrorist group that reduces the capability of that group simultaneously reduces the intensity of the contest for share and recognition. Sharp increases and decreases in brutality and violence are an observable feature of global terrorism and it is this very sharpness that is consistent with attempts to maximise brutality share rather than absolute brutality, though at times it will be difficult to distinguish between the two.

The growth of each group's share of the payoffs accumulating in aggregate to all groups in the context is critical to its individual fitness. It is within this tumult that terrorist groups emerge and fade away. Some experience very long life cycles and some experience very short life cycles. When brutality is spiralling upwards, maintenance and growth of a terrorist group's share of brutality will prompt some groups to engage in a larger number of actions or engage in actions that are more brutal. Other groups may be unwilling or unable to compete and may quickly become irrelevant as their share of activity and brutality shrinks and their share of publicity goes along with it. Members of these groups, which are in danger of losing their identities, may form new, more brutal groups, breaking away from their existing groups and leaving behind the decision-makers whose preferences are inconsistent with survival in more brutal terrorism contexts. Cycles in activity and brutality and cycles in the lifespans of terrorist groups are inextricably linked together.

Fitness and risk preference

Fitness is not detached from the group's attack method choices, its decision-making under risk and uncertainty. Whether or not the terrorist group survives depends on contextual factors and its own decisions. Decisions that are consistent with any identifiable ESS are not necessarily aligned with the group's preferences. Engaging in actions that are more brutal necessarily involves taking more risk because there is a positive relationship between fatalities inflicted and the possibility that the actual number will diverge from what was expected. The terrorist group's decision-makers may be unwilling or unable to plan and perpetrate actions in a manner that is consistent with the maximisation of the growth rate of the group's share of inflicted brutality. Although it is tempting to think that the terrorist group will always be compelled towards evolutionarily stable behaviour, the maximisation of brutality share and recognition is equivalent to a particular type of rational behaviour that not all groups will exhibit. The type of rational behaviour to which we are referring is the maximisation of *logarithmic expected utility*.

Despite being the classic representation of rational and optimal behaviour, not all expected utility maximising behaviour is consistent with fitness and survival. Blume & Easley (1992) concluded that fitness rules need not be rational and rational rules need not be fit. One type of rational behaviour that is consistent with a fitness rule based on the growth of relative share is the maximisation of logarithmic expected utility. With low and constant relative risk aversion, the terrorist group with logarithmic utility will choose actions that grow its expected share at the maximum rate. More risk averse groups or groups that exhibit increasing risk aversion, even if they maximise their utility, will avoid the types or numbers of actions necessary to grow their shares at the maximum rate. The extinction of these more risk averse groups is not guaranteed, just as the survival of any logarithmic utility maximising groups is not guaranteed. But while brutality is expanding, the share of inflicted fatalities and recognition gathered by logarithmic utility maximisers is expected to grow and the share gathered by the more risk averse groups is expected to shrink.

Let us see what happens in a dynamic context in which two groups attempt to maximise their share of inflicted brutality. Table 7.1 helps us to keep track of the

TABLE 7.1 Upward and downward brutality spirals: numbers of fatalities inflicted

A	+2	+3	+24	+0	+10	+5	+1
B	+5	+7	+17	+10	+0	+5	+0
Running total	7	17	58	68	78	88	89
Cumulative % share (A, B)	(0.71, 0.29)	(0.71, 0.29)	(0.50, 0.50)	(0.57, 0.43)	(0.50, 0.50)	(0.50, 0.50)	(0.51, 0.49)

numbers used in the example. Imagine in the first instance that a terrorist group called 'A' and one other group called 'B' initially start with zero payoffs and a zero percent share of the context:

- In period one, Group B perpetrates an attack that inflicts five fatalities while Group A perpetrates an attack that inflicts two fatalities. There is a total seven inflicted fatalities and Group B has 71 percent of the payoffs and Group A has 29 percent (approximately).
- In period two, Group A needs to inflict at least three fatalities to reach at least a half-share, even if Group B does nothing. Group B, however, wants to maintain its share at the current level and recognises that Group A must aim for at least three. If so, Group B will aim for at least seven. If this state of affairs eventuates without a further counter-response from Group A, Group A will find that its share has remained at 29 percent and it has failed, so far, to increase it.
- In period three, if Group A inflicted seven fatalities and Group B did nothing, Group A would obtain a half share. However, Group A has learned that Group B will try to maintain its share and Group A will need to 'surprise' Group B.
- If Group B expects Group A to aim for seven fatalities, Group B's response is to inflict 17 in order to maintain its share at around 71 percent. To surprise Group B (and assuming no further counter-responses) Group A must aim for at least 24 fatalities. And so on.
- Each group's attempt to survive forces the overall brutality of the context higher. The total fatalities per period in this scenario have risen from 7 to 58, and that is without further counter-responses.

Brutality spirals downwards as well as upwards. A particularly violent group may be impacted by a military retaliation lose key personnel or simply run out of resources. The brutality that characterises the context begins to fall and the process described previously works in reverse. Imagine that group B is impacted by a counter-terrorism military operation. When we left off, before the black dividing line in Table 7.1, 58 fatalities had been cumulatively inflicted and Group A had a 50 percent share:

- In period four, Group B is unable to respond as strongly as it might have and only inflicts 10 fatalities. The context is characterised by 68 fatalities and Group A falls back to a 43 percent share.

- However, in period five Group A can now maintain its share with less brutal actions than in previous periods. Group A can engage in an action that inflicts 10 fatalities and restore a 50 percent share.
- If Group B responds with five fatalities, Group A again only needs to inflict five fatalities to maintain its share.

The spiral where each successive attack must be more brutal than the last is broken and if Group B's capability is impaired altogether then it is clear that Group A can wind back its activity and still dominate.

Brutality, life cycle and contest

It is during upward spirals in brutality that the struggle for survival is most intense. When brutality is high, we must expect more brutality from terrorist groups that would seek to maintain and grow their share of inflicted fatalities and the attention that is accorded to them. Although there may be external constraints that prevent the terrorist group from perpetrating actions consistent with the growth of its share of inflicted brutality, it may also be that the group's decision-makers are unwilling to allocate resources towards such actions. In this case, it is the group's decision-making, which may be perfectly rational, and not necessarily the group's resources that prevent it from pursuing and prevailing in a contest with other terrorist groups.

Rationality or optimisation is costly, just as height is costly for plants (Conlisk 1980; Abreu & Sethi 2003). Reasoning from within the expected utility framework explains why a previously brutal group may fail to keep up with newer, even more brutal, groups during a period of upward spiralling brutality. Again, it is not necessarily any impediment to the group's resources that may be responsible but a logical and rational response to previous gains. A group that has been successful in the past and maximises a utility function that is characterised by increasing relative risk aversion will decrease its proportion of higher risk to lower risk attack methods as its payoffs accumulate. Purely because it has been brutal in the past, such a group may be less brutal in the future. If this coincides with a period of generally increasing brutality in the terrorism context, this previously dominant group will be noticeable in its decline as other groups emerge to take its place.

It is not surprising to learn that terrorist groups are more likely to claim responsibility for particular actions in contexts where there are many active terrorist groups (Hoffman, 2010). However, the matter might be more subtle than it appears in Hoffman's study. The claiming of responsibility should be expected to be a more commonly observed behaviour, not simply when the number of terrorist groups active in a context is larger, but when the brutality characterising the context is greater. Higher brutality may or may not be associated with a larger number of active groups if the majority of those groups are not particularly capable. Regardless of the political, ideological or religious objectives that terrorist groups have set for themselves, perpetrating acts of terrorism and ensuring that credit is appropriated is essential to the terrorist group's identity and survival as a *terrorist* group. The group's share of inflicted fatalities is zero if it does not receive the recognition for having inflicted them.

Cycles in terrorist brutality may be explained at least partially by the life cycle dynamics that characterise terrorist groups.[12] It is not only cyclical brutality but also spiralling brutality that captures our attention. The struggle for survival, the struggle for 'share', is consistent with a cyclicality in brutality that exhibits sharp upward and downward movements over time. When brutality in the context begins to increase, each group must become increasingly brutal and increasingly publicity savvy to survive. Not all groups will be able to follow the more brutal groups as brutality spirals upwards. This may not be due to a lack of resources but can be entirely due to rational, utility maximising, decision-making. During such periods, new groups will emerge, some born out of existing groups, as members realise that the struggle for survival is being won by others. When brutality subsides, even marginally, terrorist groups can maintain or increase their share by engaging in fewer actions or less brutal actions and brutality may spiral downwards as precipitously as it spiralled upwards, during which some groups forge and other groups lose their identity.

Resolving the problem of cycles

Although some political scientists like Martha Crenshaw (1991) and Audrey Cronin (2006) have written about the life cycle and ultimate decline of terrorist groups, the technical analysis of terrorism cycles has been dominated by defence economists. There is a long list of studies, including that of Im, Cauley & Sandler (1987), Enders, Parise and Sandler (1992), Enders & Sandler (1999, 2000, 2002) and Faria (2003), which are all very similar in nature. They all use econometric or statistical techniques that were cutting-edge at the time the studies were undertaken and they all determine that there are indeed cycles in terrorism. For example, Im, Cauley & Sandler (1987) applied spectral analysis, which is a technique for detecting periodicities in data, and found a cycle with a periodicity of 28 months in duration in the time series of all events. There is no doubt about it. Terrorist activity oscillates. Within an overarching cycle, there are oscillations for particular attack types, particular groups, particular types of groups and particular outcomes such as brutality or media attention. The problem lies in explaining why this oscillation is observed.

While we were able to list several plausible explanations at the outset of this chapter, none of these explanations is grounded in the microeconomic theory of group decision-making. Such grounding is the standard in modern economics,[13] and certainly in psychology. From a perspective of evolutionary economics and biology, the explanations fail to consider the dual interaction of micro-level decision-making and group dynamics in producing macro-level cycles. In mainstream economics (vis-à-vis defence economics), the 'proper' approach that is taught to graduate students is that econometric analysis must formally test hypotheses derived from economic theory (Summers 1991, p.129). However, as Summers

(1991, p.130) notes, successful econometric research has not been constrained by this approach and many important contributions have been made by more pragmatic applications. In the case of terrorism cycles, the detection of periodicities is an important innovation because it tells us that there is a structure to the multitude of decisions that produce the outcomes we observe. The task of searching for and presenting a theory of terrorism cycles will not be a fruitless one.

We have presented a theory of terrorism cycles, or at least the foundations for a theory, that is based on the micro foundations of terrorist decision-making and the group dynamics that emerge from selection, survival and fitness in a context characterised by a struggle with an external environment. First, we recognise that all of the oscillations that we observe are the result of decisions made in an environment characterised by risk and uncertainty. Without people making decisions, there would be no terrorism. Without risk and uncertainty, there would be no variability over time (and no surprises for either the terrorist group or law enforcement agencies). Second, we noted that 'share' rather than 'absolute' outcomes is the relevant payoff variable in an evolutionary system. There would be no need for a terrorist group to use resources to maximise absolute outcomes in a context where no other groups or an adversarial government existed. Third, we tried to find a micro foundation for maximising 'share' and discovered that evolutionary game theory provided the answer. A terrorist group that attempts to maximise a logarithmic utility function will display the evolutionarily fit characteristics consistent with maximising share. Fourth, we noted that not all groups would be characterised by logarithmic utility and for reasons that include risk aversion, will not engage in the amount or types of terrorist actions consistent with survival.

Putting all of these things together, cycles punctuated by spirals up and down in terrorist activity is a pattern that is to be expected when terrorist groups make decisions in a context where 'share' of brutality is the relevant payoff. More terrorism is necessary to maintain or grow a share during an up-spiral while less is necessary during a down-spiral. We also expect terrorist groups to exhibit life cycles, with groups more closely represented by logarithmic utility maximisation surviving the longest while those that are too risk averse or represented by some other unfit utility function fail to survive. Even groups that make perfectly rational and optimal decisions consistent with the maximisation of their utility functions may not survive if those utility functions are not fit. In a context populated by these different groups, all competing for share, we will see a pattern of cycles in both terrorist activity and terrorist group lifespans. Initial surges in terrorism will prompt additional surges, not because of any general contagion-type effect, but because each group as a decision-making unit responds to the implications for the group's survival in such changing circumstances.

That leaves one last question that we have only vaguely answered. That is, where does an initial surge in terrorism come from? We mentioned that this might come from something as simple as an unexpectedly successful attack. However, we can provide a deeper answer based on Phillips's (2011) work on terrorist group life cycles. Terrorist groups compete for grassroots supporters. Because those grassroots supporters face a real or psychological switching cost in abandoning the group to which they initially give their support, competition for grassroots support is most intense when the terrorist group first emerges and when supporters are not yet committed. When a new group enters the context, there is intense competition and terrorist activity. This can subside and re-emerge periodically as the contest continues. In a situation where there are already terrorist groups operating in a more or less stable cyclical pattern competing for share, the entry of an entirely new group or the establishment of a splinter group with its need to garner grassroots support through intense action leads to an up-spiral that initiates the processes that we have described.

Four dot points to end the chapter

- Cycles in terrorist activity, including spirals upwards and downwards in violence, might be explained by terrorist groups' efforts to maximise their 'share' of the payoffs (supporters, prestige etc.).
- The pursuit of 'share' is a fundamental concept in evolutionary game theory. In short, it is a fitness rule.
- Economists have found that not all expected utility maximisers are fit and vice versa. The maximisation of a logarithmic utility function is fit behaviour because it leads to the maximisation of share.
- When violence escalates, competition among groups for share will see an upward spiral in terrorist activity. In such periods of time, groups that are more brutal may emerge as other groups fade away.

Notes

1 Leader and Probst (2003).
2 Phillips (2011) provides a theory and explanation of this phenomenon.
3 Discussed by Enders, Parise and Sandler (1992, p.308).
4 Also see Haigh (1975).
5 See Sandler (2006).
6 Maynard Smith and Price (1973).
7 This an insight attributable to Blume and Easley (1992).
8 Eaton and Eswaran (2003, p.850) state: 'Persistent experimental findings in game theory suggest that players assess their well-being not entirely in terms of their absolute payoffs; some weight is put on relative payoffs'. Also see Bolton and Ockenfels (2000).
9 Patches of forest or jungle may be cleared by human force, by storms and wind or simply by the death of large trees that destroy a large section of the canopy as they fall.
10 For example, see Putz (1984).
11 The process may be viewed as a contest such as that described by Caruso and Schneider (2013) with elements of imitation. Within evolutionary game theory, players may decide to imitate the rule or behaviour exhibited by others. Imitation, in some cases, may be an ESS (Ohtsuki & Nowak 2008).
12 See Crenshaw (1991), Cronin (2006), Phillips (2011, 2016) and Becker (2017).
13 See, for example, Diamond (1984) and van den Bergh and Gowdy (2003).

References

Abreu, D. & Sethi, R. 2003. Evolutionary Stability in a Reputational Model of Bargaining. *Games and Economic Behaviour*, 44, 195–216.

Becker, M. 2017. Why Violence Abates: Imposed and Elective Declines in Terrorist Attacks. *Terrorism and Political Violence*, 29, 215–235.

Blume, L. & Easley, D. 1992. Evolution and Market Behaviour. *Journal of Economic Theory*, 58, 9–40.

Bolton, G.E. & Ockenfels, A. 2000. ERC: A Theory of Equity, Reciprocity and Competition. *American Economic Review*, 90, 166–193.

Caruso, Raul & Friedrich Schneider 2013. Brutality of Jihadist Terrorism: A Contest Theory Perspective and Empirical Evidence in the Period 2002–2010. *Journal of Policy Modeling*, 35, 685–696.

Cauley, J. & Im, E.I. 1988. Intervention Policy Analysis of Skyjackings and Other Terrorist Incidents. *American Economic Review Papers and Proceedings*, 78, 27–31.

Conlisk, J. 1980. Costly Optimisers versus Cheap Imitators. *Journal of Economic Behaviour and Organisation*, 1, 275–293.

Crenshaw, M. 1991. How Terrorism Declines. *Terrorism and Political Violence*, 3, 69–87.

Cronin, A.K. 2006. How Al-Qaida Ends: The Decline and Demise of Terrorist Groups. *International Security*, 31, 7–48.

Diamond, P.A. 1984. *A Search-Equilibrium Approach to the Micro Foundations of Macroeconomics*. Cambridge, MA: MIT Press.

Eaton, B.C. & Eswaran, M. 2003. The Evolution of Preferences and Competition: A Rationalisation of Veblen's Theory of Invidious Comparisons. *Canadian Journal of Economics*, 36, 832–859.

Enders, W. & Sandler, T. 1999. Transnational Terrorism in the Post-Cold War Era. *International Studies Quarterly*, 43, 145–167.

Enders, W. & Sandler, T. 2000. Is Transnational Terrorism Becoming More Threatening? *Journal of Conflict Resolution*, 44, 307–332.

Enders, W. & Sandler, T. 2002. Patterns of Transnational Terrorism, 1970 to 1999: Alternative Time Series Estimates. *International Studies Quarterly*, 46, 145–165.

Enders, W., Parise, G.F. & Sandler, T. 1992. A Time-Series Analysis of Transnational Terrorism: Trends and Cycles. *Defence Economics*, 3, 305–320.

Falster, D.S. & Westoby, M. 2003. Plant Height and Evolutionary Games. *Trends in Ecology and Evolution*, 18, 337–343.

Faria, J.R. 2003. Terror Cycles. *Studies in Nonlinear Dynamics and Econometrics*, 7, 1–9.

Friedman, D. 1991. Evolutionary Games in Economics. *Econometrica*, 59, 637–666.

Haigh, J. 1975. Game Theory and Evolution. *Advances in Applied Probability*, 6, 8–11.

Hirshleifer, J. 1977. Economics from a Biological Viewpoint. *Journal of Law and Economics*, 20, 1–52.

Hoffman, A.M. 2010. Why Groups Take Credit for Acts of Terror. *Journal of Peace Research*, 47, 615–626.

Im, E.I., Cauley, J. & Sandler, T. 1987. Cycles and Substitutions in Terrorist Activities: A Spectral Approach. *Kyklos*, 40, 238–255.

Leader, S.H. & Probst, P. 2003. The Earth Liberation Front and Environmental Terrorism. *Terrorism and Political Violence*, 15, 37–58.

Lorenz, E., 1964. The Problem of Deducing the Climate from the Governing Equations. *Tellus*, 16, 1–11.

Maynard Smith, J. 1982. *Evolution and the Theory of Games*. Cambridge: Cambridge University Press.

Maynard Smith, J. & Price, G.R. 1973. The Logic of Animal Conflict. *Nature*, 246, 15–18.

Ohtsuki, H. & Nowak, M.A. 2008. Evolutionary Stability on Graphs. *Journal of Theoretical Biology*, 251, 698–707.

Phillips, P.J. 2011. The Life Cycle of Terrorist Organisations. *International Advances in Economic Research*, 17, 369–385.

Phillips, P.J. 2016. *The Economics of Terrorism*. Abingdon, Oxon and New York: Routledge Taylor & Francis.

Putz, F.E. 1984. The Natural History of Lianas on Barro Colorado Island, Panama. *Ecology*, 65, 1713–1724.

Sandler, T. 2006. Hirshleifer's Social Decomposition Function in Defence Economics. *Defence and Peace Economics*, 17, 645–655.

Summers, L.H. 1991. The Scientific Illusion in Empirical Macroeconomics. *Scandinavian Journal of Economics*, 93, 129–148.

Taylor, P.D. & Jonker, L.B. 1978. Evolutionarily Stable Strategies and Game Dynamics. *Mathematical Biosciences*, 40, 145–156.

Van den Bergh, J.C.J.M. & Gowdy, J.M. 2003. The Microfoundations of Macroeconomics: An Evolutionary Perspective. *Cambridge Journal of Economics*, 27, 65–84.

Von Neumann, J. & Morgenstern, O. 1947. *Theory of Games and Economic Behaviour*. Princeton, NJ: Princeton University Press.

Wild, G. & Taylor, P.D. 2004. Fitness and Evolutionary Stability in Game Theoretic Models of Finite Populations. *Proceedings of the Royal Society of London,* 271, 2345–2349.

8

OVERCONFIDENCE, GENDER DIFFERENCES AND TERRORIST CHOICE

On January 29, 1974, San Franciscans woke up to the news that four people had been murdered and one injured the night before. The murders were random, stranger shootings. A gunman targeted people in three different areas of the city between 8:00 and 10:00 p.m. Police quickly connected the evening's mayhem to a string of similar crimes over the previous two months. The January crimes brought the total to ten homicides and three attempted murders. Public anxiety exploded not only because there were more murders but also because new rumours appeared that the shootings were racially motivated. All the victims had been white and eyewitnesses were now describing the killer, and his occasional driver, as black.[1]

The murders in San Francisco became known as the Zebra Murders and their perpetrators became known as the Zebra Killers.[2] The name 'zebra' comes from the name given by police to the operation set up to track down the killers: Operation Zebra. The series of homicides and attempted homicides is interesting because no single attack failed to either kill or wound a victim. This is quite rare and, in this case, stems from the killers' strict adherence to the method that they had chosen (shootings of individual victims or couples). There was no attempt to use a different type of attack method or to target groups instead of individuals. There was no attempt to 'graduate' to more elaborate attack methods. Other groups operating at the same time, by contrast, deviated from modes of operation that had been successful to embark on ultimately unsuccessful trials of attack methods, target types and strategies that might have promised more upside potential but really lay beyond the groups' capabilities. A possible explanation for these types of differences between groups is differences in their degrees of overconfidence.

Far from the mean streets of San Francisco, during the 1970s, the PFLP carried out 49 attacks that killed a total of 63 people. The average inflicted fatalities per attack was 1.31. Compare this to the Popular Front for the Liberation of Palestine General Command (PFLP-GC), a splinter group. During the 1970s, the PFLP-GC carried out 4 attacks that killed a total of 156 people. The average inflicted fatalities per attack was 39. One of the attacks of the group in 1987, in which a group member landed a hang glider near an Israeli military camp before killing six soldiers, is viewed as being a catalyst for the First Intifada. The Intifada was a period of intense violence between Israelis and Palestinians that lasted for several years until 1991. Almost 2,000 people were killed and many thousands more were injured on both sides. The PFLP-GC was far more impactful than its arguably over-confident parent organisation, the PFLP.

There are three types of overconfidence: (1) people *overestimate* their ability, performance, level of control or chance of success (Moore & Healy 2008, p.502); (2) people *over-place* themselves relative to others (Benoit et al. 2015) and (3) people have excessive certainty regarding the accuracy of their beliefs and, in particular, people are too confident that they have the correct answer (Moore & Healy 2008, p.502). This is called *over-precision* because the confidence intervals that people place around their responses are too narrow. Overconfidence of these three varieties has been found in virtually every context that researchers have explored. Svenson (1981) found that the large majority of people say that they are better drivers than average. The same finding has been repeated for intelligence, job prospects, lon-gevity, self-control, the ability to get along well with others, the quality of one's spoken expression and many consumer settings (Dunning et al. 2004; Alicke & Govorun 2005; Grubb 2015). In short, overconfidence appears to be ubiquitous (Lim 1997) and De Bondt & Thaler (1995) have declared, 'Perhaps the most robust finding in the psychology of judgement is that people are overconfident'.

For decisions involving risk and uncertainty, most of the evidence regarding overconfidence comes from calibration studies. As Brenner et al. (1996, p.212) explain:

> In a typical calibration of overconfidence subjects are presented with a series of general knowledge questions (e.g. which river is longer the Amazon or the Nile?) or prediction problems (e.g. who will win the election, the incum-bent or the challenger?). For each question, subjects select one of the two answers and assess the probability that their answer is correct. A judge is said to be calibrated if his or her probability judgments match the corresponding relative frequency of occurrence. Specifically, among all answers to which the judge assigns a given probability (say, 75%), the judge is calibrated if 75% of these answers are in fact correct. Studies of calibration have shown that people's confidence often exceeds their accuracy.

Calibration is usually depicted using a diagram of the type that we have drawn in Figure 8.1. For example, assume that the terrorist group is estimating the number of fatalities that one of its attacks will cause. Across the horizontal axis, the actual numbers of fatalities are recorded. Along the vertical axis, the terrorist group's

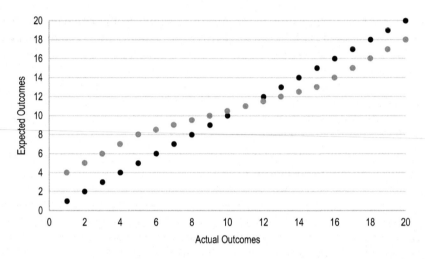

FIGURE 8.1 Perfectly and imperfectly calibrated assessments.

expectations are recorded. Perfect calibration is represented by a 45-degree line or a one-for-one correspondence between expected outcomes and actual outcomes. The questions that researchers have tried to answer is why and to what extent people's assessments diverge from such a one-for-one correspondence.

If the decision-maker's assessments are plotted against the 45-degree line, overconfidence will be indicated by assessments that sit above the 45-degree line while under-confident assessments will sit below it. As such, if the terrorist group is overconfident, its expectations of the outcomes that it can generate through its actions are too high. If the terrorist group is under-confident, its expectations of the outcomes that it can generate through its actions are too low. Interestingly, researchers have found that at low expected levels of performance, people overestimate their own level of performance (they are over-confident). At higher expected levels of performance, people underestimate their own level of performance (they are under-confident) (Moore & Healy 2008). As such, the pattern of imperfect calibration is a slight inverted s-shape that starts above and then falls below the perfect calibration line as expected outcomes increase.

The predicted and actual consequence of overconfidence is too much risk seeking. But it is not just a matter of choosing a more risky action over a less risky action. That is only part of the story. Rather, overconfidence usually means engagement in *too much* risky activity. That is, engaging in higher risk actions and doing so *too frequently*. This has been found to characterise human behaviour in a variety of settings, especially financial decision-making (Nosic & Weber 2010; Broihanne et al. 2014). If the same applies to terrorism, an overconfident terrorist group is expected to engage in too many actions relative to what would be expected from a perfectly calibrated decision-maker. In a moment, we will explain how we can tell whether the terrorist has committed 'too many' actions. For now, let us touch briefly on the issue of gender and terrorism.

If overconfidence affects the volume and frequency of violent action and if women and men have different levels of overconfidence, it might explain why females engage in violence less frequently than men (Lauritsen, Heimer & Lynch 2009; Schwartz et al. 2009). Although women are certainly active participants within terrorist groups,[3] they are vastly under-represented when it comes to actual participation in violent attacks. Over the long run, however, the total participation is not inconsequential. Between 1968 and 2012, females committed 256 acts of terrorism worldwide, 157 of which were suicide bombings. That is, around four successful female-perpetrated acts of terrorism each year since 1968 (Jordan & Denov 2007; Davis 2013; Matusitz 2019). This is a minuscule fraction of male-perpetrated terrorism. However, Jacques & Taylor (2013, p.35) make the following points:

> On November 9, 2005, a Belgium-born convert to Islam named Muriel Degauque ran into an Iraqi police patrol and detonated a bomb that killed five people and injured many others. Degauque's attack is often reported as a 'wake-up call' for forensic professionals not simply because she was the first European female to conduct such an attack, but because she was an educated, reportedly well-mannered young woman who came from a supportive family and community (Von Knop, 2007). Degauque's background contradicted widely held expectations about female involvement in terrorism, and it raised questions about how this type of offending might best be treated (Cunningham, 2003; Horgan & Braddock, 2010). Her case made clear how little is known about the risk factors associated with female-perpetrated terrorism.

Since female-perpetrated terrorism has been relatively understudied, this raises the possibility that there is a vulnerability in our law enforcement processes. Decision theory can help us to develop a picture of those aspects of behaviour under conditions of risk and uncertainty where differences between male and female perpetrators are at their most divergent. One relevant finding is that women are generally less overconfident than men. A pattern prediction is that female terrorists, though perhaps more overconfident than other women, are likely to be less overconfident than male terrorists. Female terrorists would engage in less terrorist activity than male terrorists. Although this sounds positive, there is an important clarifying point. Because their frequency of engagement in terrorism is lower, the expected outcomes over a series of female-perpetrated attacks might be higher than for male-perpetrated terrorism. Lower degrees of overconfidence among female terrorists may *increase* their expected outcomes.

Too much terrorism

Overconfidence leads to 'too much' terrorism. The problem is determining how many terrorist actions constitutes too many terrorist actions. There is no model of decision-making that designates the optimal number of actions. Researchers in other settings face the same problem. In financial markets research, for example, an overconfident investor will trade too regularly. However, there is no optimal benchmark that tells us how many trades are too many. The way that researchers have proceeded is by defining 'too many trades' as that number beyond which the investor's returns are reduced by trading. In this sense, an overconfident investor engages in excessive trading where 'excessive' is indicated by the fact that returns are actually reduced by trading (Odean 1999; Barber & Odean 2001). Analogously, then, we expect that an overconfident terrorist or terrorist group engages in actions beyond the point at which its average outcomes begin to decline. 'Too much' terrorism would be terrorist activity beyond the point where expected outcomes per attack begin to decline.

Distinguishing between overconfident groups and 'ordinary' groups is of more than mere academic interest. The outcomes that we observe in the terrorism context, including groups that capture the largest share of the most important payoffs, will be shaped to at least some degree by the relative overconfidence that characterises active terrorist groups. In a very simple but insightful model of overconfidence, Johnson and Fowler (2011) explain how overconfidence can play a role in shaping survival in contexts where there is competition for scarce resources and where conflict can ensue as rivals attempt to gain the largest share. Despite the disadvantages of misplaced confidence, including errors of judgement and reductions in expected outcomes through repeated applications, overconfidence can be an evolutionarily fit characteristic that remains stable in a population (i.e. surviving groups in that population gradually become overconfident). The primary reason for this is explained by Johnson and Fowler (2011, p.319):

> overconfidence often prevails over accurate assessment. Overconfidence is advantageous because it encourages individuals to claim resources they could not otherwise win if it came to a conflict (stronger but cautious rivals will sometimes fail to make a claim), and it keeps them from walking away from conflicts they would surely win.

How would we identify an overconfident group that engages in too much terrorism where 'too much' terrorism is activity that reduces the expected outcomes? Applying this approach, we would consider the group of four men responsible for the 'Zebra Murders' as not being at all overconfident. For six months, starting in late 1973 and continuing to April 1974, the group perpetrated 20 attacks in San Francisco. All of these were armed assaults involving either guns or knives and all of the attacks were targeted at individuals or pairs. The attacks were not spree-style shootings aimed at groups of people. In 15 of these attacks, the target was killed. In the other five attacks, the target was wounded. As the number of attacks accumulated, the outcomes remained stable. Not a single attack perpetrated by the group failed. The objective to kill or injure white people was always achieved and the average inflicted fatalities or injuries per attack remained 1.00 for the duration of the group's active period.

The Zebra Killers can be contrasted with the BLA, which by the measure identified above, oscillated in the degree of overconfidence it displayed but certainly displayed a higher degree of overconfidence than the Zebra Killers. The BLA operated at a similar period of time, with most of its actions occurring between late 1971 and early 1974. The group also set out to kill their targets, who were primarily police officers. As an indication of the group's sometime overconfidence, the group's first attack was an attempted bombing of a funeral service being held for a murdered police officer. Although it did detonate, the bomb failed to inflict any fatalities or injuries. The BLA then switched to more targeted types of armed assaults, not dissimilar to those perpetrated by the Zebra Killers. In this regard, the group was somewhat successful. Reckoning its failures and successes, the group had inflicted an average of 0.40 fatalities over the course of its first five attacks.

The average number of fatalities per attack inflicted by the BLA then increased to 0.60 by the time the group had perpetrated ten attacks. This corresponded with the group's more targeted, less ambitious, attack method choices. However, as the group continued to perpetrate actions at frequent intervals its average outcomes began to decline. By the time 15 attacks had been perpetrated, the group's average number of inflicted fatalities had declined to 0.53. It remained at 0.55 after 20 attacks. Interestingly, the group's next five attacks were specifically targeted attacks directed at police officers and carried out using pistols and automatic weapons. Three of these five attacks were perpetrated in January 1973. Five fatalities were inflicted. As a result of this, the group's average outcomes increased to a high of 0.64 fatalities per attack after 25 attacks. From this point, subsequent attacks once more decreased the average outcome, which fell back to 0.55 fatalities per attack, where it remained until the end of 1974. Whereas the Zebra Killers never deviated from their basic method of attack and never failed to inflict injuries and fatalities, the BLA, at times, looked to expand the scale of its actions into higher risk areas, such as bombing, requiring more capability than the group possessed.

Triggers for overconfidence

If people are overconfident sometimes but not at other times or if some people are overconfident all of the time while others are not, the question we must ask is what causes or triggers this overconfidence? Why aren't people always more or less perfectly calibrated in their expectations? And how plausible are these triggers for overconfidence in a terrorism context? Overconfidence may simply be inherent in the behavioural makeup of some (or most) individuals and groups and may emerge more or less spontaneously in all settings. Overconfidence has certainly been found in every setting that has been investigated. Nevertheless, there do appear to be some specific triggers for overconfidence and a few of these have been identified and studied in considerable detail. One of the most interesting is the *illusion of control*. That terrorism requires a mixture of skill and luck (rather than luck alone) makes it primed for the development of an illusion of control on the part of those who would engage in it. In fact, even if the outcomes of terrorism were purely based on luck, some individuals and groups who engage in it would still believe that the chance outcomes were subject to control. When people have an illusion of control, they are more likely to be overconfident.

The illusion of control is an expectancy of a personal success probability inappropriately higher than the objective probability would warrant (Langer 1975, p.311; Langer & Roth 1975). In general, people seem to see contingency or a causal relationship when there is none and also seem to want to attribute good outcomes to internal factors (skill) and bad outcomes to external factors (bad luck) even in cases where all of the outcomes are purely based on chance.[4] Like some of the other concepts, measurements and categories that constitute the field of overconfidence research, the boundaries between an illusion of control as a trigger for overconfidence and the possibility that an individual can be overconfident regarding the amount of control he or she actually has are blurry (Fast et al. 2012). It can be difficult to separate the two. Despite this, we have reasonable knowledge about the underlying factors that are responsible for the illusion of control.

Interestingly, 'just world beliefs' seem to play a role in shaping the illusion of control (Langer 1975, p.312). Belief in a 'just world' has attracted a great deal of research going back many years (see Lerner 1965, 1980; Lerner & Miller 1978). People who believe in a just world believe that good things happen to good people while bad things happen to bad people and everyone gets what they deserve (Langer 1975, p.312). For people who hold this view, chance is somewhat mitigated by the gravitational pull or equilibrium exerted by 'justice'. In turn, the absence of chance or its lessened impact on outcomes implies that outcomes can be predicted. If the decision-maker thinks that he or she is a good person then good things will happen. Favourable outcomes will be experienced. Being good or being on the 'right side' is the key to controlling what will happen. Hence, the illusion of control emerges.

Belief in a just world has been linked to terrorist behaviour in different ways. When people hold a belief in a just world and circumstances conflict with or shatter that belief, they can experience feelings of rage. The desire to remedy perceived injustice then becomes a stepping-stone on the pathway to terrorism (Moghaddam, 2005).[5] Beliefs in a just world can also be preyed upon by those who would seek to turn people towards terrorism. Loza (2007, p.144) explains how:

> Western civilisation with their democracy and modernity is viewed as morally corrupt. It is taught that only Islam possesses the values for a good and just world and that Muslim societies have decayed and become vulnerable to Western intrusion because Muslims have strayed from their religion. A just world will only be guaranteed and achieved by going back to true Islam.

The belief in a just world can also be used by terrorists to minimise feelings of guilt, shame or responsibility for the victims of a terrorist attack. People have a tendency to blame victims for what has befallen them (Goffman 1963; also see Loza & Clements 1991). This is the case for events such as car accidents that result in disabilities, even when the disabled person was not at fault. It was this observation that led to the formulation of the just world hypothesis (Lerner & Miller 1978, p.1030). Likewise, terrorists attribute their victims' fates to the victims themselves rather than taking responsibility for the actions they have taken as terrorists. Indeed, terrorists convince themselves that they are the real victims of oppression (Loza 2007; Rogers et al. 2007). This narrative comes through in the interviews conducted by Post et al. (2003) with terrorists aligned with groups such as Hamas, Islamic Jihad, Hizballah and Fatah.

The fact that terrorists can convince themselves that they are on the 'right side' or have a 'just cause' and that 'just outcomes' will result from their actions fosters an illusion of control that leads overconfident terrorist groups to behave as if the chance aspects of their actions are in fact controllable when they are not. Primarily, an illusion of control affects the calibration of probability assessments. These assessments will be pulled into the overconfident range, as portrayed in Figure 8.1. The illusion of control leads to overconfidence and to overoptimism. Weinstein (1980, p.808) explains:

> If an event is perceived to be controllable, it signifies that people believe there are steps one can take to increase the likelihood of a desirable out-come. Because they can more easily bring to mind their own actions than the actions of others, people are likely to conclude that desired outcomes are more likely to happen to them than to other people.

The capability of terrorist groups does determine a large part of the outcomes but the outcome of any individual terrorist attack, regardless of how well planned and executed, is subject to chance and is beyond the complete control of even the most capable terrorist group. The mixture of skill and luck fosters the illusion of control that can be magnified further by just world beliefs. Overconfident groups, believing that they can completely control the outcomes of their actions, take more risk just as the gambler places bigger bets in games where there is some skill component (Goodie 2005). The outcome, however, will be a series of attacks that gradually reduces the average outcomes recorded by the terrorist group. In time, the overconfident terrorist group is found out.

At this point, we must weigh the disadvantages of overconfidence against its potential as a strategy for evolutionary fitness. Is overconfidence a characteristic that leads some terrorist groups to dominate a context and capture a larger share of the contestable payoffs? Or is it a characteristic that leads to too much risky activity, errors of judgement and ultimate demise? Is it both of these things, depending on the context? And are overconfident groups a greater threat than groups that make judgements that are more accurate? After all, the Zebra Killers may not have been overconfident, at least relative to the BLA, but they were a very insidious threat for the period while they were active. As we shall see, the honest answer to all of these questions is that it does depend on the particular circumstances. What we do know is that overconfidence with all of its advantages and disadvantages can be expected to shape the outcomes we observe.

The advantages of overconfidence versus the costs of being found out

For a terrorist group, overconfidence can be very costly. Miscalculating the likelihood of different outcomes can lead to suboptimal decisions, too much risk taking and, ultimately, the failure of the terrorist group to survive and exert its identity. Overconfidence can also be costly to the group's status or reputation when the absence of its underlying capability is revealed. This revelation can do irreparable damage to the esteem in which the terrorist group is held by would-be recruits and grassroots supporters. These costs of overconfidence are not confined to terrorism. In all settings, overconfidence can be costly to the decision-maker. Overconfidence is costly for nations because it leads them to engage in too many conflicts and wars (Johnson 2004) and it is costly in business (Camerer & Lovallo 1999; Malmendier & Tate 2005). Why, then, do decision-makers not recognise these costs and adjust their behaviour accordingly? Why would anyone portray an overconfident self that could be exposed?

One possibility is that overconfidence provides psychological benefits that outweigh the costs (Kennedy et al. 2013). People are motivated by this favourable cost-benefit ratio to display overconfidence (Kunda 1987; Dunning et al. 1995). These benefits could be self-esteem, task motivation and persistence (Anderson et al. 2012). Another possibility, more relevant perhaps to terrorism, is that overconfidence enhances status. This might apply to both the terrorist group as a collective and the individuals that constitute it. The argument that overconfidence is so widespread because it enhances status is a relatively recent idea. If correct, there could be a status motive to overconfidence. People are overconfident because they know that overconfidence can make them appear more competent and capable to others. This idea has received some support from Anderson et al. (2012) who explain,

> If Persons A and B have equal levels of actual ability, but Person A has higher confidence than Person B, Person A will be seen as more competent and will attain higher status than Person B, even if Person A's confidence is unjustified.

There comes a time when true capability will be revealed through action. At such a time, overconfidence is dealt with harshly by others (Anderson et al. 2006). More importantly, overconfident decision-makers risk their survival. However, the matter is not as straightforward as overconfidence leading to certain extinction. Overconfidence can stop people walking away from conflicts that they would surely win. Once one considers this possibility, the results of investigations into the evolutionary stability of overconfidence begin to make sense. Initially, it seems puzzling that overconfidence with all of its costs still prevails in virtually every setting that researchers have explored. Benos (1998), for example, argues that overconfidence leads to a 'first mover advantage'. If so, an overconfident terrorist group might be expected to act sooner and more aggressively and over-allocate resources to terrorist activity in such a way that it makes it more difficult for other groups to follow and secure any significant share of recruits, grassroots supporters and other relevant payoffs. For example, Hezbollah was a first-mover in the use of suicide bombings during the 1980s, an attack method that garnered the group considerable success and was copied much later by other groups (Horowitz 2010). As such, even if the actions stemming from overconfidence are too risky, the costs of this might be offset by the value of the first-mover's advantage.

Even so, the evolutionary stability of overconfidence is tenuous and while over-confidence may survive in populations, overconfident individuals or groups may not. In Benos's (1998) model, the overconfident decision-makers set the trend with their aggressiveness and consequent first-mover advantage. Rational decision-makers find it worthwhile to follow. However, this holds only if the number of rational decision-makers is relatively small. As the number of rational decision-makers increases, the individual rational decision-maker is better off not following the trend set by the overconfident decision-maker because, as the number of imitators increase, the payoffs to overconfidence must be shared among a greater number (Benos 1998, p.373). Under these conditions, Benos (1998) shows that the payoffs accumulating to overconfident decision-makers fall more rapidly than the payoffs accumulating to rational decision-makers.

Like Benos's analysis, Johnson & Fowler (2011) associate overconfidence with a potentially beneficial form of behaviour. For Benos, this is aggression and a consequent first-mover advantage. For Johnson & Fowler (2011), overconfidence is associated with a form of 'bluffing' that enables individuals to claim more resources than otherwise. Unlike conscious bluffing, as in a poker game, the bluffing involved here is unconscious and self-deceptive. As such, it is not easily revealed by the over-confident decision-maker to others. This allows the benefits that we have been talking about to be accrued until the point at which others recognise the bluff. By that time, however, the individual or group may have had a big head start or may have built an insurmountable position within a particular environment.

The work that has been done on analysing overconfidence in different settings provides at least one way to track changes in the overconfidence of terrorists. These are the increases or decreases in the group's average fatalities (or other relevant outcomes) per attack. An overconfident group will push beyond the boundaries of its capabilities. With each successive attack, its average fatalities (or another relevant payoff) per attack decline. This is the hallmark feature of an increasingly overconfident group. When such a pattern becomes clear, law enforcement agencies may expect more risk taking by the group in the future. Just as importantly, a group that appears to have more focus and increasing average fatalities per attack may have realised the limits of its capability and mitigated its earlier overconfidence. Although such a group is likely to be less risk seeking, its targeted and competent actions may be more effective, though less poten-tially spectacular. This type of group is possibly more insidious than the overconfident group, as the example of the Zebra Killers and the BLA illustrates.

Female-perpetrated terrorism and overconfidence

Overconfidence is, as we have discussed, a practically ubiquitous human trait. It affects judgement and decision-making. If affects outcomes. It may affect fitness and survival. There are also important differences in degrees of overconfidence between males and females that are relevant to understanding how females engage in terrorism and how female terrorists make decisions. The primary result is that women are not as overconfident and do not display as much risk seeking behaviour as men (Croson & Gneezy 2009; Barber & Odean 2001; Correll 2001; Bengtsson, Persson & Willenhag 2005). The primary implication is that female terrorists will not engage in as much activity as male terrorists and, consequently, will not engage in actions beyond the point at which their expected outcomes begin to decline.

One of the most interesting questions that arises from a consideration of the implications of these findings for female-perpetrated terrorism is whether the 'terrorist identity' will overrule the male–female distinctions in overconfidence and risk seeking that characterise ordinary people. Suspecting that this might be the case in the finance industry, Beckmann & Menkhoff (2008) decided to investigate whether the differences in male–female overconfidence and risk seeking disappeared in the highly competitive risk-taking environment of professional funds management. They found, somewhat contrary to their expectations, that all of the previous findings in the economics and psychology literature were evident even in this particular context (Beckmann & Menkhoff 2008, p.367):

> Testing the 'expertise dominates gender' hypothesis surprisingly ends in a victory for the gender difference. Whether we take descriptive statistics or control for a large set of competing influences, the gender variable always shows the sign as expected from the earlier literature, i.e. women will indeed be women even in the demanding environment of fund management. However, the economic importance of the gender difference varies. First, female fund managers keep their more risk averse behaviour but on the other hand the effect is comparatively weak for the established risk measures. Second, we reject the view that women are less overconfident than men for the case of fund managers (although coefficients' signs hint at the expected direction). This finding is robust to an extension of three different measures of overconfidence, i.e. overoptimistic self-assessment, illusion of control and miscalibration. Third, evidence is consistent with the hypothesis that female fund managers shy away from competition. Fourth, the relative economic importance of the gender-related difference in explaining behaviour is sometimes small in comparison to competing influences, indicating that indeed financial expertise decreases the gender difference—but does not erase it.

Among the other findings about overconfidence, the evidence presented by Beckmann and Menkhoff (2008) also supports a conclusion that females 'shy away' from competition. Gender differences in competitiveness have been studied extensively. The results can sometimes be mixed but other studies report strong findings of more competitiveness among males than females (e.g. Hibbard & Buhrmester 2010; Gupta, Poulsen & Villeval 2011; Buser, Niederle & Oosterbeek 2014). We know from Johnson & Fowler (2011) that overconfidence can play a critical role in encouraging people to make a claim for resources that they would not otherwise win and in discouraging the abandonment of a conflict that they would surely win. The relatively lower degrees of overconfidence displayed by females shapes (and possibly determines) their competitiveness, which is also lower than male competitiveness. In a conflict over scarce payoffs, females may be less likely to compete leading us to suspect that female-perpetrated terrorism might have different objectives than simply maximising share of available resources or payoffs.

Evidence that female-male differences in overconfidence may persist in specialised contexts specifically involving conflict is also strong. In a study of the influence of overconfidence on war-games decisions, Johnson et al. (2006, p.2513) found that

> in experimental wargames: (i) people are overconfident about their expectations of success; (ii) those who are more overconfident are more likely to attack; (iii) overconfidence and attacks are more pronounced among males than females; and (iv) testosterone is related to expectations of success, but not within gender, so its influence on overconfidence cannot be distinguished from any other gender specific factor … our key finding is that males *were* overconfident; and males who were more overconfident were *more likely* to launch wars.

That is, testosterone does affect pre-game ranking but gender is the dominant explanatory factor, regardless of testosterone level. At this stage, there is no reason why we would not expect to see gender differences in overconfidence between male and female terrorists.

We are left with a similar problem to that which we came across earlier. That is, does a lower degree of overconfidence increase or decrease the threat level? Female terrorists will display less overconfidence but although this may draw them away from certain types of attacks or from high frequency engagement, it does not mean that the attacks that they do perpetrate will be any less damaging. Over time, female terrorists may be more successful in terms of maintaining a higher average payoff per attack. Whatever the case may be, overconfidence certainly makes us think differently about the threat posed by female terrorists. When approaching the task of ranking suspects for surveillance, such as the formation of a terrorism watch list, there might be a tendency to rank female suspects lower than males (based on threat assessment). However, care should be taken not to overlook the fact that while gender differences in overconfidence may make female terrorists less active and less likely to enter fiercely into the competition for a share of the payoffs that characterise the terrorism context, it does not mean that a steady, less ambitious, less risk seeking perpetrator is not a very significant threat. Female terrorists, male terrorists and terrorist groups that have a lower degree of overconfidence are a different type of threat. This is perhaps the key insight delivered by decision theory up until now.

Notes on romance, female agency and terrorism

Terrorism can be romanticised in many different ways. When this is confined to books or films, no real harm is done. But romantic notions of terrorism and the idea of romance as a foundation for behaviour in terrorist groups has been seen by some as having a force all of its own. Consider Smilansky's (2004, p.796) comments about the consequences of what he says are the Palestinians' romantic ideals of terrorism:

> In terms of just war theory, the just Palestinian aim of establishing a state of their own alongside Israel did not require terrorism: the necessity condition was not met. Historical circumstances have changed over the years, but the Palestinians have always seemed to prefer the hopes of annihilating Israel in concert with Arab states, or the romance of violent struggle, to constructive accommodation. Rather than terrorism being required in order to establish a Palestinian state, it is on the contrary the Palestinians that have repeatedly sabotaged the establishment of an independent Palestine alongside Israel, both directly, and indirectly through the influence of their choices and actions on the Israeli democratic process.

With reference to female-perpetrated terrorism, there has been a feeling even among terrorists themselves that conventional wisdom tends towards the conclusion that women enter into terrorist groups because they are following strong men and, in most cases, have romantic attachments to them (Kassimeris 2019, p.11). The most prominent example that might be used to counter this conventional wisdom is the case of Ulrike Meinhof, the German revolutionary and co-leader of the Baader-Meinhof gang, the RAF. Meinhof has sometimes been called a feminist icon (Hehn 2008), despite her own criticisms of 'bourgeois feminism' (Colvin 2011, p.110). Primarily, though, she has come to be viewed as a person who entered upon a revolutionary struggle of her own accord, through her own agency.

In 2016, Pola Roupa's daring attempt to free her fellow revolutionary Niko Maziotis achieved hit national headlines in Greece (Kassimeris 2019). As the female leader of Greece's Revolutionary Struggle, responsible for 21 attacks in Greece between 1997 and 2015, Roupa occupies an interesting position in the history of terrorism. Her story holds many parallels with that of Ulrike Meinhof. In fact, Maziotis wrote a tribute to Ulrike Meinhof in which he attempted to explain why Meinhof had become a feminist icon. In his opinion, it was because the stereotype of a female militant romantically following her love interest underground was so utterly shattered by Meinhof's story (Kassimeris 2019, p.11). What recent research in terrorism studies has shown is that female terrorists have agency. What we have shown is that there are important aspects of that agency that can be easily overlooked. Female terrorists might be responsible for far fewer attacks than men and, in general, females are less overconfident and less risk seeking than men. However, they are not always just followers or supporters and less overconfidence is not to be mistaken for ineffectiveness. On the contrary, if less overconfidence prompts more circumspection, female terrorists may attack less frequently but the payoffs per unit of risk that they bear when they do attack may be superior to that achieved by overconfident male terrorists.

Four dot points to end the chapter

- Overconfidence is a fairly ubiquitous personality trait.
- Overconfidence can produce risk seeking behaviour and, more importantly, too much risky activity (where 'too much' is activity that actually reduces expected payoffs).
- Overconfident terrorist groups engage in too much terrorism and have lower payoffs per action. However, overconfidence does have advantages, including first mover advantages as well as a kind of bluffing that enables the overconfident decision-maker to capture more resources than he otherwise would.
- There are gender differences in overconfidence. Women are less overconfident than men. While female terrorists might engage in less terrorist activity, their relative lack of overconfidence may produce higher payoffs per attack.

Notes

1 Lamberson (2016, p.201).
2 There is some debate about the group's motivations and structure. See, for example, Grabiner and Grabiner (1982, p.342) who state that no 'secret society' was ever found and no 'racial motivation' was ever proven.
3 Women have sometimes constituted around one-third of the membership of some terrorist groups. There are some prominent examples, including Germany's RAF and 2nd of June Movement. Rote Zora was almost exclusively female (Bloom 2010, p.91).
4 This is related to the clustering illusion (Frith & Frith 1972; Gilovich 1991) and 'hot hand' fallacy (Kahneman & Tversky 1972) in which people see patterns in purely random phenomena.
5 Kaiser et al. (2004) found that American students who held the strongest beliefs in a just world before 9/11 held the strongest desire for revenge following the terrorist attacks.

References

Alicke, M.D., & Govorun, O. 2005. The Better-Than-Average Effect. In M.D. Alicke, D. Dunning & J. Krueger (Eds.), *The Self in Social Judgment*. New York: Psychology Press, pp.85–106Anderson, C., Brion, S., Moore, D.A. & Kennedy, J.A. 2012. A Status Enhancement Account of Overconfidence. *Journal of Personality and Social Psychology*, 103, 718–735.

Anderson, C., Srivastava, S., Beer, J., Spataro, S.E., & Chatman, J.A. 2006. Knowing Your Place: SelfPerceptions of Status in Social Groups. *Journal of Personality and Social Psychology*, 91, 1094–1110.

Barber, B.M. & Odean, T. 2001. Boys Will Be Boys: Gender, Overconfidence and Common Stock Investment. *Quarterly Journal of Economics*, 116, 261–292.

Beckmann, D. & Menkhoff, L. 2008. Will Women Be Women? Analysing the Gender Differences among Financial Experts. *Kyklos*, 61, 364–384.

Bengtsson, C., Persson, M. & Willenhag, P. 2005. Gender and Overconfidence. *Economics Letters*, 86, 199–203.

Benoit, J., Dubra, J. & Moore, D.A. 2015. Does the Better-Than-Average-Effect Show that People Are Overconfident? *Journal of the European Economic Association*, 13, 293–329.

Benos, A.V. 1998. Aggressiveness and Survival of Overconfident Traders. *Journal of Financial Markets*, 1, 353–383.

Bloom, M.M. 2010. Death Becomes Her: The Changing Nature of Women's Role in Terror. *Georgetown Journal of International Affairs*, 11, 91–98.

Brenner, L.A., Koehler, D.J., Liberman, V. & Tversky, A. 1996. Overconfidence in Probability and Frequency Judgements: A Critical Examination. *Organisational Behaviour and Human Decision Processes*, 65, 212–219.

Broihanne, M.H., Merli, M. & Roger, P. 2014. Overconfidence, Risk Perception and the Risk Taking Behaviour of Finance Professionals. *Finance Research Letters*, 11, 64–73.

Buser, T., Niederle, M. & Oosterbeek, H. 2014. Gender, Competitiveness and Career Choices. *Quarterly Journal of Economics*, 129, 1409–1447.

Camerer, C. & Lovallo, D. 1999. Overconfidence and Excess Entry: An Experimental Approach. *American Economic Review*, 89, 306–318.

Colvin, S. 2011. Wir Frauen haben kein Vaterland: Ulrike Marie Meinhof, Emily Wilding Davison and the Homelessness of Women Revolutionaries. *German Life and Letters*, 64, 108–121.

Correll, S.J. 2001. Gender and the Career Choice Process: The Role of Biased Self-assessments. *American Journal of Sociology*, 106, 1691–1730.

Croson, R. & Gneezy, U. 2009. Gender Differences in Preferences. *Journal of Economic Literature*, 47, 448–474.

Cunningham, K.J. 2003. Cross-Regional Trends in Female Terrorism. *Studies in Conflict and Terrorism*, 26, 171–195.

Davis, J. 2013. Evolution of the Global Jihad: Female Suicide Bombers in Iraq. *Studies in Conflict & Terrorism*, 36, 279–291.

DeBondt, W. & Thaler, R.H. 1995. Financial Decision-Making in Markets and Firms: A Behavioral Perspective. In R.A. Jarrow, V. Maksimovic & W.T. Ziemba (Eds.), *Finance, Handbooks in Operations Research and Management Science*. Vol. 9. North Holland, Amsterdam, Netherlands, pp. 385–410.

Dunning, D., Heath, C., & Suls, J.M. 2004. Flawed Self-Assessment: Implications for Health, Education, and the Workplace. *Psychological Science in the Public Interest*, 5, 69–106.

Dunning, D., Leuenberger, A. & Sherman, D.A. 1995. A New Look At Motivated Inference: Are Self-Serving Theories of Success a Product of Motivational Forces? *Journal of Personality and Social Psychology*, 69, 58–68.

Fast, N.J., Sivanathan, N., Mayer, N.D. & Galinsky, A.D. 2012. Power and Overconfident Decision-Making. *Organisational Behaviour and Human Decision Processes*, 117, 249–260.

Frith, C.D. & Frith, U. 1972. The Solitaire Illusion: An Illusion of Numerosity. *Perception and Psychophysics*, 11, 409–410.

Gilovich, T. 1991. *How We Know What Isn't So: The Fallibility of Human Reason in Everyday Life*. New York: Free Press.

Goffman, E. 1963. *Stigma: Notes on the Management of Spoiled Identity*. Englewood Cliffs, NJ: Prentice Hall.

Goodie, A.S. 2005. The Role of Perceived Control and Overconfidence in Pathological Gambling. *Journal of Gambling Studies*, 21, 481–502.

Grabiner, G. & Grabiner, V.E. 1982. 'Where Are Your Papers?' 'Operation Zebra' and Constitutional Civil Liberties. *Journal of Black Studies*, 12, 333–350.

Grubb, M.D. 2015. Overconfident Consumers in the Marketplace. *Journal of Economic Perspectives*, 29, 9–35.

Gupta, N.B., Poulsen, A. & Villeval, M. 2011. Gender Matching and Competitiveness: Experimental Evidence. *Economic Inquiry*, 51, 816–835.

Hehn, K. 2008. Im Tod größer als im Leben. *Frankfurter Rundschau*, September 9.

Hibbard, D.R. & Buhrmester, D. 2010. Competitiveness, Gender and Adjustment Among Adolescents. *Sex Roles*, 63, 412–424.

Horgan, J., & Braddock, K. (2010). Rehabilitating the Terrorists? Challenges in Assessing the Effectiveness of De-radicalization Programs. *Terrorism and Political Violence*, 22, 267–291, DOI:10.1080/ 09546551003594748

Horowitz, M.C. 2010. Non-State Actors and the Diffusion of Innovations: The Case of Suicide Terrorism. *International Organisaton*, 64, 33–64.

Jacques, K. & Taylor, P.J. 2013. Myths and Realities of Female Perpetrated Terrorism. *Law and Human Behaviour*, 37, 35–44.

Johnson, D.D.P. 2004. *Overconfidence and War: The Havoc and Glory of Positive Illusions*. Cambridge, MA: Harvard University Press.

Johnson, D.D.P. & Fowler, J.H. 2011. The Evolution of Overconfidence. *Nature*, 477, 317–320.

Johnson, D.D.P., McDermott, R., Barrett, E.S., Cowden, J., Wrangham, R., McIntyre, M.H. & Rosen, S.P. 2006. Overconfidence in War Games: Experimental Evidence on Expectations, Aggression, Gender and Testosterone. *Proceedings of the Royal Society*, 273, 2513–2520.

Jordan, K. & Denov, M. 2007. Birds of Freedom? Perspectives on Female Emancipation and Sri Lanka's Liberation Tigers of Tamil Eelam. *Journal of International Women's Studies*, 9, 42–62.

Kahneman, D. & Tversky, A. 1972. Subjective Probability: A Judgement of Representativeness. *Cognitive Psychology*, 3, 430–454.

Kaiser, C.R., Vick, S.B. & Major, B. 2004. A Prospective Investigation of the Relationship between Just-World Beliefs and the Desire for Revenge after September 11, 2001. *Psychological Science*, 15, 503–506.

Kassimeris, G. 2019. Greece's Ulrike Meinhof: Pola Roupa and the Revolutionary Struggle. *Studies in Conflict and Terrorism*, Forthcoming.

Kennedy, J.A., Anderson, C. & Moore, D.A. 2013. When Overconfidence Is Revealed to Others: Testing the Status-Enhancement Theory of Overconfidence. *Organisational Behaviour and Human Decision Processes*, 122, 266–279.

Kunda, Z. 1987. Motivated Inference: Self-Serving Generation and Evaluation of Causal Theories. *Journal of Personality and Social Psychology*, 53, 636–647.

Lamberson, C. 2016. The Zebra Murders: Race, Civil Liberties and Radical Politics in San Francisco. *Journal of Urban History*, 42, 201–225.

Langer, E.J. 1975. The Illusion of Control. *Journal of Personality and Social Psychology*, 32, 311–328.

Langer, E.J. & Roth, J. 1975. Heads I Win, Tails It's Chance: The Illusion of Control as a Function of the Sequence of Outcomes in a Purely Chance Task. *Journal of Personality and Social Psychology*, 32, 951–955.

Lauritsen, J.L., Heimer, K. & Lynch, J.P. 2009. Trends in the Gender Gap in Violent Offending: New Evidence from the National Crime Victimisation Survey. *Criminology*, 47, 361–399.

Lerner, M.J. 1965. Evaluation of Performance as a Function of Performer's Reward and Attractiveness. *Journal of Personality and Social Psychology*, 1, 355–360.

Lerner, M.J. 1980. *Belief in a Just World: A Fundamental Delusion*. New York: Plenum Press.

Lerner, M.J. & Miller, D.T. 1978. Just World Research and the Attribution Process: Looking Back and Ahead. *Psychological Bulletin*, 85, 1030–1051.

Lim. R.G. 1997. Overconfidence in Negotiation Revisited. *International Journal of Conflict Management*, 8, 52–79.

Loza, W. 2007. The Psychology of Extremism and Terrorism: A Middle Eastern Perspective. *Aggression and Violent Behaviour*, 12, 141–155.

Loza, W. & Clements, P. 1991. Incarcerated Alcoholics and Rapists Attributions of Blame for Criminal Acts. *Canadian Journal of Behavioural Science*, 23, 76–83.

Malmendier, U. & Tate, G. 2005. CEO Overconfidence and Corporate Investment. *Journal of Finance*, 60, 2661–2700.

Matusitz, J. 2019. Symbolism in Female Terrorism: Five Overarching Themes. *Sexuality and Culture*, 23, 1332–1344.

Moghaddam, F.M. 2005. The Staircase to Terrorism. *American Psychologist*, 60, 161–169.

Moore, D.A. & Healy, P.J. 2008. The Trouble with Overconfidence. *Psychological Review*, 115, 502–517.

Nosic, A. & Weber, M. 2010. How Riskily Do I Invest? *Decision Analysis*, 7, 282–301.

Odean, T. 1999. Do Investors Trade Too Much? *American Economic Review*, 89, 1279–1298.

Post, J.M., Sprinzak, E. & Denny, L.M. 2003. The Terrorists in Their Own Words: Interviews with 35 Incarcerated Middle Eastern Terrorists. *Terrorism and Political Violence*, 15, 171–184.

Rogers, M.B., Loewenthal, K.M., Lewis, C.A., Amlot, R., Cinnirella, M. & Ansari, H. 2007. The Role of Religious Fundamentalism in Terrorist Violence: A Social Psychological Analysis. *International Review of Psychiatry*, 19, 253–262.

Schwartz, J., Steffensmeier, D., Zhong, H. & Ackerman, J. 2009. Trends in the Gender Gap in Violence: Re-evaluating NCVS and Other Evidence. *Criminology*, 47, 401–425.

Smilansky, S. 2004. Terrorism, Justification and Illusion. *Ethics*, 114, 790–805.

Svenson, O. 1981. Are We All Less Risky and More Skilful Than Our Fellow Drivers? *Acta Psychologica*, 94, 143–148.

Von Knop, K. 2007. The Female Jihad: Al Qaeda's Women. *Studies in Conflict and Terrorism*, 30, 397–414.

Weinstein, N.D. 1980. Unrealistic Optimism about Future Life Events. *Journal of Personality and Social Psychology*, 39, 806–820.

9

EXPECTED UTILITY AS A MEASUREMENT TOOL IN THE TERRORISM CONTEXT

Classical criminology assumes that criminals are rational beings who weigh the costs and benefits of their actions. Gary Becker (1968) produced the first fully-fledged theory of crime based on rational behaviour. His research led to an upsurge of interest in the economics of criminal behaviour [see, for example, Isaac Ehrlich (1973), Ann Witte (1980), Ehrlich and George Brower (1987), James Andreoni (1991), Richard Freeman (1996), Steven Levitt (1997), Pablo Fajnzylber et al. (2000), inter alia.[1]

In his well-known work, Becker (1968) deals with the decision to engage in criminal activity or, as he calls it, a determination of the supply of offenses. He makes use of the orthodox model of decision-making under risk and uncertainty: expected utility theory. But when Becker (1968) says that the offender maximises expected utility and when he sketches an outline of the offender as a rational decision-maker, he uses expected utility theory more as a logical-formal construct than as a theory of measurement. Becker never actually measures utility. The same is true of Enders and Sandler's (2002) application of Becker's approach to the analysis of terrorist behaviour. The utility that the terrorist group expects to accrue from different actions is never measured. Expected utility theory is simply used as a way to structure the terrorist group's decision-making process and predict some basic patterns. For example, that the expected utility of terrorism vis-à-vis legitimate activity can be impacted negatively by government security initiatives and, if the terrorist group seeks to maximise expected utility, such security initiatives may result in a re-ordering of its preferences in favour of legitimate activities. And so forth.

To go beyond the basic patterns that speak only of the choice between terrorism or crime and legitimate activity, expected utility theory could be used as it was intended. That is, to *measure* (see Fishburn 1989, p.138). The principal idea and principal result presented by von Neumann & Morgenstern (1947) is that if a small number of seemingly self-evident rules or axioms[2] are obeyed during the decision-making process, a utility function exists that allows for the preference ordering of some set of risky prospects (gambles or risky actions). Terrorist actions such as bombing, armed assault and hostage taking are risky prospects $x, y, \ldots$ with payoffs measured in some unit, say media attention, and occurring with some probability. For example, there might be a 5 percent chance that an assassination will generate more than 1,000 column inches of newspaper coverage. Economists would say that terrorist actions like bombing and armed assault and others form a set X and we use the symbol > to indicate that the terrorist prefers one action to another. A utility function u that orders the terrorist actions on X is:

$$\text{for all } x, y \in X, x > y \Leftrightarrow u(x) > u(y)$$

For all terrorist actions in the set, one action x is preferred to another y if and only if (denoted by $\Leftrightarrow$) the utility function yields a higher value for x than for y. Von Neumann & Morgenstern (1947) set out to show that such a function or, rather, class of functions exists. The result, expected utility theory, is a contribution to representational measurement theory (see Boumans 2007), a branch of mathematics and logic that aims to establish a correspondence between some type of magnitudes (e.g. mass, velocity, dollars) and numbers (e.g. 1, 2,…). In expected utility theory, von Neumann & Morgenstern (1947) establish such a correspondence between payoffs (which might be monetary, fatalities, column inches or minutes of media attention etc.) and utility numbers where the magnitude of the former corresponds to the order or magnitude of the latter. If we 'weight' the utility numbers for each possible outcome by the probability that the outcome occurs and then add up all these weighted utilities, we get the expected utility for the action:

$$EU = \sum_{i=1}^{n} u(x_i)(p_i)$$

The perfectly rational terrorist group would choose the attack method with the highest expected utility. Even if we don't believe that the terrorist group would choose optimally—by now it should be clear that such a belief has a reasonably high likelihood of being wrong on any given occasion—the expected utility theory provides the benchmark against which actual decisions can be compared. The preliminary step, computing $u(x_i)$, is also important because it allows us to see how utility changes with changes in outcomes. One of the key reasons why expected utility theory exists is that the mathematical expectation or expected value of a gamble does a poor job of explaining human decision-making. People do not choose the option with the highest expected value. Rather, utility increases at a decreasing rate as outcomes increase and the decision-maker will usually prefer a sure payoff to a gamble with an expected value of the same amount. We can put these ideas into action by exploring the relationship between utility and payoffs to one of the most notorious terrorists of the twentieth century, Carlos the Jackal.

Measuring the Jackal's utility

Ilich Ramirez Sanchez or Carlos the Jackal was responsible for multiple terrorist attacks during the 1970s and 1980s. And we can measure the utility[3] of each of those attacks. That a terrorist's preferences for types of terrorism or different attack methods or different targets are *measurable* is probably the most paradigm shattering implication of expected utility theory. The way that this works, as explained, is to convert payoffs (any units) into utility numbers using a utility function. The use of a utility function, which doesn't contravene any of the axioms of expected utility theory, preserves the decision-maker's preferences. What preferences? What does a utility function, which is only a mathematical object, have to do with human behaviour and human preferences? The answer lies in the 'mappings' that have been established between aspects of human behaviour and properties of mathematical objects, including but not limited to utility functions (Phillips 2007).

On the surface, utility functions seem to be basic mathematical objects. But there are links (metaphors, really) that can be established between these objects and human behaviour. One utility function that we can use is the logarithmic utility function, $\ln(x)$. This is a popular choice in economics and some economists have even argued that all utility is logarithmic (e.g. Rubinstein 1976). One reason why it is popular is that it is straightforward. Simply, the utility number associated with any particular payoff is the natural logarithm of that payoff. For example, the utility number associated with six fatalities is $\ln(6) = 1.792$. For payoffs 1 through 20, the set of utility numbers is plotted in Figure 9.1. The graph reveals another of the reasons for the popularity of the logarithmic function. That is, as payoffs increase utility increases but at a decreasing rate. This 'diminishing marginal utility' is a fundamentally important concept in economics and the economist can see it reflected in the mathematical properties of the logarithmic function.

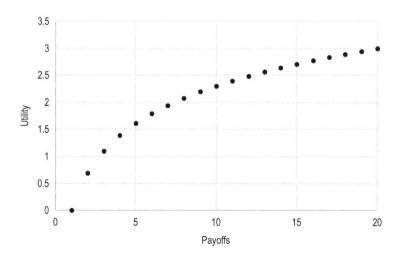

FIGURE 9.1 Logarithmic utility, payoffs 1–20.

More importantly, the concavity of the utility function implies risk aversion. The reason for this is quite simple. In economics, a risk averse decision-maker is formally identified as one who rejects a fair gamble (one whose price is equal to its mathematical expectation or expected value). The risk averse person rejects such a gamble because the expected utility of the gamble is less than the utility that the decision-maker would receive if he or she were paid the gamble's expected value up-front. This can be the case only if the utility function is concave. In Figure 9.2, a concave utility function is drawn along with some information about a gamble. The gamble has two payoffs, x_1 and x_2, and a mathematical expectation or expected value of $E(x)$. For example, if $x_1 = 12$ and $x_2 = 24$ and there is a 2/3 chance of x_1 and a 1/3 chance of x_2, the expected value is 16. Let us say that the decision-maker was asked to pay 16 to participate. This payment to participate provides the decision-maker with a chance of either 12 or 24. The expected utility of the gamble is $E(u)$. Notice, though, that this is less than $u\big[E(x)\big]$, the utility of the expected value if it were received up-front without having to participate in a gamble. The difference between $E(u)$ and $u\big[E(x)\big]$, which leads to the rejection of a fair gamble, can emerge only when the utility function is concave. Hence, if a utility function is concave, it is interpreted as representing risk aversion. This is how a mathematical property like concavity can come to represent an economic property such as risk aversion. A decision-maker whose preferences are represented by a logarithmic function (Figure 9.1) is therefore seen as a risk averse decision-maker.

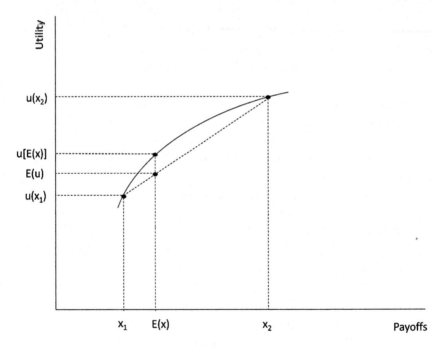

FIGURE 9.2 The concave utility function of a risk averse decision-maker.

The practical implications of this begin to emerge once utility is measured in some concrete setting, such as terrorism. As an example, let us concentrate on Carlos the Jackal's post-1975 attacks and in particular the series of attacks that he perpetrated in 1982 and 1983. Carlos had already gained notoriety through attacks carried out under the auspices of the PFLP. Most notably, his raid on the OPEC headquarters in Vienna in late 1975 which, in fact, led to his separation from the PFLP. After settling in East Berlin with the help of the East German secret police, Carlos attacked a number of targets in Europe. In early 1982, two of his collaborators, including his wife Magdalena Kopp, were arrested in Paris. Carlos's demands for her release were not met. Now began a series of retaliatory attacks that we shall focus our attention on here in order to show how utility can be measured. The motivation for these attacks was quite different from his other attacks, as they were not directly tied to his overarching narrative of the Palestinian cause (though he did try to link them to French airstrikes on PFLP training camps in Lebanon). These attacks were:

- The bombing of the Le Capitole train on March 29, 1982, with 5 dead and 77 injured.
- The car bombing of a Paris-based newspaper on April 22, 1982, with 1 dead and 63 injured.
- The bombing of the French consulate in West Berlin on August 25, 1983, with 1 dead and 22 injured.
- The bombing of the Gare Saint-Charles railway station in Marseille on December 31, 1983, with 2 dead and 33 injured.
- The bombing of the Marseille-Paris TGV train also on December 31, 1983, with 3 dead and 12 injured.

Assuming that Carlos's preferences are reflected by a logarithmic utility function, the utility associated with each of the outcomes can be measured. If we use the logarithmic utility function to compute the utility numbers associated with the total outcomes of each attack (injuries + fatalities), we can see the results in Figure 9.3. The diminishing marginal utility and risk aversion properties are embedded within the logarithmic function itself but what is interesting is that once we have run the calculations and transformed the outcomes into utility numbers, the relative differences in utility across attacks become more apparent. Obviously, an attack with higher outcomes generates higher utility but at a diminishing rate. Proportionally, there is less and less to be gained by larger and larger attacks. Carlos, in this series, actually worked backwards from two higher impact attacks to three lower impact attacks. There was also a yearlong gap between the second attack and the third. Carlos then stopped these types of attacks altogether (even before his 'exile' to Syria in 1985).[4]

With logarithmic utility, the biggest increases in utility come as outcomes increase from zero to 10. Utility then begins to flatten out. The Le Capitole bombing inflicted five times as many injuries and fatalities as the Marseille-Paris TGV bombing and yet

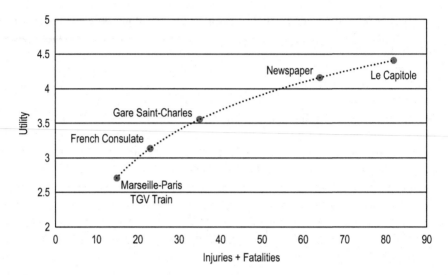

FIGURE 9.3 Utility measurements of Carlos's 1982–1983 attacks.

in moving from the TGV bombing to the Le Capitole bombing, there is only around a two-thirds differential in utility to be gained. Although this is a very old concept in economics, diminishing marginal utility has some interesting interpretations and implications that have been developed within psychology since the 1970s. In fact, while the economists have tried to remove psychology from the diminishing utility concept, psychologists have been doing the opposite. When it is linked with various psychological factors, diminishing marginal utility might account for some of the patterns in this series of Carlos's attacks. For example, affective habituation where stimuli have diminishing affect; self-control, which is easier to exercise when one is more 'satisfied' and goal motivation that decreases as steps are taken towards achieving the goal (Berkman, Kahn & Livingston 2016). Generally, we would expect de-escalation rather than complete disengagement (in the short run at least), gaps between attacks (especially after more successful actions) and, in the longer run, disengagement from activities that are directed towards specific goals. This does not mean that a terrorist like Carlos will disappear altogether but if a particular sub-series of the terrorist's overall attack series is directed towards a specific goal, this sub-series may be subject to the patterns that we have identified and these patterns may be explained by diminishing marginal utility augmented with other psychological concepts. We now turn to another question. Why did Carlos choose bombing instead of some other attack method? More generally, why do terrorists choose one type of attack over another?

The measurement of expected utility

Let us say that the terrorist group aims to inflict fatalities by perpetrating a terrorist action and chooses an attack method based on how well the group believes that the attack method will help it to achieve this operational objective.[5] Again, fatalities are the immediate outcome of terrorism but the same analysis can be undertaken using any payoff or index of payoffs that is deemed relevant. The GTD lists a number of attack methods and categorises the terrorist events from 1970 to 2014 accordingly.[6] Which attack method will the terrorist group choose from among those listed by the GTD if maximising the expected utility, not expected value, of fatalities is the objective of the decision-making process? Expected utility theory allows us to answer this question by giving us a method of computing or measuring the expected utility for each attack method and comparing the results. If the theory yields an accurate prediction of the outcome of the terrorist group's decision-making process, the attack method that is characterised by the highest expected utility will be the one that the terrorist group will choose or, perhaps more realistically, will be the attack method towards which the terrorist group's preferences gravitate over time.

The GTD reports that there were more than 100,000 terrorist attacks (globally) between 1970 and 2014. This is more than enough information for us to form reasonable estimates about the number of fatalities that we might expect to result from each type of attack method.[7] For each attack method, the expected or average outcome and the standard deviation can be computed. These statistics provide the foundation for the determination of the probabilities of outcomes and, ultimately, the expected utility for each action. Assuming a normal distribution, it is a relatively straightforward matter to compute the expected utility for each attack method. The outcomes (fatalities) are transformed into utility numbers using a logarithmic utility function, $\ln(x)$. The utility numbers are weighted by the relevant probabilities (read from the probability distribution) and the weighted utilities are then summed to obtain the expected utility for each attack method. Once these steps have been completed, all that remains is to order the attack methods in terms of their expected utility and determine which attack method sits atop the preference ordering.

The exact number of fatalities inflicted by any attack methods in any particular attack event is a discrete random variable. The probability of inflicting exactly one fatality, two fatalities and so forth can be found by using the probability mass function that describes each attack method.[8] For an attack method such as armed assault, which has an expected number of fatalities of 4.16 and a standard deviation of 13.73, the probability of inflicting exactly 10 fatalities, for example, is approximately 3-in-100 attacks while the chance of inflicting exactly 20 fatalities is approximately 1-in-100. By transforming the numbers of expected fatalities into utility numbers then weighting each by the probability that the particular number of fatalities will be inflicted and then summing over all outcomes, the expected utility of each attack method is eventually arrived at. The expected utilities for the attack methods are reported in Table 9.1.

In this case, armed assault is prescribed by expected utility theory. Some terrorists will choose this. Some will choose to do something else. Others will start by choosing something else but drift towards the prescribed choice. By saying that the terrorist group might drift towards choosing the attack method with the highest

TABLE 9.1 The expected utility of alternative attack methods: GTD, 1970–2014

Attack method	Average inflicted fatalities	Standard deviation of fatalities	Expected utility (logarithmic utility)
Armed assault	4.16	13.73	0.977
Assassination	1.32	1.83	0.466
Bombing	1.72	6.78	0.897
Facility	0.42	7.52	0.775
Hijacking	7.49	89.03	0.189
Hostage (barricade)	2.94	14.92	0.888
Hostage (kidnapping)	2.08	22.76	0.654

expected *utility* (armed assault in this example), we are saying indirectly that it is not necessarily the case that the terrorist group will choose the attack method with the highest expected *value* or average outcome (hijacking). Such a choice would pay no heed to the risk involved in such an action, which in the case of hijacking is very high. Hijacking is the attack method with the most variable outcomes since 1970. Expected utility theory incorporates both the expected outcomes and risk into the measurement procedure, implying that risk averse decision-makers will trade off risk and reward and only choose higher risk alternatives if the reward is commensurate. We see, therefore, that it would be a mistake for law enforcement only to consider the expected outcomes of terrorist actions whilst overlooking the risk that the terrorist group must bear in attempting to perpetrate a terrorist action.

Some people might object on the grounds that the process that we have just worked through does not align with what decision-makers actually do when they make a decision. This is a completely valid standpoint but if it is meant to imply that expected utility theory is wrong because it does not describe the actual decision-making process, then we must point out that the alignment of expected utility theory with the actual decision-making process is not relevant to the validity of the theory as a prescriptive model of human decision-making. Expected utility theory is not a descriptive model of human behaviour (Schoemaker 1982).[9] If expected utility theory is used for a different purpose than it was intended, we should expect that the theory would run into trouble the moment that a decision-maker failed, for example, to weight the utility of each outcome by its exact probability of occurrence. This is best kept in mind because it is too easy to slip into a critique of a mathematical theory on the grounds that it is unrealistic and in doing so overlook the fact that the realism of assumptions is not a permissible criterion on which to judge a model that was built with a purely particular purpose in mind. Of course, as we said at the beginning, expected utility theory provides the correct ordering in each context. As a prescriptive model, it is completely correct. We should also point out that a significant percentage of people (around 40 percent) make choices that are consistent with the choices that expected utility theory prescribes (see, e.g., Hey & Orme 1994). This is why some economists like to use expected utility theory as a predictive model.

Allowing measurements to be impacted by 'biases'

Behavioural economics is an attempt to generalise orthodox economics. Its distinct feature is its use of psychology and its purpose is *description* of how decision-makers arrive at a choice.[10] Some people might think that orthodox economics was wrong and behavioural economics has corrected its mistakes. This is not so. As a prescriptive model, orthodox economics is correct. It is just a matter of how and under what conditions one wishes to use it. One should not expect good results if a prescriptive model is used as a descriptive model. Ultimately, neither orthodox nor behavioural economics is perfect. Both are still works in progress. In fact, the dominant model of orthodox economics, expected utility theory and the dominant model of behavioural economics, prospect theory, seem to work well in concert to explain various aspects of human behaviour (Harrison & Rutström 2009). Overlooking this 'coexistence' leaves us open to serious error (Harrison & Rutström 2009, p.134):

> One of the enduring contributions of behavioural economics is that we now have a rich set of competing models of behaviour in many settings, with expected utility theory and prospect theory as the two front-runners for choices under uncertainty. Debates over the validity of these models have often been framed as a horse race, with the winning theory being declared on the basis of some statistical test in which the theory is represented as a latent process explaining the data. In other words, we seem to pick the best theory by 'majority rule'. If one theory explains more of the data than another theory, we declare it the better theory and discard the other one. In effect, after the race is over we view the horse that 'wins by a nose' as if it was the only horse in the race. The problem with this approach is that it does not recognise the possibility that several behavioural latent processes may coexist in a population.

It is clear, then, that we should not want to close the door completely on any of the models of decision-making that have been developed. Rather, we want to use each of their strengths in a complementary way and we might be surprised to find just how similar the preference orderings from the different types of models are. In a comprehensive study of 23 datasets, 2,000 choice patterns, across several models of decision-making, including prospect theory, expected utility theory and expected value, Harless & Camerer (1994) concluded that there is no definitive answer to the question which theory is best. As they say (1994, p.1286):

> We cannot give a more definitive answer to the question of which theory is best because people use theories for different purposes. A researcher interested in a broad theory, to explain choices by as many people as possible, cares less for parsimony and more for accuracy; she might choose mixed fanning or prospect theory. A decision analyst who wants to help people make more coherent decisions, by adhering to axioms they respect but sometimes wander from, might stick with EU or EV.

The primary advantage of a descriptive model of choice like prospect theory is not necessarily a more 'correct' set of preference orderings but a richer theoretical framework with which to describe patterns of behaviour. Expected utility theory provides a part of the picture but it must be complemented by other frameworks in order that we may say more about the decision-makers in any context. For descriptive models, we must look among the generalisations of expected utility theory that have been developed since the late 1970s. The most prominent of these is prospect theory and its later, more robust derivation, cumulative prospect theory (CPT). Developed by Kahneman & Tversky (1979), prospect theory includes several aspects of the decision-making process that are absent from expected utility theory. These are: (1) the assessment of outcomes from the perspective of a *reference point*; (2) the *non-linear weighting* of probabilities; (3) *risk-aversion* in the domain of gains and (4) risk seeking prompted by *loss aversion* in the domain of losses.

We can re-run the calculations from before using the CPT framework in place of the expected utility theory framework. To do so, we must first assume a particular reference point. Let us say that the terrorist group has a reference point of five fatalities and views anything less than this as a loss. Second, we have to assume that the values for the various parameters of the model determined by Tversky and Kahneman (1992) are broadly generalisable. Although the process of determining the orderings becomes more convoluted as a result, the end product is a preference ordering that reflects some of the features of the actual decision-making process observed in experiment after experiment by behavioural economists and psychologists. The pertinent question that arises concerns the extent to which the result varies from the preference ordering we computed using expected utility theory. With a reference point of five fatalities, the preference orderings determined using prospect theory are not dramatically different from the preference orderings determined using expected utility theory. The true advance of the behavioural model is not computational but as we might expect from a descriptive model, the richer descriptions that it facilitates. Some of the richest descriptions, though, are not isolated within prospect theory but come from comparing and contrasting the results of each of the models of decision-making.

The rankings derived from prospect theory are subject to the reference point and the rankings may diverge further and further away from or, conversely, converge closer and closer to the expected utility rankings depending on the reference point against which outcomes are assessed. According to prospect theory, a decision-maker who is essentially the same in all respects as he was before may view the same set of alternatives differently if his reference point changes. Within expected utility theory, the decision-maker represented by any particular utility function views the same set of alternatives unchangingly within a given period of time.[11] The possibility of changing perspectives is one of the strengths of prospect theory and allows us to consider situations in which the terrorist group initially views the attack methods from one perspective only to change perspectives following some event. For example, the reference point of five fatalities may derive from this number being slightly above the average that is usually observed in terrorist actions in general. Following a particular attack by a rival group that inflicts seven fatalities, the terrorist group may revise its

TABLE 9.2 The prospect value of alternative attack methods

Attack method	Prospect value, reference point = 5 fatalities	Cumulative prospect theory rank	Expected utility theory rank
Armed assault	43.13	3	1
Assassination	12.16	7	6
Bombing	64.44	1	2
Facility	63.05	2	4
Hijacking	27.50	6	7
Hostage (barricade)	42.81	4	3
Hostage (kidnapping)	37.05	5	5

own reference point upwards. This may change the order of the group's preferences. It should always be kept in mind that the expected utility theory measures are the absolutely correct measurements in each particular context. The decision-maker's preferences may diverge from the expected utility orderings to the extent that factors not encompassed within expected utility theory impact the decision-making process or to the extent to which the decision-maker errs.[12]

Returning to the rankings in Table 9.2, we can see that the orderings are not much different regardless of whether one applies prospect theory or expected utility theory to the attack methods under consideration. Bombing moves from second place to first for a CPT decision-maker with a reference point of five fatalities while armed assault moves from first place to third. The reason for the difference, bearing in mind that armed assault is the optimal choice for a log utility maximiser, is the different perspective that the CPT decision-maker brings to the assessment of the alternatives. The reference point is the primary factor shaping the decision-maker's perspective towards bombing and away from armed assault. Armed assault is expected to inflict more fatalities than bombing but the variability is greater.[13] While armed assault is associated with a higher probability (about one in two) of inflicting *at least* five fatalities, the outcomes are far less certain. Bombing gives a marginally lower probability (about one in three) of inflicting at least five fatalities but the outcomes are far less variable. The CPT decision-maker would like to bear just enough risk to ensure that the possibility of exceeding the reference point is sufficiently attractive. Bombing is the attack method that achieves this objective. If the reference point were different, a different attack method would be chosen. A higher reference point would require the selection of a riskier attack method.

Dynamic measurements in the face of innovations

A security initiative such as metal detectors makes hijacking much more difficult and reduces the average inflicted fatalities over time. If we use expected utility as a logical framework without measurement we might be tempted to conclude that this will reduce the expected utility of the attack method, once and for all. However, while the expected utility may decline, the position of hijacking on any preference ordering is relative to the other attack methods. Hijacking may have a lower expected utility than before but this might or might not affect its position in the terrorist group's preference ordering. Only measurements that consider the alternatives can allow us to reach such a conclusion. All of the decision theory frameworks consider both payoffs and their variability. A decline in payoffs may reduce the expected utility or prospect value but if risk declines as well, the attack method might still be a preferred alternative. Furthermore, the preference orderings are not static. Hijacking occupies a low position in the rankings computed here but it need not occupy this position forever more. Measurements must be retaken. Also, if attack methods have a low rank when they are considered individually it does not necessarily mean that the attack method will never be used. It could still form a fundamental part of an efficient combination of attack methods.

We imagine expected utility as a measurement tool being used routinely by law enforcement. The primary rationale for this is simply that expected utility provides the correct measurements and correct rankings of risky prospects. Before attempting to determine what the terrorist might choose to do, would it not be desirable to know what would be optimal for him to do under current and fore-cast or imagined conditions? The second step in this application is not to then work backwards from this optimal decision to a terrorist's prospective decision by subjective judgements alone but by winding back the optimality of the deci-sion by introducing the decision-making biases incorporated into the prospect theory. Systematic decision-making biases that lead to divergences from expected utility maximisation stem from reference points, loss aversion, probability weighting and diminishing sensitivity. Law enforcement agencies will potentially have some insights at least into possible reference points that terrorists might use. This com-bination of law enforcement insight and technical decision theory can produce another set of 'less than optimal' orderings of risky prospects and so on until an array of possible decisions along with their likelihoods is produced.

While our measurements of expected utility and prospect value have been computed for choices of attack methods with payoffs measured in terms of inflicted fatalities, expected utility and prospect value can be measured over any payoffs for any type of risky prospect. It is also the case that the location of attacks is an obviously important consideration. A ranking over locations can be measured by applying the same approach. Different locations might be associated with different levels of media attention (Pohl 2015, 2017) or different expected levels of inflicted fatalities. Once this association has been determined analytically, it is then a straight-forward matter to determine the expected utility or prospect value for alternative terrorist target types or target locations. As Phillips (2016) explains, the potential target location for a planned attack may be based on a reference point location deriving from a recent attack or prominent previous attack. There is virtually no limit to the use to which models of the decision-making process can be put in exe-cuting the task of anticipating, pre-empting and pursuing terrorist offenders.

Four dot points to end the chapter

- Utility theory is a theory of measurement.
- We can use utility theory to convert the payoffs to terrorist attacks (media attention, grassroots supporters, recruits, territory, fatalities etc.) into utility numbers to provide a more nuanced measurement of the relative attractiveness of different terrorist actions to terrorist groups. Terrorist groups don't simply choose the action with the highest absolute payoff.
- Both expected utility theory and prospect theory can be used to work out preference rankings or orderings of risky prospects, including attack methods. We can see how different assumptions about the terrorist decision-maker change these rankings.
- Expected utility theory and prospect theory can be used together. The latter provides us with more pattern predictions. Together, both theories provide us with a useful analytical framework with which to inspect human decision-making, including our own.

Notes

1 Di Tella and Schargrodsky (2004).
2 For example, transitivity. If you prefer A to B and B to C then you must prefer A to C.
3 It should be noted that measurements of utility we refer to are strictly within the framework of von Neumann and Morgenstern's (1947) expected utility theory.
4 Also, his wife was not released from prison until 1985.
5 The following example can be re-worked with any payoff, including media attention (see Pohl 2015).
6 We have chosen this period deliberately, before the 'unarmed assaults' of 2015 and 2016 discussed in a previous chapter.
7 These estimates do need to be recalculated every so often to incorporate innovations in terrorist behaviour and law enforcement. However, like batting averages, once a reasonable number of results have been recorded, the average is not very sensitive to new observations.
8 This gives the probability that some variable, in this case inflicted fatalities, is exactly equal to some number. A basic statistics program can be used to run the calculation.
9 Schoemaker (1982) also notes that expected utility theory can be used prescriptively. That is, as a model that prescribes the correct choice. Thaler (2016), for example, notes that he himself would use expected utility theory to help him make the correct choice. This is a strong endorsement from one of the most cited of all of the behavioural economists.
10 The alternative purposes of economic models were discussed by Schoemaker (1982) in one of our favourite papers.
11 To be precise, the views of which we speak concern the payoffs and probabilities that characterise the alternatives. If these change, both the PT and expected utility measurements will change. Both measurements can also change over time as gains and losses accumulate. The difference between the two theories is that PT and CPT measurements may change based on a changed perspective or reference point even if the underlying payoffs and probabilities and everything else remains the same.
12 Prospect theory does not address the possibility of 'mistakes' and as such does not represent a benchmark against which decisions can be judged in terms of optimality or

correctness. Within PT and CPT, the decision-maker fully understands the situation and deals with it in particular ways that lead to divergences from expected utility theory. It is not mistakes that lead to such decisions. By contrast, one can certainly use the expected utility measurements as a clear benchmark against which to assess decisions and judge divergences as 'mistakes' if one so wishes.

13 On the basis of average fatalities and standard deviation for the period 1970–2014.

References

Andreoni, J. 1991. Reasonable Doubt and the Optimal Magnitude of Fines: Should the Penalty Fit the Crime? *RAND Journal of Economics*, 22, 385–395.

Becker, G. 1968. Crime and Punishment: An Economic Approach. *Journal of Political Economy*, 76, 169–217.

Berkman, E.T., Kahn, L.E. & Livingston, J.L. 2016. Valuation as a Mechanism of Self Control and Ego Depletion. In E.R. Hirt, J.J. Clarkson, & L. Jia (Eds.), *Self Regulation and Ego Control*. London: Academic Press (Elsevier), pp. 255–279.

Boumans, M. 2007. *Measurement in Economics: A Handbook*. Amsterdam: Elsevier.

Di Tella, R. & Schargrodsky, E. 2004. Do Police Reduce Crime? Estimates Using the Allocation of Police Resources after a Terrorist Attack. *American Economic Review*, 94, 115–133.

Ehrlich, I. 1973. Participation in Illegitimate Activities: A Theoretical and Empirical Investigation. *Journal of Political Economy*, 81, 521–565.

Ehrlich, I. & Brower, G. 1987. On the Issue of Causality in the Economic Model of Crime and Law Enforcement: Some Theoretical Considerations and Experimental Evidence. *American Economic Review*, 77, 99–106.

Enders, W. & Sandler, T. 2002. Patterns of Transnational Terrorism, 1970 to 1999: Alternative Time Series Estimates. *International Studies Quarterly*, 46, 145–165.

Fajnzylber, P., Lederman, D., & Loayza, N. 2000. Crime and Victimisation: An Economic Perspective. Economia, Fall, 1, 219–230.

Fishburn, P.C. 1989. Retrospective on the Utility Theory of von Neumann and Morgenstern. *Journal of Risk and Uncertainty*, 2, 127–158.

Freeman, R. 1996. Why Do So Many Young American Men Commit Crimes and What Might We Do about It? *Journal of Economic Perspectives*, 10, 25–42.

Harless, D.W. & Camerer, C.F. 1994. The Predictive Utility of Generalised Expected Utility Theories. *Econometrica*, 62, 1251–1289.

Harrison, G.W. & Rutström, E.E. 2009. Expected Utility Theory and Prospect Theory: One Wedding and a Decent Funeral. *Experimental Economics*, 12, 133–158.

Hey, J.D. & Orme, C. 1994. Investigating Generalisations of Expected Utility Theory Using Experimental Data. *Econometrica*, 62, 1291–1326.

Kahneman, D. & Tversky, A. 1979. Prospect Theory: An Analysis of Decision under Risk. *Econometrica*, 47, 263–291.

Levitt, S. 1997. Using Electoral Cycles in Police Hiring to Estimate the Effect of Police on Crime. *American Economic Review*, 87, 270–290.

Phillips, P.J. 2007. Mathematics, Metaphors and Economic Visualisability. *The Quarterly Journal of Austrian Economics*, 10, 281–299.

Phillips, P.J. 2016. *The Economics of Terrorism*. Abingdon, Oxon and New York: Routledge Taylor & Francis.

Pohl, G. 2015. Media and Terrorist Choice: A Risk-Reward Analysis. *Journal of Applied Security Research*, 10, 60–76.

Pohl, G. 2017. Terrorist Choice and the Media. Unpublished PhD Thesis, University of Southern Queensland, Australia.

Rubinstein, M. 1976. The Strong Case for the Generalised Logarithmic Utility Model as the Premier Model of Financial Markets. *Journal of Finance*, 31, 551–571.

Schoemaker, P.J.H. 1982. The Expected Utility Model: Its Variants, Purposes, Evidence and Limitations. *Journal of Economic Literature*, 20, 529–563.

Thaler, R.H. 2016. *Misbehaving: The Making of Behavioural Economics*. New York: W.W. Norton.

Tversky, A. & Kahneman, D. 1992. Advances in Prospect Theory: Cumulative Representation of Uncertainty. *Journal of Risk and Uncertainty*, 5, 297–323.

Von Neumann, J. & Morgenstern, O. 1947. *Theory of Games and Economic Behaviour*. Princeton, NJ: Princeton University Press.

Witte, A. 1980. Estimating the Economic Model of Crime with Individual Data. *Quarterly Journal of Economics*, 94, 155–167.

10

DECISION-MAKING WITH MORE THAN ONE REFERENCE POINT

In January 2000, Al-Qaeda operatives gathered secretly in Malaysia for a planning meeting. The Central Intelligence Agency (CIA) was watching. Among the participants was Khalid al-Mihdhar, one of the hijackers who would later help to crash American Airlines flight 77 into the Pentagon. By the time the meeting disbanded, the CIA had taken a photograph of al-Mihdhar, learned his full name, obtained his passport number, and uncovered one other critical piece of information: al-Mihdhar held a multiple-entry visa to the United States. It was twenty months before the September 11, 2001, terrorist attacks on the World Trade Centre and the Pentagon. George Tenet, the director of central intelligence (DCI), later admitted that the CIA should have placed al-Mihdhar on the State Department's watch list denying him entry into the United States. It did not until August 23, 2001, just nineteen days before the terrorist attacks and months after al-Mihdhar had entered the country, obtained a California motor vehicle photo identification card (using his real name), and started taking flying lessons.[1]

How do reference points affect law enforcement decision-making? Prospect theory depicts the decision-maker as being reference point dependent. More recently, it has been discovered that people make decisions with more than one outcome reference point in mind. The general predictions of prospect theory still hold when more than one outcome reference point is introduced. That is, people become risk seeking in the domain of losses (below a reference point) and risk averse in the domain of gains. But with multiple outcome reference points, these aspects of decision-making may change dynamically as a decision-making process unfolds. Rather than simply becoming risk averse once the single outcome reference point has been exceeded, the decision-maker may become *risk seeking above* an outcome reference point. This apparent contradiction can be explained by introducing a second or third outcome reference point. We can then say that the individual is risk seeking above one outcome reference point because he or she is still below another outcome reference point. There will be a sort of oscillation in risk preference as the decision-maker approaches any of the multiple reference points and either falls short or exceeds it.

There are many types of law enforcement decisions that could be examined in this regard. We will concentrate on the task of ranking or prioritising suspects. This could be a task that has to be completed as soon as possible after a terrorist attack with the objective of identifying and pursuing the perpetrators or identifying 'cell' members. Or, it could be a task that is never completed as such. The development of terrorism watch lists has seen the ongoing prioritisation and reprioritisation of potential or known terrorists. The sheer size of the terrorism watch lists in Europe and the United States along with the unfortunate number of cases where offenders whose names have been on watch lists have, nonetheless, managed to perpetrate an act of terrorism, make the management of terrorist watch lists one of the most important counter-terrorism tasks.

There have been cases where, although numerous red flags were raised, eventual offenders were never listed on watch lists at all. These oversights permitted these offenders to plan their terrorist actions relatively unimpeded. Of course, public discourse following such an attack focuses on the question of why the person was not identified as a threat. In early 2019, Brenton Tarrant perpetrated New Zealand's most deadly mass shooting when he attacked mosques in Christchurch. There were 51 people killed and a further 50 injured. The suspect had developed an interest in fringe movements as well as an interest in historical battles between Christians and Muslims. He also appears to have made provocative statements in various online environments that could be viewed, especially with the benefit of hindsight, as being signals of intent. He was not, however, at any time under the watch of law enforcement or intelligence agencies. He had purchased his weapons legally. The general explanation offered in cases where a watch listed person or a non–watch listed person perpetrates an attack is that the volume of information is large and separating signals from noise in such a context is extremely difficult. This is true. But even with perfect information, law enforcement agencies will make prioritisation errors. It is important that this be recognised in order for it to be addressed.

Reference point dependence in decision-making can influence suspect identification and prioritisation in various ways. We explained how reference point dependence and the other important features of prospect theory shape this task in our paper, 'Terrorism Watch Lists, Suspect Ranking and Decision-Making Biases' (Phillips & Pohl 2019). A reference point in this context might be viewed as a set of remembered characteristics. To the extent that the most serious terrorism threats are posed by individuals whose characteristics match those of the reference point, the prioritisation of suspects may be more or less optimal. Because a reference point focuses the attention of the decision-maker, potential offenders with characteristics that place them at a greater 'distance' from the reference point, will not figure as prominently in law enforcement assessments. More concerning though is the fact that diminishing sensitivity away from the reference point means that changes in behaviour exhibited by suspects that are more 'distant' do not seem as important. As such, a potential terrorist offender might initially be seen to be a long way from the set of reference characteristics and be placed further down the list of potential threats (or not listed at all). This initial mistake may then be compounded by the failure to recognise and adjust to changes in the suspect's exhibited behaviour.

Introducing multiple reference points allows us to consider not only the ways in which different suspect (outcome) reference points may interact to shape suspect ranking but also the ways in which different organisational career goals within law enforcement agencies may shape law enforcement behaviour. After 9/11, it became apparent that many organisational factors had played at least some role in impeding the analysis and interpretation of the available intelligence and, in particular, had hampered the sharing of intelligence across agencies. Multiple reference point theories allow us to consider, for example, a situation in which a law enforcement agent or investigative team approaches its tasks with status quo, minimum requirements and aspirational career reference points in mind. The team's behaviour will oscillate as it experiences losses or gains relative to these reference points, leading to potentially suboptimal rankings of suspects and misallocation of surveillance and other resources.

The reference point concept: from single to multiple

The reference point concept makes its first appearance in Kahneman & Tversky's (1979) original prospect theory paper after 11 pages of analysis and discussion (on p.274). The authors explain how people will code outcomes as gains and losses rather than as final (absolute) states. They identify the status quo as the most likely candidate for a reference point but suggest that different factors, including problem framing and expectations, may influence it as well. The reference point is depicted several pages later as the point around which the value (utility) function inflects, with a convex risk seeking portion to the left in the domain of losses and a concave risk averse portion to the right in the domain of gains. Even though oscillating utility functions were not new (e.g. Friedman & Savage 1948), Kahneman and Tversky's (1979) asymmetrical S-shaped utility function captured the attention of a generation of young behavioural economists. The oscillation in risk preferences allows deeper behavioural narratives to be constructed and a wider range of behaviour to be explained. For example, in finance people tend to hold their losing investments too long and sell their winning investments too soon. This can be explained as a manifestation of risk seeking over losses and risk aversion over gains.

Kahneman & Tversky (1979) identified the status quo as a likely candidate for a decision-maker's reference point. Later, Lopes (1987) and, later still, Heath, Larrick & Wu (1999), argued that reference points could just as easily be 'goals' or 'aspirations'. Lopes developed what she called *SP / A* theory for security-potential-aspirations. It is a variant of expected utility theory and prospect theory but with greater emphasis on feelings rather than cognition. In Lopes' theory, people are guided by fear and hope in attempting to achieve their aspiration level. Heath, Larrick & Wu (1999) do not develop a decision model as such but use prospect theory to shed more light on the psychology of goals. They ask, for example, what makes goals motivating. And why do people feel worse when they fail to reach their goals? Their answer is formed by treating goals as reference points. Of course, these developments simultaneously show the importance of non-status-quo reference points and diminish the standing of the status quo as 'the' reference point. This expands our narratives and the scope of our pattern prediction still further to include goal-related concepts such as persistence, motivation, effort and performance (Heath, Larrick & Wu 1999, p.80).

In the 1990s, researchers began to combine different sorts of reference points into single decision-making models. These extensions of prospect theory included reference points as goals (G), the status quo reference point (SQ) and also minimum survival-type reference points called 'minimum requirements' (MR). For example, Sullivan & Kida (1995) combined SQ and G to explore investment managers' behaviour. They found that the managers considered both reference points in a single risky decision-making task. When managers' performance was such that they found themselves above the SQ, they became risk averse, especially if there was a chance that performance could dip back below SQ. However, if they were well above SQ, such that there was little chance of slipping back below it, they became risk seeking with reference to G. It was confirmed that decision-makers can indeed use multiple reference points in a single task, sometimes with surprising results (Boles & Messick 1995; Koop & Johnson 2012). Theoretically, the main frameworks that can be found in the literature are Lopes' (1987) *SP / A* theory, March & Shapira's (1992) variable risk preference model and Wang & Johnson's (2012) tri-reference-point theory. In the remainder of this chapter, we draw on various features of these frameworks to explain how multiple reference points can shape law enforcement behaviour and decision-making.

Multiple reference points in an investigative context

When decision-makers orient towards a reference point and are close to it, they are risk seeking below it and risk averse above it. In a law enforcement context, the pursuit and pre-emption of terrorist offenders is performed under conditions of risk and uncertainty. This includes the prioritisation or ranking of suspects for terrorism watch lists. A reference point here might derive from the offender characteristics. In this case, a typical offender or an offender that has been the subject of a recent investigation forms the basis for the reference point and other potential suspects are assessed against it. At some stage, but not always, the investigative team will receive feedback about the accuracy of their suspect ranking when an offender perpetrates or attempts to perpetrate an act of violence. At such a point in time, the investigative team enters the domain of gains or the domain of losses. In the domain of gains, the team takes a much more conservative approach to the ranking process. In the domain of losses, the team becomes more risk seeking, revising their rankings in line with developments and perhaps recalibrating to a new reference point.

Such reference point dependence is centred on the terrorist but what if the investigative team has an internal or organisational reference point? For example, a reference point derived from the recent success of another or rival team and their subsequent enhancement in career level or status. Investigative teams work in organisations that have cultures, incentive structures, career pathways, informal and real authority, turf wars and power dynamics that are analogous to those that can be found in every other type of organisation. After 9/11 much discussion was focused on the role of culture within intelligence agencies in *creating* the conditions for systematic intelligence failures. This is discussed in detail by Davies (2004). Davies (2004) argues that the distinct national cultural 'traits' of the Americans and the British are so strong as to shape the outcomes, successes and failures, of American and British intelligence. Intelligence agencies are the products of the cultures in which they exist. They are not somehow removed from such influences.

The discourse on organisational culture within the intelligence community reached a fever pitch following the 9/11 attacks. So much so that some authors have urged more circumspection. Bean (2009) could unequivocally state, 'Post-9/11 studies of US intelligence routinely attribute a cause of intelligence failure to the "dysfunctional", "conflictual" or "fragmented" organizational cultures of US intelligence agencies'. It had become the standard explanation and the primary emphasis in efforts to reform intelligence. Bean (2009, p.479) lists no fewer than ten scholarly papers contributed from various perspectives asserting that culture played a strong role in the failure to detect and pre-empt the 9/11 attackers: Treverton (2003), Dahlstrom (2003), Turner (2004), Davies (2004), Cooper (2005), Garicano and Posner (2005), Johnston (2005), Jones (2006), Marrin (2007) and Zegart (2007). Bean (2009) sees a danger in attributing failures or identifying as the locus of intelligence failures 'systems' and 'cultures' rather than individuals or groups who have specific responsibilities. This, Bean argues (2009, p.481), is, '…the latest manifestation of a 60 year-old institutional struggle over the meanings of accountability and the relationships between intelligence systems, cultures, and individuals'.

The implications of this ongoing debate are significant (see O'Connell 2006). In the midst of this cacophony, however, a few authors spent some time considering the role that decision-making processes play in creating the conditions for intelligence failures. Garicano & Posner (2005) and Meszerics & Littvay (2009) are two of the more prominent examples. Garicano & Posner (2005), for instance, suggest that the unanimous conclusion on the state of Iraq's weapons programs before the 2003 invasion was an outcome of groupthink ultimately due to poorly designed organisational structures. In a similar but slightly different way, Meszerics & Littvay (2009) focus on analytic failures where wrong conclusions are reached and which cannot be explained by organisation factors such as poor information sharing. Their primary concept is 'pseudo-wisdom' introduced by Deutsch & Madow (1961) to distinguish between situations in which people advance within an organisation by making correct decisions essentially by chance and situations in which truly wise people advance. Of course, if an individual reaches an important decision-making position without actually being 'wise', unfavourable outcomes may result.

These papers represent steps towards the individual decision-making processes that produce intelligence reports but do not go so far as to explore more fully their implications.

Most of these ideas, including culture and incentives, can be interpreted through a prospect theory framework. The four features of prospect theory, reference point dependence, probability weighting, loss aversion and diminishing sensitivity combine to introduce 'biases' into decision-making even where the decision-makers have perfect information. As mentioned previously, we could frame an analysis of terrorist suspect ranking around a reference point based on an archetypal terrorist suspect to show how such a reference point combined with these other features of the decision-making process can produce suboptimal prioritisations of suspects. In such an analysis, we would not even have to introduce any of the contextual features that we have just been discussing to find that there are plenty of ways in which decision-making in law enforcement agencies can go wrong (and plenty of ways to attempt to mitigate the problems). Viewing these internal organisational features through a prospect theory lens, however, allows us to reinterpret them and identify their significance as factors that shape the decision-making process of individual law enforcement agents and teams.

Imagine, first, that the individual agent or investigative team (or intelligence team) has a single composite reference point that encompasses the team's current organisational status quo on all relevant matters. Essentially, a *status* status-quo (SSQ). We might modify the standard S-shaped utility function to illustrate the situation (Figure 10.1).

It is not the case that the individual agent or team seeks only organisational status or career advancement. Of course, we could be confident in saying that all agents would gladly forgo such things to prevent a terrorist action. However, this trade-off is never in play. No one gets the chance to trade a career step for the prevention of a terrorist attack. In reality, individuals and teams *do* work in organisations and *do* operate in an incentives structure. Successful individuals and teams *will* receive enhanced status and it cannot be denied that this is a relevant, if secondary or even subconscious, consideration in their work. In fact, the status of individual, team and agency is a consideration. Inter-agency rivalries, sometimes with long and complicated histories, were identified as one of the sources of poor inter-agency communication before 9/11. Parker & Stern (2005, p.316) make the following observation:

> Some analysts emphasize the role of several high-profile espionage cases during the 1990s in exacerbating the already acerbic relationship between the CIA and the FBI. For example, Mark Riebling (2002) suggests that fallout from cases such as the infamous Aldrich Ames and Robert Hanssen affairs fuelled animosity and mistrust between the agencies. FBI officials were tasked to investigate its sister agency in the former case and conducted what Riebling (2002:454–455) describes as a 'vicious and indiscriminate' 'inquisition' in search of possible additional moles within the agency. The inquiries

FIGURE 10.1 S-shaped utility function with a SSQ reference point.

were implemented in a fashion that greatly antagonised the mainstream CIA, wreaked havoc with the staff, and, not least, produced tremendous resentment. In February 2001, the CIA would have a chance to return the favour following the arrest of FBI agent Robert Hanssen on charges of spying for the Soviets. According to Riebling (2002:468), the 'Hanssen effect' would have devastating consequences: 'Until CIA officers could be sure that there was not another Hanssen within the bureau, they would hesitate to share sensitive information.' Thus, the cumulative effect of such mutual suspicion and resentment was to further constrict the information flow in the critical months prior to 9/11.

Once we have framed the situation in this way, we see it transformed. The team's current status is a status quo. In performing its functions, the team has the chance to experience improvements or reversals. Let us say that the team's sole function is the ranking and surveillance of terrorist suspects according to the level of threat that the potential offenders are thought to represent. Let us also say, for simplicity, that the team will experience three possible outcomes: (1) a ranked[2] suspect perpetrates an attack. This is a loss for the team. (2) No ranked suspect perpetrates an attack. This maintains the status quo. (3) A ranked suspect is apprehended in the planning phase of an attack. This is a gain for the team. Outcomes (1) and (3) place the team in the domain of losses or gains. The team's subsequent rankings may now be influenced by either risk seeking or risk averse behaviour. Within the agency, however, it is not just the team's own actions that result in gains and losses. A rival team may experience gains, which may place the team in the domain of losses relative to that rival team. Once more, risk seeking behaviour may be observed as the team attempts to recover lost ground. Prospect theory tells us that outcomes regarding organisational status that are close to the reference point are felt more acutely than outcomes that are further away. Each individual and team will be most sensitive to changes at or around their own current level rather than more remote developments. Events within the intelligence agency are also subject to diminishing sensitivity.

In Garicano and Posner's (2005, p.155) analysis of intelligence failures, career incentives were viewed as a significant factor:

> Career incentives can encourage herding. When an employee's career depends on evaluations by superiors, the employee will have an incentive to echo the opinions of superiors (the 'yes men' phenomenon of Prendergast, 1993) and also not to update prior beliefs, lest it make the employee appear unreliable (changing one's mind means acknowledging an error). In effect, the analyst herds with his own prior judgments. The tendency is greater with more experienced managers because they have a longer track record, meaning that any bold departure they make is more likely to contradict a position they've taken in the past. Only if they can credibly claim that their information is new can they change their minds without losing reputation. The need to be seen to be consistent plays a role even at the agency level. The CIA defended the curveball intelligence long after it was discredited, fearing how an acknowledgment of error would look to senior management at the CIA and to policymakers.
>
> *WMD Commission (2005, p. 107)*

Under the same conditions that we have just described, we could introduce a second reference point. Rather than SSQ, this one could be status goal (SG). Now, the individual or team, in performing their tasks, takes two reference points into consideration. If the team is above SSQ but not securely so, the team might be expected to be risk averse as it tries to protect its gains. However, if it has achievements that ensure that it will certainly remain positively beyond the SSQ, it may become risk seeking with reference to SG. Depending on where the team is situated relative to SSQ and SG, the team will exhibit different behaviour. This is depicted in Figure 10.2.

These behavioural patterns hold for any particular decision task, any individual decision-maker or team of decision-makers as well as for the organisation or agency as a collective. As we discuss in a moment, the agency's directors can be expected to exhibit risk aversion or risk seeking when they find themselves either side of a reference point that is related to the overarching direction in which they are leading the agency and their aspirations or goals regarding it. Their broader policy decisions can influence the risk preferences of the organisation as a whole, instilling a more

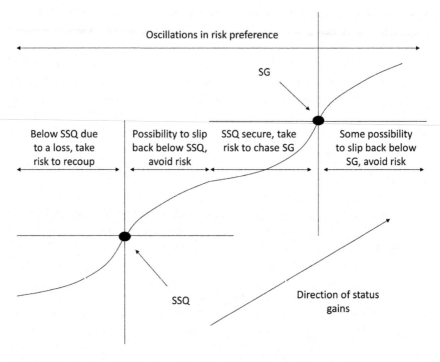

Oscillations in risk preference

SG

| Below SSQ due to a loss, take risk to recoup | Possibility to slip back below SSQ, avoid risk | SSQ secure, take risk to chase SG | Some possibility to slip back below SG, avoid risk |

SSQ

Direction of status gains

FIGURE 10.2 S-shaped utility function with dual reference points.

or less risk-taking culture as the case may be. The status of an individual, team or the whole agency may usually be expected to oscillate around SSQ reference point. Sometimes, external events provide the opportunity to move rapidly to a point above or below SSQ. Intelligence failures like those that preceded 9/11 may plunge an entire agency into the domain of losses below SSQ. One could expect the leadership and perhaps the individual personnel within that agency to take more risk in subsequent periods in order to recoup their losses. The aggressive actions of the CIA post-9/11 are not inconsistent with this pattern prediction. Conversely, a different type of event can elevate an agency quickly above SSQ and possibly above SG while still other events can have ambiguous effects. The Cuban missile crisis worked both ways, first elevating and then diminishing the CIA's reputation (Robarge 2009). It is possible that an analysis of the Agency's decisions following the crisis might lead to a conclusion that they were more volatile than usual, now conservative, now more risk taking.

As interesting as this might be, let us return to our specific topic of interest. That is, suspect prioritisation. Risk aversion and risk seeking in suspect ranking may be interpreted in different ways. Most straightforwardly, each potential suspect is characterised by a particular probability that he or she will perpetrate an attack. A risk seeking investigative team might be expected to make the mistake of pursuing lower probability offenders, their attention having been drawn to the less likely events and their probability weighting exaggerating the likelihood. Being responsible for pre-empting an offender who would normally not be considered a likely threat would enhance the status of the team more than pre-empting an offender who every other team knows to be a serious threat. Conversely, a risk averse investigative team might make the opposite mistake. A risk averse team concentrates on the higher probability offenders, simultaneously ensuring that the worst outcome is avoided (i.e. a 'clear and present danger' perpetrates an attack) while at the same time maximising their chances of remaining in the domain of gains by pre-empting further high-probability offenders.

Resolving this potential problem is not easy. The organisational reforms initiated after 9/11 and basic processes that ensure peer reviews of certain decisions and appropriate incentives structures require vigilant maintenance. We must not overlook the role of the government and its political leaders in shaping the behaviour of government agencies, including intelligence and law enforcement agencies. For example, during the 1970s the CIA was under immense pressure from political leaders and many policy decisions placed considerable restraints on the Agency (Johnson 1997). The decisions of investigative teams and case officers are affected by high-level government policy decisions. Placing a whole agency in the domain of losses (or gains) might prove to be counterproductive in ways that are not at all obvious. Micro-level risk seeking (or risk averse) behaviour stemming from being forced into the loss (or gain) domain will not be detectable at the macro level and while such behaviour might result in big mistakes that do become visible to political decision-makers, the results of many small miscalculations from periods where an agency has been shunted off-course might simmer in the background for years.

A note on slack

In their discussion of the influence of multiple reference points on the decision-making process, March and Shapira (1992) explore the relationship between resource availability and the reference point. In studies of risk taking, it had been discovered that people in organisations take more risk when there is more 'slack'. That is, when there are resources in excess of current aspirations (e.g. Libby & Fishburn 1977; Antonelli 1989; Wehrung 1989). The opposite holds. This relationship of risk-taking to slack has important implications for any single or multiple reference point model. The decision-maker, as we have explained, does not want to fall below a reference point. If the SSQ has been surpassed, risk aversion prevails. However, if the decision-maker closes in on the higher, SG, reference point, risk seeking can emerge. The amount of resources that are available in an organisation, including an intelligence organisation, acts either as a check on this risk-taking behaviour or as an encouragement to it. More than this, the availability of resources and the amount of slack can focus the attention of the decision-maker on either SSQ or SG.

Practically, most intelligence organisations operate without much slack relative to the amount of work that could be done. Suspect ranking is a prime example.

Given sufficient resources, all watch listed individuals could be watched all of the time. There will never be such resources available and so there are always constraints and, mostly, not much slack. On the contrary, then, we might say that there will be a general tendency within such organisations towards risk aversion and a general focus of attention on the lowest of the two (or more) reference points. However, this conclusion overlooks the very real jostling and lobbying for resources that characterises government departments and agencies. Although the availability of current resources may act as a check on risk-taking or an encouragement to it, various factors, including the particular agency's successes and failures, determine the amount of future resources that might be made available to the agency or, indeed, its continued independent existence vis-à-vis potential amalgamation.

At the agency level, then, far beyond the individual operational decisions of investigators, agents and teams, the subtle interplay of aspirations and resources may shape an organisation-wide preference for more or less risk, as the case may be. For the agency and those who lead it, there may be a shifting focus of attention between the survival of the agency (a lower reference point) and the aspirations that are held for it. The available slack, granted to the agency by government policymakers, turns attention in one direction or the other. As March & Shapira (1992, p.174) explain,

> Consequently, aggregate risk-taking behaviour in a population [agency-wide] is attributable partly to the way the [risk-taking] process affects the accumulation of resources, partly to the way it distributes risk-takers to success and failure (in terms of their own aspiration levels) and partly to the way it allocates attention between the two reference points.

An agency's resources may shape its aggregate risk behaviour but its risk behaviour may shape the agency's resources. These sorts of complexities are not easily spotted unless intelligence and law enforcement agencies are viewed as collections of decision-makers.

Four dot points to end the chapter

- In the original version of prospect theory, the reference point is zero or the status quo.
- Later research expanded the reference point concept to include goals and expanded the number of reference points that can shape a decision-maker's behaviour.
- Within organisations, various career-oriented and organisational-oriented reference points lead to oscillations in risk preferences, from risk seeking to risk averse and back again.
- Sometimes, the position of individuals, teams and whole agencies relative to these reference points may be determined by broader organisational or governmental decisions.

Notes

1 Zegart (2005, p.78).
2 Although failing to find and rank a terrorist suspect also represents an error and potential for loss, we are assuming for the moment that no known suspect is unranked and the team is not in error for not having ranked a suspect about whose existence the team was unaware.

References

Antonelli, C. 1989. A Failure Induced Model of Research and Development Expenditure: Italian Evidence from the Early 1980s. *Journal of Economic Behaviour and Organisation*, 12, 129–180.
Bean, H. 2009. Organisational Culture and US Intelligence Affairs. *Intelligence and National Security*, 24, 479–498.
Boles, T.L. & Messick, D.M. 1995. A Reverse Outcome Bias: The Influence of Multiple Reference Points on the Evaluation of Outcomes and Decisions. *Organisational Behaviour and Human Decision Processes*, 61, 262–275.
Commission on the Intelligence Capabilities of the United States Regarding Weapons of Mass Destruction. 2005. Report of the Commission on the Intelligence Capabilities of the United States Regarding Weapons of Mass Destruction. Washington, DC: Government Printing Office. Available at (www.wmd.gov/report/wmd_ report.pdf).
Cooper, J. 2005. *Curing Analytic Pathologies: Pathways to Improved Intelligence Analysis.* Washington, DC: Center for the Study of Intelligence.
Dahlstrom, E. 2003. *Intelligence and Law Enforcement: Bridging the Cultural Divide* Washington, DC: National War College.
Davies, P.H.J. 2004. Intelligence Culture and Intelligence Failure in Britain and the United States. *Cambridge Review of International Affairs*, 17, 495–520.
Deutsch, K.W. & Madow, W.G. 1961. A Note on the Appearance of Wisdom in Large Bureaucratic Organisations. *Behavioural Science*, 6, 72–78.
Friedman, M. & Savage, L.J. 1948. The Utility Analysis of Choices Involving Risk. *Journal of Political Economy*, 56, 279–304.
Garicano, L. and Posner, R. 2005. Intelligence Reform Since 9/11: An Organizational Economics Perspective. *Journal of Economic Perspectives*, 19, 151–170.
Heath, C., Larrick, R.P. & Wu, G. 1999. Goals as Reference Points. *Cognitive Psychology*, 38, 79–109.
Johnson, L.K. 1997. The CIA and the Question of Accountability. *Intelligence and National Security*, 12, 178–200.
Johnston, R. 2005. *Analytic Culture in the U.S. Intelligence Community: An Ethnographic Study.* Washington, DC: Center for the Study of Intelligence.
Jones, G. 2006. It's a Cultural Thing: Thoughts on a Troubled CIA. *Orbis*, 50, 23–40.
Kahneman, D. & Tversky, A. 1979. Prospect Theory: An Analysis of Decision under Risk. *Econometrica*, 47, 263–291.
Koop, G.J. & Johnson, J.G. 2012. The Use of Multiple Reference Points in Risky Decision-Making. *Journal of Behavioural Decision-Making*, 25, 49–62.
Libby, R. & Fishburn, P.C. 1977. Behavioural Models of Risk Taking in Business Decisions: A Survey and Evaluation. *Journal of Accounting Research*, 15, 272–292.
Lopes, L.L. 1987. Between Hope and Fear: The Psychology of Risk. *Advances in Experimental Social Psychology*, 20, 255–295.
March, J.G. & Shapira, Z. 1992. Variable Risk Preferences and the Focus of Attention. *Psychological Review*, 99, 172–183.

Marrin, S. 2007. At Arm's Length or at the Elbow? Explaining the Distance between Analysts and Decision-Makers. *International Journal of Intelligence and Counterintelligence*, 20, 401–414.

Meszerics, T. & Littvay, L. 2009. Pseudo-Wisdom and Intelligence Failures. *International Journal of Intelligence and Counter Intelligence*, 23, 133–147.

O'Connell, A.J. 2006. The Architecture of Smart Intelligence: Structuring and Overseeing Agencies in a Post-9/11 World. *California Law Review*, 94, 1655–1744.

Parker, C.F. & Stern, E.K. 2005. Bolt from the Blue or Avoidable Failure? Revisiting September 11 and the Origins of Strategic Surprise. *Foreign Policy Analysis*, 1, 301–331.

Phillips, P.J. & Pohl, G. 2019. Terrorism Watch Lists, Suspect Ranking and Decision-Making Biases. *Studies in Conflict & Terrorism*, 42, 898–914.

Prendergast, C. 1993. A Theory of 'Yes Men'. *American Economic Review*, 83, 757–770.

Riebling, M. 2002. *Wedge, from Pearl Harbor to 911: How the Secret War between the FBI and CIA Has Endangered National Security*. New York: Touchstone.

Robarge, D. 2009. CIA in the Spotlight: The Central Intelligence Agency and Public Accountability. *Journal of Intelligence History*, 9, 105–126.

Sullivan, K. & Kida, T. 1995. The Effect of Multiple Reference Points and Prior Gains and Losses on Managers' Risky Decision-Making. *Organisational Behaviour and Human Decision Processes*, 48, 131–146.

Treverton, G. 2003. Terrorism, Intelligence and Law Enforcement: Learning the Right Lessons. *Intelligence and National Security*, 18, 121–140.

Turner, M. 2004. A Distinctive U.S. Intelligence Identity. *International Journal of Intelligence and Counter Intelligence*, 17, 42–61.

Wang, X.T. & Johnson, J.G. 2012. A Tri-Reference-Point Theory of Decision-Making under Risk. *Journal of Experimental Psychology*, 141, 743–756.

Wehrung, D.A. 1989. Risk Taking over Gains and Losses: A Study of Oil Executives. *Annals of Operations Research*, 19, 115–139.

Zegart, A. 2005. September 11 and the Adaptation Failure of U.S. Intelligence Agencies. *International Security*, 29, 78–111.

Zegart, A. 2007. *Spying Blind: The CIA, the FBI, and the Origins of 9/11*. Princeton, NJ: Princeton University Press.

11

A GUIDE TO THE TERRORISM STUDIES CONVERSATION

It is a wondrous coincidence that all human knowledge and experience can be completely and accurately expressed in binary digital terms.[1]

Reputations for organisational intelligence are built on capabilities for securing, analysing, and retrieving information in a timely and intelligent manner. This practical consciousness of the importance of the information is mirrored by research intended to understand and improve the uses of information by human beings.

Feldman and March (1981, p. 171)

Once the need to maintain a vigilant watch on new developments in the academic literature is realised, there remains the challenge of dealing with an incredible amount of new and existing information. The most likely people to be tasked with these responsibilities and carry them out successfully are analysts with graduate qualifications or analysts who are ex-academics with PhDs and research experience. Even so, just like writing craft, qualifications and education and experience and even some degree of research success do not necessarily translate into successful information gathering, organisation and dissemination technique. There is always room for improvement. For example, there are certain aspects of writing craft that might be hit upon by accident or subconsciously at times but which must be made the subject of conscious and deliberate implementation for a writer to take his or her craft to the next level and consistently deliver publishable outcomes. The same is true of information gathering and the foundational skills of research.

On a deeper level, the search process and the problem solving methodology underlying it may be shaped by the decision-making process, leading to suboptimal or erroneous outcomes. Each analyst tasked with 'search' or 'search and solve', in all likelihood, already has an intuition about the result. This can be a positive thing because following hunches might work out well. But hunches do not always work out well. In any case, it is best to be aware of the effect that intuition is having on the task. Kahneman (2011, p.97) introduces his readers to the idea of 'answering a different question'. That is, confronted with a particular question, people have the tendency to replace it with an easier one. The 'target' question is the one that the decision-maker intends to answer while the 'heuristic' question is the simpler question that is answered instead. Part of the reason why this can result in substantial biases is that the easier heuristic question might be more prone to being shaped by moods and feelings. For example, if one asks whether terrorism studies academics have developed any insights into a particular problem, an affect heuristic might be applied in which a dislike of 'impractical' people determines the answer to an easier question such as whether academics have produced anything worthwhile. This may be micro-directed in the sense that an analyst might generally value research but has strong feelings about one or more of the disciplines that contribute to terrorism studies. An analyst with an economics background and an aversion to psychology may provide good reports about what economists have said but overlook or down-play what psychology academics have found.

Indeed, as Feldman & March (1981, pp.177–178) point out, organisations are arenas for exercising social values, for displaying authority and for exhibiting proper behaviour and attitudes with respect to intelligent choice. Information gathering is a symbol for intelligent choice. Good decision-makers use information. This commitment to the visible symbols of intelligent choice can introduce unex-pected problems and departures from what decision theorists would expect to be optimal information gathering processes. Essentially, *visible* features of information use become particularly important. Being seen to gather, hold and use more infor-mation than everyone else is usually key to creating a positive reputation within an organisation. Of course, decision-makers can acquire a legitimacy that is somewhat artificial simply by displaying these visible trappings of information gathering and utilisation. According to Feldman & March (1981, p.178),

> Using information, asking for information, and justifying decisions in terms of information have all come to be significant ways in which we symbolise that the process is legitimate, that we are good decision-makers, and that our organisations are well managed.

We briefly present an overview of the task of accessing and using information produced by the research community. In particular, we think that the situation is best viewed as an ongoing conversation, though in some parts the chatter has died down considerably. For example, there was for a long time a lot of discussion about the meaning of terrorism. Obviously, having no unanimously agreed upon definition played no role in slowing down the discourse in general. Terrorism studies grew exponentially all through the time these people were conversing. Though there are now far fewer people talking about definitions, the record of their conversation can still be accessed. Approaching a growing discourse requires a different methodology than would be applied to a conversation that has slowed or ceased. Our first step is to explain where and how the record of 'the conversation' can be accessed. After this, we direct our attention to ways in which heuristics and biases can influence the task of finding information or answers to particular questions within the never-slowing stream that flows continuously from the research community.

The record of scholarly conversation

The truly extraordinary thing about the modern research conversation, in all fields, is its accessibility. To almost anyone, at any time. For the most part, the conversation has always taken place within the scholarly journals for each discipline, a select number of conferences and their published proceedings, and books published by individual scholars once they had collected their ideas and thoughts and once their investigations had reached the point where a longer narrative could be presented. The record of the conversation was kept in hard copies of these publications, on university library bookshelves. Where space and budget considerations were such that economies had to be sought, microfilm was the alternative to storing volume upon volume of journals. Subscriptions were expensive and it is doubtful that the educated man on the street ever had much access to the scholarly discourse. He had to wait until it was distilled into textbooks or into popular books that he might find at the bookstore or into magazines on science, business or the arts that he could pick up at the newsstand or subscribe to at a reasonable rate.

At the turn of the 21st century, the record of the conversation was still stored in these ways. Even for people with access to the university libraries, finding information was cumbersome. Since the journals were valuable, university libraries would rarely loan them out. Interested readers either had to read the articles on the spot or pay for photocopies, provided the library had the facility. Probably the most efficient way for researchers to remain up to date with developments was to trust that the major journals would carry cutting-edge work and maintain an awareness of the latest articles published in those journals. The journals would carry book reviews and one could purchase or order for the university library catalogue any book that might look interesting enough to warrant closer inspection. It was lucky if one stumbled across an important article in a more obscure journal. For the most part, scholars who published off the beaten track would find it virtually impossible to secure readers and citations. They were simply wallflowers to the conversation being carried on by others.

Accessibility worked both ways. Readers might have found it difficult but so too did authors. The major journals controlled the bulk of the readership. Accessing readers committed to those journals was challenging. Each journal has an editorial style, more or less strictly applied, and authors whose work fell outside of the scope of the major journals were forced into becoming potential wallflowers, unless they really hit the conference circuit and took up mailing pre-prints to other scholars. The residual consequences of this are still visible today. Any scholar with enough research experience will tell you of an article that she has found recently that was published long ago but which is still inaccessible in e-copy, even for a fee. Not surprisingly, even if the article has all the hallmarks of a significant piece, its readership and citations are miniscule. One cannot help but feel somewhat sorry for the authors who produced such good work but which only relatively few people have had the pleasure of reading.

In the space of around five years, much of this changed in ways that were unimaginable to the majority of students, academics and researchers as they celebrated New Year's Eve 1999. The journals began publishing digital copies in addition to their paper copies. These were available, at first, through databases subscribed to by university libraries, especially ProQuest and Ebsco. The capabilities of these databases were relatively crude and it would take some time before older articles could be digitised and made available. In some cases, just alluded to, this is yet to be accomplished. There were some search tools available but these too were crude. The advances, though, were rapid. Soon, the journals became searchable by keyword and, much more significantly, the true extent of the conversation began to be recorded by the inclusion of 'cited in' and 'cited by' links. These provided, for the first time, an instant insight into the extent of a particular conversation and the relevance of a particular article to it or the reverence attached to a particular article by scholars. Further developments along these lines allowed researchers to reveal for themselves and others the intricate architecture of academic conversation and to do so with less time and effort and potential error than ever before.

In the mid-2000s, with this development in full swing, there was a transition period that was not without its challenges. As late as 2005, some prominent journals still accepted submissions by post. Others had moved to accepting email submissions to the editor or editor's office. The flow of correspondence was in a state of flux as people's awareness of journals, previously catering to a small group of readers and publishing the work of a relatively small number of scholars, found themselves receiving submissions from outside quarters. Scholars looking for somewhere to publish their work had found the journal mentioned online and decided to send them a paper. The manuscript submission portals were in a state of infancy and it would take many years to streamline the process. Indeed, single password logins for different journals using the same manuscript submission platform were a rarity until the late 2010s. Journals with submission processing infrastructure built in the old days were swamped with increasing numbers of submissions from all corners of the world while authors tried to figure out whether it was worth exploring an outfit they had not heard of before or whether it might be best to take their chances with the established players.

Of course, what happened next is fairly predictable. By 2010, the number of journals had exploded in a new democracy and free market of ideas. Anyone could start a journal and anyone did. Traditionally, journals had allayed their publication costs by relying on the generosity of a sponsoring university and the guaranteed income from university library subscriptions plus, not unusually in economics, a non-refundable submission fee paid by the author (regardless of the outcome of the referees' decision). Now, new start-ups sensed a profit opportunity and charged not a submission fee but a publishing fee should the paper be accepted. Needless to say, the acceptance rates were in most cases very near 100 percent at some (but certainly not all) of these journals. A great sifting process had to begin in which the shadier outfits were gradually weeded out or starved of decent submissions by the growing awareness of their true nature among students and established academics. A good estimate of how long this took is probably around five years or until around 2015. It should be noted, though, that a strong case could be made for the efficiency of ideas in this new freer marketplace. Freely available to readers who were more interested in the quality of the work than in the quality of the journal and who were smart enough to sort the wheat from the chaff, many useful ideas that would not have seen the light of day found a place in the conversation. That is, rather than being refereed by a few people, articles would be refereed by the entirety of their prospective audiences. The critically important factor underpinning this argument is that most of the start-up journals, even those that were later found to be somewhat shady or at least very relaxed about the standards applied to the articles they published, almost always had ISSNs and were knitted into the fabric of the conversation by being 'listed'.

The best known of the 'journal listers' is Scopus. Scopus was launched in 2004 by the Dutch publishing company (and now data analytics and information company) Elsevier. The general idea was to 'list' journals and to keep a record of the abstracts of articles that they published. The database gradually evolved into an increasingly elaborate record of the conversation across tens of thousands of journals and authors. Later, Scopus developed a set of article and author metrics to provide numbers against which to assess the impact of a paper or an author on the conversation. Academics use a variety of these metrics to compare themselves to others. They choose the metrics that paint them in relatively the best light. You might have a low *h*-index but your latest paper is in a journal with a high impact factor or vice versa. As far as the conversation is concerned, however, the most important features of the databases remain one of the earliest innovations. This is the 'cited in' and 'cited by' facility that allows researchers who find one thread of the conversation to find more and more still.

While Scopus is proprietary (not all its features can be accessed for free by the broader public) and journals-centric, we know that much conversation takes place outside of the journals that Scopus lists or outside of journals altogether. Preceding somewhat the great explosion in the number of journals was a great explosion in the number of conferences. Only relatively few conference proceedings are listed by Scopus and for the most part readers will not find links to this part of the conversation through Scopus. There are also multitudinous volumes of working papers, waiting in queue to be published (or not) by listed journals. These working papers are available in separate repositories, which we will mention in a moment, but their links to the published conversation are becoming increasingly developed as search engines include them within the 'cited in' and 'cited by' listings. This leads us to what is perhaps the greatest of all the innovations in this space, Google Scholar. Also launched in 2004, Google Scholar has a much wider reach than Scopus and its features, though not as extensive as Scopus' analytics, are freely available to anyone, anywhere.

The record of the conversation is mostly accessible now through Google Scholar. Some might even say that Google Scholar is the record of the conversation. The most recent available research comparing Google Scholar with other Academic Search Engines and Bibliographic Databases (ASEBDs) concluded that Google Scholar is the most comprehensive, with almost 400,000,000,000 records (Gusenbauer 2019). Because Google Scholar looks like Google, most people are familiar with how it works and most academics use it rather than a rival service like Microsoft Academic (van Noorden 2014). Using Google Scholar rather than Google itself limits the search to scholarly papers. Nevertheless, a degree of skill is required to use it effectively. Like walking into a party where the conversation is in full swing, it takes a while to figure out what is going on, where best to stand, which groups to approach and who is talking about the most relevant things. Google Scholar includes the full spectrum of research items: working papers, author versions, published papers, conference proceedings, abstracts of books and so on. It works by trawling publishers but also the host of repositories that contain all sorts of academic material.

There exists a multitude of such repositories holding working papers, conference papers and published papers. The leading platform was the Social Science Research Network (SSRN), which was founded in 1994 and held tens of thousands of articles in a freely and publicly accessible online database by 2005. In addition, one would be hard pressed to find a university without an online repository of works published by academics associated with the institution. Most of these came online during the early 2000s. In various countries, these repositories form part of the research reporting to the relevant government departments. That is, as a place to record what the university's researchers have produced and when. The fact that these repositories also hold 'author versions' of published articles means that much of the published work, hitherto available only by subscriptions to journals, could at least be read, though not in its final typeset form. Developments that are more recent include the commercial academic 'social networks', especially ResearchGate, founded in Germany in 2008, and Academia.edu, founded in San Francisco in 2008. Both platforms host tens of millions of published papers, working papers and conference papers. All of these entries, in SSRN, university repositories and academic social networks, are encompassed by Google Scholar.

Accessing the conversation at the right point

Terrorism studies is multidisciplinary. Focusing on just one of the disciplines that contributes to it will result in potentially important work being overlooked or potential solutions to particular problems not being identified. Like most similarly multidisciplinary fields, there is no single best access point to the literature for anyone seeking a fairly complete account of the conversation on a particular topic or the answer to a potential problem. What follows is an extremely brief account, based on a carefully noted (essentially auto-ethnographic) process about how footholds can be established and the account of the relevant conversation gradually pieced together. Starting anew, without much prior knowledge of a particular problem area, this process must be applied iteratively, combined with careful review of the articles found, for anywhere up to several months. In most cases, it will take at least two or three weeks to develop an understanding of the conversation that is at such a level that one can be confident that not too much has been missed. Nevertheless, items will continue to turn up and it might be sometime longer before one can say that only relatively unimportant conversation pieces remain outstanding.

What we shall do here is present the approach that we have taken to piece together the conversation around a particular type of (potentially) violent behaviour: protests. This is a good example because it is a long but relatively straightforward conversation. We are interested specifically in the economic theory of counter-protest behaviour. If we wanted to develop such a theory, we need to know to what extent it has already been attempted. It could be that there is no opportunity for new work at all. The best place to start, then, is with Google Scholar and a search that involves variants of 'economic theory of protest behaviour'. You will find that a slight variant such as 'economic theory of protests' yields a different ordering of articles or, potentially, a set of different articles. So too does 'the economics of protests'. Each of these, though very similar, is a distinct entry point into the conversation. The first yields articles concerned with reasons (from a somewhat economics perspective) why people protest (among other things). The second yields articles that are concerned with specific protests, almost case studies, especially those with an economics origin (e.g. protests against austerity in Greece). The third yields a miscellany of articles, none of which is immediately relevant. What we learn quite quickly, however, is that the particular type of analysis that we wanted to see applied to the decision to protest (and counter-protest) is not obviously part of the conversation and the term 'collective action' is prominent among the results.

The 'economics' part of the search has to be jettisoned at this point, at least for now. Searching now using variants of 'theory of protest behaviour', we find something that piques our interest. A paper titled 'Towards a Theory of Protest' by none other than Kenneth Boulding (1967), a well-known economist. Unfortunately, the paper was published in an obscure journal and has been rarely cited. There is no real thread of literature running from this starting point and, more importantly, he takes a very general approach that does not yield any of the theoretical applications that we were looking for. However, our search appears to have yielded the first signs of a coherent conversation. That is, a set of papers, relatively highly cited, with contributions from the same authors. We have found amongst our list of results the names Meyer, Staggenborg, Stekelenburg and Klandermans repeated more than once. Their papers are relatively recent, starting in the 1990s. Unless they were the first authors to investigate protest behaviour, which is doubtful given the dates, we must be missing something. Perhaps, using the term 'collective action' will yield older, more seminal, investigations. Upon trying this, we find the author name

P.E. Oliver (1993) listed against several entries and in the abstract excerpt to one of the articles, we see the sentence, '…This review begins with a brief summary of the historical grounding of collective action theory in Mancur Olson's work'. Mancur Olson (1965), another well-known economist from about the same era as Boulding, once more piques our interest. At this stage, we have several current researcher names, about ten papers to review, a fair suspicion that economists have not applied a great deal of sophisticated decision theory—expected utility theory and its generalisations—to protest action and the Mancur Olson lead to follow up.

It is clear that a complete picture of the literature will not be found through Google Scholar alone. Once we reach this point, it is necessary to start reading the articles. Additional searches will emerge from that reading and so on. Mancur Olson's work was one of the seminal pieces in the literature dealing with protest movements (a new search variation). Searching 'Mancur Olson review' will yield survey articles that contain further hints about the origins and evolution of the field of study. These include important pieces by Wilson, Lipsky and Gamson. Gradually, it emerges that the study of protest behaviour is predominantly the domain of comparative sociology. If we circle back, using what we have learned, to our search for economics material, we find that 'economics of collective action' is a relatively small field of study, primarily in the domain of labour economics and concerned with labour strikes. We also see the broad structure of conversation taking place against the context. The early literature was produced during and immediately after the great protest waves and riots of the 1960s and 1970s. The next generation of researchers built on the foundations that were established at that time and developed additional insights by studying problems that are more specific or by directing new tools to old problems.

We also see, by careful reading of the collected material, that although the work of another noted economist, Thomas Schelling, is used by some researchers who are interested in protest waves, it is really Olson who has contributed most to shaping the themes of rational choice that characterise parts of the literature on protests. This influence of economics, the idea that protesters balance benefits and costs, runs through much of the material that surfaces by iterative searches. In general, though, protest behaviour has not figured prominently as a problem within the economics literature and we do not find many of the more modern tools of economic theory applied to it. The broad sweeps of theory that emerged during the 1960s and 1970s have been complemented since by a large number of more specific investigations based on the data that is now more easily collected and analysed. Active conversations about theory are still to be found, especially as they pertain to parts of protest behaviour that were missed in earlier years. For example, counter-movements are understudied vis-à-vis social movements and the interactions between social movements and counter-movements and the dynamics of those interactions are understudied and under-theorised as well. If we were looking for our place in the conversation, we have found it.

We were interested in determining whether economists had applied the theory of decision-making under risk and uncertainty to the study of protest behaviour.

While there are strong rational choice themes throughout the literature, the application of models such as expected utility theory and prospect theory to protest and counter-protest behaviour is not clearly evident and the economics literature contains relatively little about the precise type of behaviour and theoretical application in which we are interested. This provides an opening for contributing such an application but any such application has to be a part of the conversation about protest behaviour in general. In total, about 60 works (books and articles) make up the heart of this particular conversation. There are many others that fall towards the periphery for one reason or another. For example, case studies of particular protest movements might or might not be relevant depending on the theoretical points explored through the empirical work. Notice, though, that even if one's focus is a particular field (economic theory), it is necessary to encompass as much of the conversation as possible. In this case, comparative sociology is the dominant field of study and any biases that one might have towards other disciplines must be curtailed.

We have sketched here the broad outlines of an approach. In reality, this process of sifting iteratively took several weeks, with much time spent reading the material that was uncovered with each sweep through Google Scholar. For every relevant article, we estimate that we came across at least three dozen more entries in Google Scholar that were irrelevant or led nowhere. That is, for the 60 pieces that form the heart of the conversation in this field, we covered in one way or another more than 2,000 additional artefacts. The academic search engines capture nearly everything. These include papers from journals of varying quality, papers of varying quality regardless of where they were published, working papers, presentations, unfinished pieces and pieces from completely different fields of study that get caught up in our word searches. The apparent ease with which Google Scholar can present us with the conversation might lead some to conclude that a picture of the conversation in any field can be built from an academic search engine alone. This is far from being the case. One needs to start somewhere and then build iteratively with intelligent searches based on careful review of the names and works that gradually emerge. For every minute spent with Google Scholar, several hours must be spent with the material that it helps to turn up.

Formally, the process that we have described is a combination of strategy and heuristics. Amazingly, one of the best, detailed explanations of the search procedure that we have outlined can be found in Harter & Peter's (1985) paper: 'Heuristics for Online Information Retrieval'. This is amazing because the paper was written in 1985, 20 years before Google Scholar. While the systems available at the time were rudimentary by comparison, many of the main principles retain their validity. What is interesting about Harter and Peter's paper is that they partition the search task into two parts: (1) an overarching strategy and (2) a set of tactics, which they call heuristics. Both are essential to the successful completion of the search task. The heuristics that they list, dozens in all, applying to various stages of the search task, include things such as 'serendipity is important for effective retrieval', 'don't assume perfect indexing' and 'do not become overly committed to search terms and concepts you think are the best'. Either consciously or unconsciously, researchers will be applying some set of heuristics or other whenever they engage with a database.

Harter & Peters' (1985) complete article makes for useful reading, decades after it was first published. The main theme that runs through their discussion is that a spirit of genuine open-mindedness and inquiry is essential and that a flexible, heuristics-based approach in which the researcher adjusts and interacts with the ebb and flow of the search results is the best way to achieve the desired outcomes. As we tried to explain earlier in our brief sketch of a particular search, one starts somewhere and then iteratively adjusts and modifies the search as new themes, authors and search terms emerge and as old ones have to be discarded after proving fruitless or running their course. The use of heuristics is certainly necessary. The thing that we have not yet discussed and to which we now turn is how these heuristics may introduce biases into our results. An information gathering task, like any problem solving task, is susceptible to decision-making biases that can severely limit the value of the results.

Using Google Scholar and decision-making biases

> The study of information in organisations, like the study of choice with which it is often closely allied, involves a dialectic between students of information behaviour on the one hand and information engineers (or economists) on the other ... For students of behaviour, the problem is to understand actual human encounters with information.
>
> *Feldman & March (1981, p.171)*

Feldman and March recognise, as do all scholars in the broad field of 'information theory', that information and its use is intimately linked with decision theory, including theories of decision-making under risk and uncertainty. Indeed, they provide references to Tversky & Kahneman (1974), Slovic, Fischhoff & Lichtenstein (1977) and Nisbett & Ross (1980). They do so because they are concerned with explaining the departures from the 'classical' model of information use and organisational choice. That is, people within organisations make choices in a context of risk and uncertainty. They use information to help them make better choices. They search for information and use information to the extent that the benefits of doing so outweigh the costs. The value of information is calculated and recalculated dynamically based on needs, costs and benefits. As we know, these decisions are not likely to be carried out optimally. People make errors of judgement and errors of evaluation. For our present discussion, we are concerned with how these errors emerge during the information gathering process.

Kahneman & Tversky's research program is called 'heuristics and biases'. From the title, we can see from where they think biases emerge. From the use of heuristics. Harters & Peters (1985) referred to heuristics. By heuristics, they meant rules or methods of discovery. Heuristics have long been deemed essential to the method of research (Lakatos 1970). In Kahneman & Tversky's work and in the fields of psychology and behavioural economics, heuristics refer to shortcuts or 'fast thinking' methods that people use to reduce cognitive effort or to generate a solution, though not necessarily the best or even a good solution, to a complex problem (Grandori 2010, p.480). For example, when asked to assess the likelihood of being killed by a terrorist attack in New York City, people will base their answer on the ease with which they can recall terrorist attacks in that city in which people were killed. If many events are easily recalled, the estimate of the probability of dying in a future attack will be higher and vice versa. This is the availability heuristic. It is one of the several heuristics that were introduced to scholars by Tversky & Kahneman (1974). Just as they do when completing any other problem, human beings can be expected to apply heuristics and unwittingly introduce biases when they use Google Scholar and other ASEBDs.

In most respects, the idea that people experience cognitive biases while searching for information in an ASEBD is a particular case of a broader problem. This is, broadly speaking, the problems associated with information in organisations. Much work was done following 9/11 regarding the communication and sharing of information. Here we are interested in the gathering of information. Both gathering and sharing information have been studied extensively by management scientists. They have found that gathering, communication and sharing of information are characterised by behaviours that are not consistent with the classical view developed by information theorists. Departures from the classical model have many explanations. The simplest is that organisations (and the people in them) are systematically stupid (Feldman & March 1981, p.174). One can imagine frustrated decision theorists, information theorists and management scientists spending many hours as consultants within organisations watching with horror as all aspects of the information system deviate from the 'optimal' at virtually every turn. Stupidity is no doubt an explanation that would be at the top of their lists.

It is not much of an explanation, though. Feldman & March (1981, pp.175–176) found at least five other explanations within the management science and decision science literature as to why organisations depart from the classical information models: (1) organisations have too much information and face an information glut; (2) the information available to organisations is systematically the wrong kind of information; (3) organisations offer incentives for gathering more information than is optimal. Because organisations face uncertainty and decisions are judged post hoc, decision-makers know that they will face criticism for failing to anticipate a particular outcome. This criticism can be mitigated or avoided by collecting more information than necessary; (4) organisations gather information that does not have apparent immediate decision consequences and (5) information within organisations is subject to strategic misrepresentation. To these five explanations, Feldman & March add their own. That is, as mentioned earlier, collecting and being seen to use information is a symbol of intelligent choice. All of these factors result in too much information being gathered.

Feldman & March (1981) are aware of the possibility that heuristics and biases likely play a role as well but do not explicitly engage with Kahneman & Tversky's work. Schwenk (1986), writing for *Academy Management Review*, comes closer to exploring the problem of the role of heuristics and biases in information gathering when he addresses the interconnected problem of information and cognitive biases within organisations as it specifically relates to commitment to a course of action. In particular, Schwenk argues that personal and very vivid information combined with a high volume of information can induce a representativeness heuristic that draws decision-makers' attention away from important statistical data that would lead to a different choice. In a completely decontextualised experiment, Jones & Sugden (2001) found that decision-makers exhibit a positive confirmation bias when acquiring information. When testing an existing belief people search for evidence confirming it. This certainly suggests that information gathering may be shaped by cognitive biases. But despite some of these leads, quite surprisingly, the study of heuristics and biases as they emerge during information gathering tasks, and especially with regard to the use of ASEBDs, is very much understudied.

In their 1974 paper, Tversky & Kahneman introduced us to three heuristics:

1. Representativeness
2. Availability
3. Anchoring

Each of these concerns the decision-maker's ability to determine the probability of some uncertain or risky outcome. Rather than apply the rules of statistical inference correctly, people tend to rely on heuristics. As a result, their estimates are often biased. In trying to determine the likelihood that object A belongs to or is drawn from class or process B, people tend to reach a decision based on the degree to which A is representative of B. This heuristic is illustrated by the famous 'Linda Problem' in which subjects are presented with the description of a person called Linda and are ultimately asked to assess whether it is more likely that Linda is a bank teller or a feminist and a bank teller. Because certain aspects of the description of Linda point to an interest in feminism, decision-makers often say that the latter is more likely. Of course, this violates certain rules of statistical inference. A 'feminist and a bank teller' cannot have a higher probability than 'a bank teller' since the set of bank tellers includes feminist and non-feminist bank tellers. In assessing chances, people might also make use of the availability heuristic. In Tversky & Kahneman's research program, availability refers to the ease with which instances can be called to mind. As mentioned previously, the likelihood of a terrorist attack might be assessed by the ease with which attacks can be recalled. Anchoring is a little bit more complicated. The key to anchoring is the idea that people make estimates of something by starting with some initial value and making an adjustment. The initial value is called the anchor because it is often difficult to shift. People tend not to adjust their estimates far enough from the anchor.

How can these sorts of fast thinking shortcuts lead to biased decisions and outcomes in the context of searching for information using ASEBDs? Lau & Coiera (2007) took some general steps that might give us some hints. Focusing on medical scenarios, they looked into information retrieval where a subject had to use a search engine to find information to answer a particular clinical question. They found that anchoring did play a role in shaping the results of information retrieval tasks. The participants in their study displayed a statistically significant relationship between their pre-search answers and their post-search answers. This is very similar to the confirmation bias reported by Jones & Sugden (2001). It is the first formal evidence that heuristics and biases might be present when people approach information gathering tasks. Usually, most of our attention has focused on the use of information to solve problems but, of course, information gathering is itself a problem and people use various techniques, experiences, prior knowledge and, seemingly, heuristics in order to solve information gathering problems.

Kahneman & Tversky (1979) proceeded to encompass within a model of decision-making under conditions of risk and uncertainty, some of the decision-making 'quirks' that they had observed and documented from about the mid-1960s onwards. Prospect theory can serve as a theoretical framework within which to think about the influence of decision-making processes on the task of searching through the scholarly literature either to remain up to date with developments or to solve a particular problem. Prospect theory decision-makers are characterised by reference point dependence, loss aversion, risk aversion in the domain of gains, risk seeking in the domain of losses and non-linear probability weighting. Searching for information is subject to risk and uncertainty, not just regarding the information that might or might not be found but also the context in which the search itself takes place and the organisational outcomes that may be experienced by the information gatherer. Different people within the organisation will view problems through one lens or another. Solutions that are found in the literature of one field may need to be communicated to people who apply a different lens to the situation. Once someone, for example, comes to view every strategic problem through a game theory lens, it will be difficult for him or her to see a problem any other way.

In any organisation, the information gatherer faces risks associated with the search itself and the context. The information gatherer approaches the task as a human decision-maker. He or she has limited time and limited capacity. The decision-maker can be tasked with one of two problems. First, the task might be to maintain a watch on the latest research. Second, the task might be to look for a solution to a particular problem. The reader might be expecting us to say that the reference point in this case might be the decision-maker's field of expertise (say, the political science literature) or a particular field of study or even a particular journal where he or she has found viable information before. These more closely resemble anchors than reference points. A reference point in prospect theory is the point that divides gains and losses. A reference point relates to outcomes. It can be the status quo or it can be a goal or expectation. Here, the way in which the decision-maker sets the reference point, consciously or unconsciously, is critically important because it frames the entire search process. A status quo reference point might be set at 'zero knowledge' or some positive amount of knowledge. That is, the degree to which the information gatherer believes that they already have the answer. A goal or expectation reference point is more open-ended. It might be set at some amount of knowledge or information that will be gained during some period of search time.

Relative to this reference point, the information gatherer finds himself in the domain of gains or the domain of losses as the search proceeds. These are perceived gains and losses, though, and may not be real. Here, the relevant payoffs are measured in terms of information. The value of the information is a matter of perception, at least in part. How colleagues and superiors view the information that has been gathered is important. It might be valued, as Feldman & March (1981) found within the organisations they studied, for its own sake, regardless of the content. As such, an information gatherer may perceive herself to be in the domain of gains and, as far as the organisational response to the gathered information is positive, may actually have some justification for this belief. Unfortunately, no valuable information or knowledge may have been gathered, just noise. Or vice versa. The information gatherer may perceive himself to be in the domain of losses because the results of his search are not valued by his peers and yet he might really have found useful information. The information gatherer's response in each case may have significant effects on the state of information and information flow within the organisation.

Scholarly research findings that are salient to law enforcement and intelligence agencies tasked with pre-empting and pursuing terrorist offenders can be found across the literatures of at least a half-dozen distinct disciplines and are scattered through probably a hundred different journals. Some of these disciplines and journals may seem the most unlikely of places to find innovative results. In fact, one cannot concentrate on particular journals. Even the most elite journals in a field may not carry the most cutting-edge results for any number of reasons. The odds of a successful search and the odds that colleagues and superiors will view the search as a success weigh on the information gatherer's mind. Probability weighting distorts his or her assessment of the odds in both cases. The volume of academic research that is published on any given topic makes every search in which there is something important at stake a task involving decision-making under conditions of risk and uncertainty.

Loss aversion, slack and search

Risk preference in prospect theory is 'reflective' around the reference point. The reference point divides the domain of gains and the domain of losses and is the dividing point between risk averse and risk seeking behaviour. Information gathering within an organisational context is an activity undertaken under conditions of risk and uncertainty. On balance, the risks lie more with the task of finding solutions or insights into particular problems than with the task of remaining up to date with developments, though something could certainly be missed. Concerning a search for particular insights or solutions, there is a risk that the search will actually fail or fail within a period of time allowed. There is also a risk that the results of the search will be perceived to have failed by either the information gatherer or his or her peers and managers. The question is whether risk aversion or risk seeking behaviour in this context is more conducive to successful information gathering. There is also the question of what factors lead the information gatherer to become more risk averse or more risk seeking. Within the prospect theory framework, risk seeking behaviour emerges when decision-makers feel themselves to be confronting actual or expected losses or when problems or contexts are framed negatively. Within an organisation, people are also observed to take more risk when there is more 'slack'. That is, when there are resources in excess of current aspirations (e.g. Libby & Fishburn 1977; Singh 1986; Antonelli 1989; Wehrung 1989). The opposite holds.

First, we must address the question of whether risk seeking is a positive or negative influence on successful information gathering. This question can be best answered by drawing parallels between information gathering and creativity and innovation. The link between risk preferences and innovation and creativity has been carefully studied over many years. There are many similarities between the types of behaviour and the types of organisational situations that we have been discussing and the behaviour and situations identified by managerial scientists studying risk taking, innovation and creativity. Generally, risk taking has been positively linked to innovation. Because bolder initiatives are necessary to achieve innovative results, risk-taking decision-makers achieve more innovation (March & Shapira 1987; March 1996; Ling et al. 2008; Latham & Braun 2009; Garcia-Granero et al. 2015). Concerning creativity, Garcia-Granero et al. (2015, p.1095) explain:

> One fundamental idea is that creative behaviour is about challenging the status quo of a given aspect of the organisation. From the employee's point of view, the consequences of such challenges are uncertain. In fact, those employees displaying creative behaviours may face negative consequences if they fail.

They go on to explain how people with new ideas may come into conflict with co-workers (also see Zhou & George 2001; Janssen 2003). Hence, it takes somewhat of a risk seeking mindset to be truly creative in an organisational context.

It might very well be the case that some tension with colleagues and supervisors can act as a spur to innovation and creativity. This is because the information gatherer's risk preferences are shaped by the way they perceive or frame a problem. Losses loom larger than gains. People feel a loss more acutely than they feel a gain of the same amount. People will take risk to avoid losses. When they perceive themselves to be in the domain of gains, people become conservative and risk averse. When they perceive themselves to be in the domain of losses, they become more risk seeking in an attempt to recoup their losses and recover lost ground. It is interesting to discover that departments at Stanford University introduced more innovations into their teaching and course offerings when confronted with financial adversity (Manns & March 1978). As a matter of circumstance, then, an information gatherer may be driven by his or her risk preferences to a more innovative and creative pursuit of a solution or information in the scholarly literature. A degree of competitiveness and rivalry within the organisational culture might be conducive to effective search. However, it is important that this not be allowed to get out of hand. A very obvious and completely satisfactory solution may be available from a very traditional part of the literature. A risk seeker might too easily overlook this fact when driven to find a more innovative solution. It is not a black and white issue.

Beyond a competitive culture, the organisation might initiate more targeted risk seeking behaviour among its information teams by providing one section of the team with 'slack'. Organisations with more slack exhibit more risk taking. This might be as simple as providing a section with more team members or more time to gather the required information. It might also go hand in hand with a loosening of centralised controls, which tend to emerge in decision-making structures when managers are worried about competition or costs (Pfeffer & Leblebici 1973). The information gatherers are human decision-makers who, unlike some of the representative agent frameworks of pure economic theory, are players interacting with each other and the environment or stage on which they find themselves. They use heuristics, make biased judgements, overweight and underweight probabilities, assess their gains and losses against a reference point and exhibit different degrees of risk aversion or risk seeking behaviour depending on whether they perceive themselves to be in the domain of gains or losses. To some degree, these aspects of decision-making can be controlled or mitigated or even directed to the advantage of the agency but before any of the downsides can be avoided and before any of the upsides might be manufactured, intelligence agencies and law enforcement agencies must be aware that the human decision-making process has likely survived intact, with all of its quirks, through even the most rigorous recruitment procedures and subsequent training.

Four dot points to end the chapter

- Heuristics and biases influence the task of information gathering and reporting. Researchers can find themselves in the domain of gains or the domain of losses and they might become more cavalier or more conservative in their pursuit of information.
- The academic literature is more accessible than ever, but it is also very multi-disciplinary. Combined with the volume of information that is now available, this context is certainly susceptible to heuristics and biases.
- Although not usually viewed as a gamble or risky prospect, searching for information whenever something important is at stake or depends on the outcomes of the search is essentially a decision-making process applied under conditions of risk and uncertainty.
- In the presence of risk and uncertainty, diversification has usually been found to be a worthwhile strategy. Multidisciplinary research and information teams

are one way in which diversification can be introduced to reduce the risk of error and, possibly, increase the rewards accruing to those organisations with a strong commitment to research engagement.

Note

1   William O. 'Bill' Baker, Bell Labs (quoted in Gertner 2012, p.251).

References

Antonelli, C. 1989. A Failure Induced Model of Research and Development Expenditure: Italian Evidence from the Early 1980s. *Journal of Economic Behaviour and Organisation*, 12, 129–180.

Boulding, K.E. 1967. Towards a Theory of Protest. *ETC: A Review of General Semantics*, 24, 49–58.

Feldman, M.S. & March, J.G. 1981. Information in Organisations as Signal and Symbol. *Administrative Science Quarterly*, 26, 171–186.

Garcia-Granero, A., Llopis, O., Fernandez-Mesa, A. & Alegre, J. 2015. Unravelling the Link between Managerial Risk-Taking and Innovation: The Mediating Role of a Risk-Taking Climate. *Journal of Business Research*, 68, 1094–1104.

Gertner, J. 2012. *The Idea Factory: Bells Labs and the Great Age of American Innovation*. London, UK: Penguin.

Grandori, A. 2010. A Rational Heuristic Model of Economic Decision Making. *Rationality and Society*, 22, 477–504.

Gusenbauer, M. 2019. Google Scholar to Overshadow Them All? Comparing the Sizes of Twelve Academic Search Engines and Bibliographic Databases. *Scientometrics*, 118, 177–214.

Harter, S.P. & Peters, A.R. 1985. Heuristics for Online Information Retrieval: A Typology and Preliminary Listing. *Online Review*, 9, 407–424.

Janssen, O. 2003. Innovative Behaviour and Job Involvement at the Price of Conflict and Less Satisfactory Relations with Co-Workers. *Journal of Occupational and Organisational Psychology*, 76, 347–364.

Jones, M. & Sugden, R. 2001. Positive Confirmation Bias in the Acquisition of Information. *Theory and Decision*, 50, 59–99.

Kahneman, D. 2011. *Thinking, Fast and Slow*. New York: Farrar, Straus, Giroux.

Kahneman, D. & Tversky, A. 1979. Prospect Theory: An Analysis of Decision under Risk. *Econometrica*, 47, 263–291.

Lakatos, I. 1970. Falsification and the Methodology of Scientific Research Programmes. In I. Lakatos & A. Musgrave (Eds.), *Criticism and the Growth of Knowledge*. Cambridge: Cambridge University Press, pp.91–196.

Latham, S.F. & Braun, M. 2009. Managerial Risk, Innovation, and Organisational Decline. *Journal of Management*, 35, 258–281.

Lau, A.Y.S. & Coiera, E.W. 2007. Do People Experience Cognitive Biases While Searching for Information? *Journal of the American Medical Informatics Association*, 14, 599–608.

Libby, R. & Fishburn, P.C. 1977. Behavioural Models of Risk Taking in Business Decisions: A Survey and Evaluation. *Journal of Accounting Research*, 15, 272–292.

Ling, Y., Simsek, Z., Lubatkin, M. & Veiga, J. 2008. Transformational Leadership's Role in Promoting Corporate Entrepreneurship: Examining the CEO-TMT Interface. *Academy of Management Journal*, 21, 557–576.

Manns, C.L. & March, J.G. 1978. Financial Adversity, Internal Competition and Curriculum Change in a University. *Administrative Science Quarterly*, 23, 541–552.

March, J.G. 1996. Learning to be Risk Averse. *Psychological Review*, 103, 309–319.

March, J.G. & Shapira, Z. 1987. Managerial Perspectives on Risk and Risk Taking. *Management Science*, 33, 1404–1418.

Nisbett, R. & Ross, L. 1980. *Human Inference: Strategies and Shortcomings of Social Judgment*. Englewood Cliffs, NJ: Prentice Hall.

Oliver, P.E. 1993. Formal Models of Collective Action. *Annual Review of Sociology*, 19, 271–300.

Olson, M. 1965. *The Logic of Collective Action: Public Goods and the Theory of Groups*. Cambridge, MA: Harvard University Press.

Pfeffer, J. & Leblebici, H. 1973. The Effect of Competition on some Dimensions of Organisational Structure. *Social Forces*, 52, 268–279.

Schwenk, C.R. 1986. Information, Cognitive Biases and a Commitment to a Course of Action. *Academy Management Review*, 11, 298–310.

Singh, J.V. 1986. Performance, Slack and Risk Taking in Organisational Decision Making. *Academy of Management Journal*, 29, 562–585.

Slovic, P., Fischhoff, B. & Lichtenstein, S. 1977. Behavioural Decision Theory. *Annual Review of Psychology*, 23, 1–39.

Tversky, A. & Kahneman, D. 1974. Judgement under Uncertainty: Heuristics and Biases. *Science*, 185, 1124–1131.

Van Noorden, R. 2014. Online Collaboration: Scientists and the Social Network. *Nature*, 512, 126–129.

Wehrung, D.A. 1989. Risk Taking over Gains and Losses: A Study of Oil Executives. *Annals of Operations Research*, 19, 115–139.

Zhou, J. & George, J.M. 2001. When Job Dissatisfaction Leads to Creativity: Encouraging the Expression of Voice. *Academy of Management Journal*, 44, 682–696.

12
INFORMATION CASCADES AND THE PRIORITISATION OF SUSPECTS

Deep into the night of April 19, 1989, New York City police officers were called to a macabre scene at the north end of Central Park: a twenty-eight-year-old woman named Trisha Meili had been raped and beaten so brutally that, it was later determined, she lost three-quarters of her blood. (She was coma-tose for twelve days, and remained in the hospital for several months.) Antron McCray, Korey Wise, Yusef Salaam, Kevin Richardson, and Raymond Santana, five young men from upper Manhattan, aged between fourteen and sixteen, were apprehended by the police, following the first reports of the attacks in the park that night. After hours of police questioning, four of them confessed, on video, to taking part in the attack. In two trials, in 1990, Santana, Wise, Richardson, McCray, and Salaam were convicted of the attack, even though there was no physical evidence tying them to it, only their supposed confessions, which contradicted one another. They were sentenced to terms of between five and fifteen years. The accused came to be known as the Central Park Five.[1]

On the night of April 19, 1989, there was mayhem in Central Park as roaming groups of youths, perhaps 30 in total, beat and harassed 8 different victims. While the mayhem unfolded, Trisha Meili was being beaten and raped by a single serial offender elsewhere in the park. Police rounded up a large number of the suspected perpetrators. Five of them were charged with the assault on Meili. They became known as the Central Park Five. Although they confessed to crime during police questioning (without their lawyers present), they were exonerated 12 years later when the true perpetrator confessed and his confession was confirmed by DNA evidence. Among other things, the case demonstrates that people sometimes make false confessions under the pressure of police questioning (Russano et al. 2005).

More importantly, false confessions can appear plausible if they fit into a broader frame constructed by investigators and may compound problems caused by confirmation bias or, more generally, tunnel vision.[2] Findley (2010) discusses the similar case of Marvin Anderson. Despite vigorously maintaining his innocence, Anderson was convicted in 1982 of robbery, abduction and rape of a 24-year-old woman in Hanover, Virginia. During the assault, the rapist had told the victim that he had a white girlfriend. Marvin Anderson was the only black man that police knew who had a white girlfriend. This fact seemed to be enough to precipitate a series of decisions that led to the arrest and, ultimately, conviction of Anderson even though the evidence pointed more strongly towards another man. It was 20 years before DNA evidence would prove Anderson's innocence.

Cases like the Central Park Five have inspired a growing literature on the effect of decision-making biases on the investigative decision-making process. The most prominent of the biases that have been examined in the investigative context is confirmation bias and tunnel vision. Tunnel vision leads law enforcement to focus on one offender or one offender type while paying less attention to others. Confirmation bias leads the investigator to gather or weight more heavily evidence that supports a previously held hypothesis. After introducing the concept of confirmation bias and explaining its deeper relationship with the updating of beliefs as new evidence comes to hand, we move on to explore a related but distinct phenomenon called 'information cascades'. An information cascade occurs when people find it optimal to ignore their own private information. If this happens during a watch listing or suspect prioritisation task, errors could cascade across jurisdictions and through investigative teams or law enforcement agencies.

Decision-making biases and investigations

Gross & O'Brien (2008) found that there was a wrongful conviction rate over the period since 1970 of at least 2.30 percent *among defendants sentenced to death*. Risinger's (2006) estimate is that 3.30 percent of people who received the death penalty for murder and rape have been wrongly convicted. Although it may be tempting to attribute wrongful convictions to incompetence or, worse, corruption, the truth is that wrongful convictions are usually the product of a decision-making process where, at each step along the way, only the best of intentions are held by the investigators, prosecutors, judges and juries (O'Brien 2009, p.315). Although a number of factors combine to explain the worrying statistics about wrongful convictions, researchers have devoted a lot of attention to confirmation bias. This is a subconscious tendency to gather or weight more heavily evidence that supports a particular hypothesis or previously held belief (Nickerson 1998; O'Brien 2009). Confirmation bias and, more generally, tunnel vision, have emerged as the primary explanations for wrongful convictions.

The evidence that investigations can be influenced by decision-making bias relies upon the general findings in psychology (i.e. that human decision-makers have been found to exhibit systematic patterns) along with some specific context-relevant studies. For example, Ask & Granhag (2007) found that investigators discounted the credibility of witnesses who did not confirm a particular hypothesis about a particular suspect. In training scenarios, police trainees have also been found to discount evidence that conflicted with a previously held hypothesis (Kerstholt & Eikelboom 2007; Ask, Rebelius & Granhag 2008). Salet (2017) found similar problems in four major investigations. More recently, judges who had previously decided to detain a suspect before or during a trial appear to exhibit confirmation bias in their subsequent guilt assessments if they preside over the defendant's trial (Liden, Gräns & Juslin 2019).

Given the available evidence, researchers such as Findley (2010), rather than calling for more research into whether tunnel vision is found within the investigative context, have called for more research into measures that might counter tunnel vision in the law enforcement and justice communities.[3] On the contrary, some researchers (e.g. Snook & Cullen 2008) have questioned the practice of extending the results of psychology experiments to particular settings and are unwilling to accept that findings in laboratory settings or certain contexts can be generalised to other groups of human decision-makers. We think that this debate emerges because the deep human roots of the observed patterns of behaviour discovered by psychologists are not always made clear. This lack of depth of explanation, which makes it seem as though confirmation bias is a tendency among some people rather than anything more substantial, introduces doubts about the application of decision theory to a new context. The roots of confirmation bias run deep and it is really this deepness that allows its application to new contexts.

The deep roots of cognitive biases: the case of confirmation

The deep logical roots of tunnel vision can be found in Bayesian probability and the ways in which people update their beliefs—or should update their beliefs—as new evidence emerges. To see how this works, we first have to introduce Bayes' rule. Bayes' rule allows us to compute the probability of an event conditional on some other piece of information. For example, imagine that there are two urns full of gold and black balls. Urn 1 contains 80 gold balls and 20 black balls. Urn 2 contains 50 of each. An umpire rolls a die. If the die roll is 3 or higher, the umpire draws from urn 2, otherwise urn 1. The umpire rolls a die and draws a ball *without the player being able to see either the die roll or the action of drawing the ball*. The player has to guess which urn the ball was drawn from.

Without seeing the ball, the player would estimate the likelihood of the ball having been drawn from urn 1 as 1/3 (i.e. the probability given by the die roll). The player's prior probability or hypothesis that the ball is drawn from urn 1 is 1/3. Now, let's say that the player is given some additional evidence. He is shown the ball that was drawn. It is a gold ball. How should he change is prior probability estimate of 1/3 in light of the new evidence? Bayes' rule can be used to determine the optimal updating of the player's belief from 1/3 to some other probability, which could be higher or lower:[4]

$$P(Urn\ 1|\ Gold) = \frac{P(Gold|\ Urn1)\ P(Urn1)}{P(Gold)}$$

This equation, Bayes' rule, can tell us the probability that the ball was drawn from urn 1 conditional on the fact that the ball is gold. We have to work out the three different probabilities that are on the right-hand side of the equation. First, the probability that the umpire has drawn from urn 1 is just the probability of rolling 1 or 2 on the die. That is, $P(Urn1)$. This probability is 1/3. The probability of drawing a gold ball given urn 1, $P(Gold| Urn1)$, is the fraction of gold balls in that urn. This probability is 80/20 or 4/5. These two probabilities make up the numerator in the above equation but we do not yet have the denominator, $P(Gold)$. This is the unconditional probability of drawing a gold ball from either urn. This is equal to the total probability of drawing a gold ball:

$$P(Gold) = P(Gold| Urn1)P(Urn1) + P(Gold| Urn2)P(Urn2)$$
$$= \frac{4}{5} \times \frac{1}{3} + \frac{1}{2} \times \frac{2}{3} = 3/5$$

With the values computed, Bayes' rule can now be used. As such, the probability that the umpire has drawn the gold ball from urn 1 is:

$$P(Urn1| Gold) = \frac{4/5 \times 1/3}{3/5} = 4/9$$

Given that the ball is gold, there is a 4/9 chance that it was drawn from urn 1. Given the evidence (gold ball), the player should update his belief that the ball was drawn from urn 1 from 0.33 (1/3) to 0.44 (4/9).

The fact that Bayes' rule can be interpreted as a logical depiction of optimal learning or updating in the light of new information means that Bayes' rule can be attributed a deeper meaning. Indeed, it has come to play an important role in confirmation theory. That is, the theory of how scientists confirm their hypotheses. Departures from this procedure are called confirmation biases. How these biases can arise, even in pure science, and how optimal decision-making must be in order to avoid them is what really gives us confidence in the application of confirmation bias to an investigative context (or any other context involving human decision-making).

In order to use Bayes' rule for hypothesis and theory testing, we can work in terms of hypothesis and evidence instead of urns and coloured balls. Let us imagine a case where a scientist is evaluating a hypothesis based on evidence and that as new evidence emerges in a series of trials the scientist updates her evaluation. The scientist starts, for whatever reason, including gut feel, experience, intuition or some preliminary real knowledge about the state of affairs, with a prior probability, $P(H)$, or belief in the likelihood that the hypothesis, H, is true. The probability is prior to her becoming aware of any particular evidence, E. Now as evidence comes in, she updates her belief changing her prior probability to what is called a posterior probability, $P(H|E)$. That is, the probability that H is true given that evidence E is observed. The transition from $P(H)$ to $P(H|E)$ involves a change of beliefs. If the scientist updates her beliefs in accordance with Bayes' rule then she has engaged in Bayesian updating. An optimal rule for updating beliefs in the context of evidence and hypothesis is given by Bayes' rule:

$$P(H|E) = \frac{P(E|H)P(H)}{P(E)}$$

Let's say that a piece of scientific equipment reveals one of two outcomes, 'alpha' and 'omega'. If the machine is working properly, 'alpha' is revealed 10 percent of the time and 'omega' 90 percent of the time. When the machine malfunctions, it always reveals 'omega'. One way to find out whether the equipment is functioning correctly is to call in the machine's manufacturer and ask them to send out a technician. Another way is to simply run a test and see whether both 'alpha' and 'omega' are revealed. Let H be the hypothesis that the equipment is malfunctioning and let the opposite, $\neg H$, be the hypothesis that the equipment is functioning correctly. The scientist believes that there is a 60 percent chance that H is true (the equipment is malfunctioning). That is, her prior probability $P(H)$ is 0.60. A test has been carried out and the result is 'omega'. That is, E is 'the result is omega'. What probability, $P(H|E)$, should she assign to H now that some evidence has come in? $P(E|H)$ must be equal to 1 because the equipment always reveals 'omega' when it malfunctions. The last piece of the equation is $P(E)$. Here, $P(E) = P(E|H)P(H) + P(E|\neg H)P(\neg H)$. Therefore:

$$P(H|E) = \frac{1 \times 0.60}{1 \times 0.60 + 0.90 \times 0.40} = 0.625$$

This means that in light of the evidence, 'omega', the scientist should update her prior belief from 0.60 to 0.625. The evidence 'omega' increases the likelihood that the equipment is malfunctioning but because we expect 'omega' most of the time anyway, this evidence does not dramatically change the prior probability. The scientist cannot yet be sure. She runs another test and this time the result is 'omega' again. She can further update her beliefs as follows:

$$P(H|E) = \frac{1 \times 0.625}{1 \times 0.625 + 0.90 \times 0.375} = 0.649$$

A second revelation of 'omega' increases her posterior probability even further. At some point, if 'omega' keeps coming up, the scientist's posterior probability converges on 1.00 and she believes that it is absolutely certain that the equipment is malfunctioning. Wherever the decision-maker starts, from whichever prior belief, Bayesian updating provides an optimal (prescriptive) updating rule. Human decision-makers are not perfect when it comes to learning from new information. It is important to note that like Herbert Simon's boundedly rational decision-makers (Simon 1957), the scientist may not have time to run repeated tests. She might have to stop after two or three tests. In our example, if she stopped testing after two tests and concluded that the equipment is malfunctioning, she would still have a very significant possibility of being wrong. Investigators too cannot investigate forever.

In this example, the optimal updating of the scientist's beliefs should give due weight to the fact that a correctly functioning piece of equipment reveals 'omega' most of the time.[5] The equipment can still function correctly and yet yield a string of 'omega' results. Such a string of results might lead the scientist to conclude too soon that her hypothesis is true. If this occurred, the scientist might be said to have succumbed to confirmation bias. She was too eager to view each 'omega' result as evidence in support of her hypothesis. This detour into probability theory was essential to our discussion of confirmation bias because confirmation bias can be formally defined in this context as the tendency to interpret the evidence 'omega' as support for the prior, $P(H)$, and to conclude too soon that the hypothesis is true. Confirmation bias is a sub-optimal updating of beliefs as new evidence becomes available. One can easily see how this might upset a scientific inquiry or an investigative process.

In an investigative context, the flow of evidence should see an adjustment process occur whereby the investigators adjust their priors. Regardless of where the investigators start in terms of $P(H)$, they should adjust their beliefs, though not necessarily to complete certainty, $P(H|E) = 1$, or uncertainty, $P(H|E) = 0$, as the evidence mounts one way or the other. That is, the investigator who believes that there is a 50 percent chance that the suspect is guilty might optimally adjust this belief to 80 percent as evidence is collected. Or he might adjust his belief optimally to 20 percent. Wherever the investigator starts, Bayes' rule provides the optimal adjustment or updating process. Confirmation bias in this case is a possible explanation for the failure to adjust optimally to new evidence. If, for example, the investigator believes that there is a 50 percent chance of guilt, $P(H) = 0.50$, and evidence arrives that should see this adjusted downwards to 0.37 and yet the investigator's posterior probability adjusts to 0.45 or remains the same or increases to 0.55, then there is a possibility of confirmation bias. If one thinks about confirmation bias in this context, one can see how plausible it is to extend the findings of decision theory to a context such as criminal investigation, suspect prioritisation or watch listing.

We turn now to a problem that goes beyond confirmation bias yet which has related and similar consequences. This is the possibility of an *information cascade*. According to Bikhchandani, Hirshleifer and Welch (1992, p.994), 'An information cascade occurs when it is optimal for an individual, having observed the actions of those ahead of him, to follow the behaviour of the preceding individual without regard to his own information'. Information cascades interrupt and disrupt the assessment of outcomes, probabilities and the updating of beliefs. They can result in behaviours that are analogous to herding. Information cascades, when they are fragile, can also be responsible for fads or a drastic change in behaviour. It can be the case that a terrorism suspect may be prioritised (or deprioritised) as information about him cascades through the investigative team. It can also be the case that a sudden change in the investigative team's opinion of the suspect may be experienced when a fragile information cascade 'breaks'.

Information cascades

Information cascades have three key characteristics: (1) imperfectly informed decision-makers follow those that came before; (2) this can be optimal, rational behaviour and (3) once a cascade starts, the aggregation or pooling of information ceases. This is a fascinating phenomenon. To set the scene, let us present Bikhchandani, Hirshleifer & Welch's (1992, p.994) example. This example also highlights the possibility that an information cascade may form in the type of literature survey process that we discussed in the previous chapter:

> An information cascade occurs when it is optimal for an individual, having observed the actions of those ahead of him, to follow the behaviour of the preceding individual without regard to his own information. Consider the submission of this paper to a journal. The referee will read the paper, assess its quality, and accept or reject it. Suppose that a referee at a second journal learns that the paper was previously rejected. Under the assumption that the referee cannot assess the paper's quality perfectly, knowledge of the prior rejection should tilt him towards rejection. Suppose now that the second journal also rejects and that when the paper is submitted to a third journal, the third referee learns that the paper was rejected at two previous journals. Clearly, this further raises the chance of rejection.

Cascades can be correct or incorrect. They do not always have to result in wrong decisions. In economics, information cascades have been used to explain a variety of phenomena, including bank runs, financial crashes, consumer decisions, the adoption of medical procedures, types of shows television stations broadcast, political preferences,[6] criminals' decisions to commit a crime[7] and hiring decisions at firms (Kübler & Weizsäcker 2004, p.425). According to Bikhchandani, Hirshleifer & Welch (1998, p.151), even unexpectedly good book sales find an explanation with information cascades:

> In 1995, management gurus Michael Treacy and Fred Wiersema secretly purchased 50,000 copies of their business strategy book The Discipline of Market Leaders from stores across the nation. The stores they purchased from just happened to be the ones whose sales are monitored to select books for the New York Times bestseller list. Despite mediocre reviews, their book

made the bestseller list. Subsequently, the book sold well enough to continue as a bestseller without further demand intervention by the authors. Presumably, being on a bestseller list helps a book sell more because consumers and reviewers learn from the actions of previous buyers.

In a laboratory setting, information cascades have been found to be quite prevalent though not ubiquitous. Anderson & Holt (1997) found that information cascades emerged in 87 of the 122 experimental settings in which cascades were possible. These results have been replicated by two independent studies: Hung & Plott (2001) and Willinger & Ziegelmeyer (1998). It is generally accepted, therefore, that information cascades exist and will emerge more often than not when conditions are amenable.

Let us say that we have a series of investigators each deciding whether to prioritise a particular suspect. The decision is 'prioritise' or 'not prioritise' where 'prioritise' involves taking a particular action and 'not prioritise' involves no further action. Each investigator has some private information about each suspect but since this information is not perfect, no one knows for sure whether the suspect should be prioritised. Each investigator can observe the action taken by each investigator who has already made a decision but cannot observe an investigator's private information. What happens next really depends on the outcome of a tussle between the information content contained in the observed behaviour of others and the private information held by each investigator. This sort of scenario can arise in practice, especially with intelligence sharing across agencies or jurisdictions. An investigator can see that a suspect has been placed into a particular law enforcement system, for example, or has been given some sort of marker that indicates that the suspect has been prioritised but cannot see the full information (if any) behind the other investigators' decisions.

An information cascade, as the name implies, is just a flow of information that heads in a particular direction. In our example, the flow can be in the direction of 'prioritise' or 'not prioritise'. Once the cascade starts, the flow becomes a torrent. A droplet of information starts with the first decision-maker's choice. This is too little to start a torrent on its own. The second decision-maker adds a little more information in the same direction, increasing the chance of creating a torrent, or he adds some information to the opposite direction and both little droplets sit more or less idly, awaiting a third decision-maker. This can go back and forth indefinitely and neither collection of droplets becomes the fountainhead for a single, dominant torrential flow of information through the remaining decision-makers. Alternatively, there will accumulate enough droplets in one direction to overwhelm the other and start an information cascade in that direction.

The most important factor that determines how likely it is that a cascade will start is the quality of private information held by the investigators. If it's perfect, then of course everyone chooses in the same (correct) way, an information cascade begins immediately and it flows in the correct direction. If the information is completely and perfectly wrong, everyone chooses the same (wrong) way, an information cascade begins immediately and it flows in the incorrect direction. If the information is intermediately imperfect in some way, then the oscillation between decision-makers begins. Under these conditions, it is possible that a cascade does not form at all or, as we just mentioned, enough droplets will accumulate in one direction to become sufficient to start either a correct or an incorrect cascade. Regardless of the quality of the information, a cascade can start as soon as two decision-makers in a sequence choose in the same direction. These might be the first two decision-makers.

The Bayesian updating process is always in danger of being swept away by a cascade. People generally do not update their beliefs exactly in accordance with Bayes' law for many different reasons, including their reliance on heuristics and the time pressures that they face. The pathway from prior belief to complete belief in the correctness of a hypothesis is a steady one that relies upon the collection of evidence. When you are assessing a hypothesis at the same time that others are doing so too and you can see what their choice is, it is possible for your updating process to be swept along, not by the evidence but by the observed choices of others. This might be in the right direction but it might also be in the wrong direction. When information cascades are thought of as a torrent of information sweeping the Bayesian updating process along with it, it becomes easier to see how information cascades can be expected to emerge in most settings at some point. If we are interested in getting to the bottom of the patterns of behaviour that lead to incorrect suspect prioritisations (or de-prioritisations), it is important to understand how the flow of information through a sequence of decision-makers can lead to particular outcomes, sometimes correct, sometimes undesirable, despite the best or worst intentions of each individual decision-maker.

Fragile cascades and dissemination of intelligence

Once started, a cascade becomes stronger as the number of people following along increases. However, the original torrent might rely on a fountainhead of just a few decision-makers. Such a cascade is more fragile than one that grows more slowly on a deeper foundation. For example, a cascade of wearing Reebok Pumps might commence at a high school following just a few fashion leaders. However, the cascade is based on a shallow foundation. As more and more students wear the shoes, the fashion or style information that is carried by their collective decisions doesn't have any additional value. Many people wearing the shoes adds nothing further to the desirability of the shoes and, in fact, leads to fragility. Some new piece of information such as a sports star muffing an important shot and blaming it on his shoes might destroy the information cascade (Bikhchandani, Hirshleifer & Welch 1992, p.1004).

In general, a fragile cascade can be broken by a decision-maker with high-precision information even if that decision-maker comes in late (i.e. he might be decision-maker # 20). The other way in which a cascade may break is when correct, highly informative, information becomes available to all of the decision-makers.

When they no longer have to rely on private signals, the structure within which the cascade forms is weakened. Within a counter-terrorism context, the availability of such information can reverse an incorrect cascade encompassing particular suspects or suspect types. Importantly, this has a flipside. The dissemination of noisy or partially correct information may lead to undesirable outcomes. This might be particularly relevant to law enforcement agencies weighing up whether or not to release information to other agencies. Doing so might stop what was actually a correct cascade.

One of the more interesting problems arises when different agencies (within or across jurisdictions) have their own, potentially incorrect or noisy, information about potential suspects and can also observe the treatment of a potential suspect by another agency. Just because a single agency places an individual on a watch list, it does not mean that every other agency will follow suit. This is why suspects might be free to cross jurisdictions without much scrutiny even though an agency has placed their name on a watch list. One agency's decision does not start a cascade. However, it might take only two agencies to start an information cascade and if this is an incorrect cascade, many subsequent errors across jurisdictions may result. The fragility of cascades is something that must be considered before an individual agency 'announces' information about a suspect or suspect type. Cascades are fragile with regard to new information becoming available to all relevant decision-makers. Releasing information too early may precipitate an incorrect cascade or even disrupt a correct cascade.

Four dot points to end the chapter

- Confirmation bias and tunnel visions have been suggested as possible explanations for wrongful convictions.
- The deep roots of confirmation bias are not always made clear. Bayes' rule is an optimal rule for updating one's beliefs as new information comes to hand. A person might conclude far too soon that his or her hypothesis is correct. Divergences from this optimal updating of beliefs underlie biases such as confirmation bias. It is not just that people exhibit tunnel vision. It's deeper than that. People do not always optimally update their beliefs in light of the available evidence.
- Information cascades can lead to similar problems. A cascade can start within a very basic setting and it can begin as early as decision-maker #3.
- Information cascades can be correct or incorrect, fragile or strong. A fragile but correct cascade is something that one must be careful not to break.

Notes

1 Jelani Cobb in *The New Yorker*, April 19 2019.
2 Snook and Cullen (2008, p.26) identify confirmation bias as one of several heuristics that constitutes tunnel vision. The others are the satisficing heuristic, the elimination-by-aspects heuristic and the 'take the best' heuristic.

3 However, some of the measures might be so unobtrusive that they could be applied without fear of major disruption or negative consequences. For example, the basic task of preparing a schematic overview of the evidence, a simple sketch with pen-and-paper, may help reduce tunnel vision (Rassin 2018).
4 Example adapted from Just (2014, pp.161–162).
5 If a properly functioning piece of equipment revealed 'alpha' 30 percent of the time and 'omega' 70 percent of the time (instead of 10 percent and 90 percent), the revelation of 'omega' would lead to a more rapid increase in the prior probability.
6 Lohmann (1994) argues that the collapse of communism in East Germany in 1989 was partly due to an information cascade.
7 Kahan (1997).

References

Anderson, L.R. & Holt, C.A. 1997. Information Cascades in the Laboratory. *American Economic Review*, 87, 847–862.
Ask, K., & Granhag, P.A. 2007. Motivational Bias in Criminal Investigators' Judgements of Witness Reliability. *Journal of Applied Social Psychology*, 37, 561–591.
Ask, K., Rebelius, A., & Granhag, P.A. 2008. The 'Elasticity' of Criminal Evidence: A Moderator of Investigator Bias. *Applied Cognitive Psychology*, 22, 1245–1259.
Bikhchandani, S., Hirshleifer, D. & Welch, I. 1992. A Theory of Fads, Fashion, Custom and Cultural Change as Informational Cascades. *Journal of Political Economy*, 100, 992–1026.
Bikhchandani, S., Hirshleifer, D. & Welch, I. 1998. Learning from the Behaviour of Others: Conformity, Fads and Informational Cascades. *Journal of Economic Perspectives*, 12, 151–170.
Cobb, J. 2019. The Central Park Five, Criminal Justice and Donald Trump. *The New Yorker*, April 19. www.newyorker.com/news/daily-comment/the-central-park-five-criminal-justice-and-donald-trump
Findley, K.A. 2010. Tunnel Vision. Conviction of the Innocent: Lessons from Psychological Research. University of Wisconsin Legal Studies Research Paper No. 1116. Available at SSRN: https://ssrn.com/abstract=1604658.
Gross, S.R. & O'Brien, B. 2008. Frequency and Predictors of False Conviction: Why We Know So Little and New Data on Capital Cases. *Journal of Empirical Legal Studies*, 5, 927–962.
Hung, A.A. & Plott, C.R. 2001. Information Cascades: Replication and Extension to Majority Rule and Conformity-Rewarding Institutions. *American Economic Review*, 91, 1508–1520.
Just, D.R. 2014. *Introduction to Behavioural Economics*. Hoboken, NJ: Wiley.
Kahan, M. 1997. Social Influence, Social Meaning and Deterrence. *Virginia Law Review*, 83, 276–304.
Kerstholt, J.H. & Eikelboom, A.R. 2007. Effects of Prior Interpretation on Situation Assessment in Crime Analysis. *Journal of Behavioural Decision-Making*, 20, 455–465.
Kübler, D. & Weizsäcker, G. 2004. Limited Depth of Reasoning and Failure of Cascade Formation in the Laboratory. *Review of Economic Studies*, 71, 425–441.
Liden, M., Gräns, M. & Juslin, P. 2019. Guilty, No Doubt. Detention Provoking Confirmation Bias in Judges' Guilt Assessments and Debiasing Techniques. Psychology, *Crime and Law*, 25, 219–247.
Lohmann, S. 1994. The Dynamics of Informational Cascades: The Monday Demonstrations in Leipzig, East Germany, 1989–1991. *World Politics*, 47, 42–101.

Nickerson, R.S. 1998. Confirmation Bias: A Ubiquitous Phenomenon in Many Guises. *Review of General Psychology*, 2, 175–220.

O'Brien, B. 2009. Prime Suspect: An Examination of Factors That Aggravate and Counteract Confirmation Bias in Criminal Investigations. *Psychology, Public Policy and Law*, 15, 315–334.

Rassin, E. 2018. Reducing Tunnel Vision with a Pen and Paper Tool for the Weighting of Criminal Evidence. *Journal of Investigative Psychology and Offender Profiling*, 15, 227–233.

Risinger, M.D. 2006. Innocents Convicted: An Empirically Justified Factual Wrongful Conviction Rate. *Journal of Criminal Law & Criminology*, 97, 761–804.

Russano, M.B., Meissner, C.A., Narchet, F.M. & Kassin, S.M. 2005. Investigating True and False Confessions within a Novel Experimental Paradigm. *Psychological Science*, 16, 481–486.

Salet, R. 2017. Framing in Criminal Investigation: How Police Officers (Re)Construct a Crime. *Police Journal: Theory, Practice and Principles*, 90, 128–142.

Simon, H.A. 1957. *Models of Man*. New York: John Wiley & Sons,.

Snook, B. & Cullen R.M. 2008. Bounded Rationality and Criminal Investigations: Has Tunnel Vision Been Wrongfully Convicted? In D.K. Rossmo (Ed.), *Criminal Investigative Failures*. Boca Raton, FL: CRC Press, pp.71–98.

Willinger, M. & Ziegelmeyer, A. 1998. Are More Informed Agents Able to Shatter Information Cascades in the Lab? In P. Cohendey, P. Llerena, H. Stahn & G. Umbhauer (Eds.), *The Economics of Networks: Interaction and Behaviours*. Heidelberg: Springer-Verlag, pp.291–305.

13
EVERYDAY DECISION-MAKING

The policeman must, from a single human hair, be able to describe the crime, the weapon and the criminal and tell you where the criminal is hiding. But ... If he catches the criminal, he's lucky; if he doesn't, he's a dunce. If he gets promoted, he has political pull; if he doesn't, he's a dullard. The policeman must chase bum leads to a dead end, stake out 10 nights to tag one witness who saw it happen but refuses to remember. He runs files and writes reports until his eyes ache to build a case against some felon who'll get dealt out by a shameless shamus or an 'honourable' who isn't. The policeman must be a minister, a social worker, a diplomat, a tough guy, and a gentleman. And of course he'll have to be a genius ... For he'll have to feed a family on a policeman's salary.[1]

In Becker's (1968) analysis, 'policemen' are just a part of the costs of apprehending criminals. They are resources that can be directed by society towards a problem in order to increase the probability that a criminal will be detected and apprehended. In abstraction as well as in reality, there is significant element of truth to this. But there is no everyday decision-making here. There is no tiredness from long shifts, no competition among investigative teams, no conflict, no danger and no endless stakeouts in cold cars or standing in shopfront doorways sheltering from the wind and trying to warm the hands with a cup of coffee.[2] Most importantly, there are no investigative decisions. Police resources are allocated at some cost and this has some effect on increasing the chance that the criminal will be apprehended and, thereby, reducing to some degree the incentive to commit a crime. For example, police would be posted at a stakeout location and tasked, without the complication of boredom or other such factors, to observe known criminals or suspected or known criminal targets such as commercial locations with a history of attempted break-ins.

Or they would be given the job of stopping and frisking individuals, called a Terry stop,[3] around a particular neighbourhood (see Gelman, Fagan & Kiss 2007).

Stakeouts and Terry stops, however, involve decision-making under risk and uncertainty. Ferguson (2012, p.287) explains:

> In non-warrant situations, prediction is also a critical element of analysis. Police officers regularly take action in anticipation of criminal activity. Stakeouts, ongoing surveillance, and undercover investigations focus not only on past crimes, but also future crimes. On the street, a Terry stop based on reasonable suspicion that 'criminal activity may be afoot' is at base a prediction that the facts and circumstances warrant the reasonable prediction that a crime is occurring or will occur. Again, the controlling legal standard speaks in terms of predictive considerations. In others words, to justify a stop, the police have to predict that a person is actively committing a crime. That prediction comes from the available information, which in turn involves a judgement about the information's quality, source, and reliability among other factors.

According to the Fourth Amendment in the United States, police must have a reasonable suspicion that a crime has, is or will be committed by the suspect before the person can be stopped and that the suspect is armed before he or she can be frisked.[4] Police must use their judgement under conditions of risk and uncertainty in estimating the likelihoods along with the other variables that need to be considered in these types of operations. None of these everyday decisions is given much prominence in the economic analysis of crime, at least not in its classical form following Becker (1968).

In the economic analysis of terrorism and counter-terrorism, the situation is the same. There are decision-making scenarios, of course, but these are not everyday scenarios. Predominantly, the scenarios that are studied are the exceptional or high-profile situations that attract attention but which do not constitute the relentless everyday of counter-terrorism law enforcement. As a case in point, consider the survey of the economics of counter-terrorism prepared by Schneider, Brück and Meierrieks (2015). The word 'strategy' appears in the article 11 times while the word 'decision' appears once, and that is with reference to strategic decision. The word 'rational' appears 25 times. This is primarily because the contexts are exceptional and with exceptionality comes the structure and logic that either characterises these more sophisticated events, which are the end product of relatively sophisticated planning, or has come to characterise them by extensive study and modelling. Hostage situations, embassy attacks, mass casualty suicide bombings and so forth.

Everyday policing involves decision but not a lot of strategic *interaction* with criminals, at least not in the formal sense that the word 'strategic' is used in economics and political science. In counter-terrorism, hostage takings and hijackings, in particular, are exceptional events that can be modelled as games of strategy. Being archetypal terrorist events, these have been subjected to the most analysis. And one of the most obvious analytical tools to apply is game theory. Concerning the everyday, the matter is somewhat different. A game theorist *can* deal with 'strategic' interaction between police and criminals (e.g. Tsebelis 1990) but this still rarely touches the everyday of police work or counter-terrorism. This strategic inter-action involves strategic reasoning (see Ghosh, Meijering & Verbrugge 2014). This is different from simply taking the actions of the opposing party into consider-ation. Rather, it involves thinking about what the other side is thinking about and considering such things as, 'if they do that, then I'll do that, but they'll anticipate that, so I'll do this'. It involves making a plan of action, a strategy. When both sides do this to some degree, there is a game of strategy.

Strategic interaction, though, is not the only way in which people interact. In fact, it is probably the least common way. People do consider each other's actions and the actions of one person affect the actions of other people but this is simply the essence of human action in a society. The decision-makers do not think about what the other decision-makers are thinking about and so on in a chain of reasoning. If someone wants a coffee but sees that it is 8.30 am and the coffee shop is likely to be crowded, he/she will either decide it is worth waiting until later to go to the coffee shop, worth waiting in line at the coffee shop or not worth going at all. The decisions of others influence his/her decision, but it is not a strategic interaction. A game theorist could complicate the situation but it is not necessary to do so.[5] More problematically, when the only interaction between decision-makers that we perceive is strategic in the game theory sense, we are left with treating individuals as isolated from each other on the one hand or as strategically interacting on the other. Such an approach completely overlooks the ordinary behaviour that characterises everyday life where people's actions affect others but not as the result of strategy on anyone's part.

In this chapter, we want to explore the everyday of terrorist and law enforce-ment decision-maker 'interactions'. That is, a situation where the decisions of each party might affect the other but where there is no strategic interaction (thinking about thinking) and certainly no common knowledge of the other party's ration-ality because there might not be any (see Sugden 2001, p.113). Law enforcement agencies put in place some counter-terrorism initiative or other, obviously thinking that it will have some positive effect. Terrorists react (or not) by changing some aspect of their behaviour (or not). This action and reaction, however, is not a 'you move, he moves, you move' situation or a 'simultaneous' move situation. It is real, authentic action played out on a social stage where the actors are real and they *think* and *feel*. Law enforcement agencies do not *know* that their initiative will have a positive effect. They think that it will. They feel that it will. They hope that it will. They fear that it won't. They overestimate its chances of success, or underestimate it. They gauge it against a reference point. The terrorist group responds with similar thinking, feeling, hoping and fearing. Law enforcement agencies' decisions affect the terrorists groups' decisions and vice versa but it is not a game of strategy. It is simply human action and reaction guided by a decision-making process subject to biases and emotions.

Everyday decisions, everyday decision-makers

Everyday decision-making is messy. Much messier than the well-structured risky prospects from which both the expected utility decision-maker and prospect theory decision-maker traditionally chooses. And much, much messier than the highly structured games of strategy that are constructed by classical game theorists. Risky prospects with outcomes x_i occurring with probability p_i are a part of everyday life and the expected utility decision-maker deals with them in one way while a prospect theory decision-maker deals with them in another way. Part of what makes every day risky prospects messy is other people. This is not other people acting strategically but simply acting like humans, getting in each other's way, generally being understandable but not completely so, generally being predictable to each other but not completely so, choosing too quickly, choosing too slowly, being too emotional or not emotional enough, not being analytical or being too analytical and, in general, proving to be spanners in the works. The decision-maker confronts the humanity of others and others confront the humanity of the decision-maker. Everyday decisions are made in the maelstrom of it all.

Messy risky prospects. Normally, the economist who wants to make things a little bit messy will introduce noise or uncertainty or incomplete information or some such thing into a formal, structured model. By contrast, we just introduce the idea that people are people and that includes people who work at law enforcement agencies and people who decide to join a terrorist group or who choose to do violence. People make risky prospects messy. From the perspective of law enforcement, a set of counter-terrorism measures produces outcomes x_i with some probability p_i. The terrorists against whom these measures are directed are people and their actions and reactions change the expected outcomes and the probabilities. From the perspective of the terrorist group, attack methods produce outcomes x_i (fatalities or media attention etc.) with probability p_i. The law enforcement agents trying to stop them are people and their actions affect the outcomes and the probabilities. In thinking about the possible outcomes and their chances, each decision-maker is susceptible to cognitive biases and emotions. Furthermore, each side influences the other both by making rational, smart decisions and by making emotional decisions. This is what we mean by everyday messiness.

One thing, often overlooked, that makes human decision-making messy is that humans second guess themselves, rate themselves and assess themselves against some *internal* reference point. For example, the person who thinks that they are sometimes too vocal at meetings might resolve to be quieter next time or the person who thinks that they are too negative might resolve not to be pulled into negative discussions about their workplace around the water cooler. These perceptions of self are not necessarily shared by others. The person's opinions may be valued and might not be seen as domineering and the gossip around the workplace water cooler might be a useful source of information for others or at least not seem as negative to them as it does to the person who is reflecting on their own contribution. Nevertheless, following a team meeting or a water cooler discussion, the person may feel as though they did or did not meet the reference point for behaviour that they had set themselves. This sort of self-referencing behaviour may be associated with self-signalling (see Bodner & Prelec 2002).

There are aspects of the self that the individual does not know. For example, when the time comes to attack, will the terrorist lose his nerve? Some terrorists do, some don't. A prospective terrorist may be unsure as to which category he may fall into. As such, a prospective terrorist may view his decision to continue meeting with associates despite a detectable police presence as a signal (to himself) of his own courage or dedication. There are things about themselves that law enforcement agents do not know for sure either. It is only in the taking of action that a particular trait might be revealed (Bodner & Prelec 2002). Before an action is taken, however, there is only the likelihood that we are who we would like to be (or not). We know, of course, that people are very bad at estimating likelihoods. Is there a high or a low probability that the terrorist will follow through with a plan? He might not know for sure himself and his assessment of the likelihood is probably biased. And even if the probability assessment was correct, he might overweight or underweight it if his decision-making process is best described along the lines of prospect theory.

Everyday decision-making does not usually involve a 'fork in the road' choice. That is, a choice of one action at one point in time. It is messier than that. Hastie (2001, p.665) provides an alternative image:

> The image of a decision maker standing at a choice point like a fork in a road and choosing one direction or the other is probably much less appropriate for major everyday decisions than the image of a boat navigating a rough sea with a sequence of many embedded choices and decisions to maintain a meandering course toward the ultimate goal.

While this type of image has given rise to constructions such as the 'problem space', the really crucial point was recognised by Shackle (1961). This is the fact that human decision-makers create their choices. They create the alternatives and then make a choice. They are not always hemmed in by available, pre-existing alternatives. Terrorists sometimes create something completely new. Law enforcement agencies continuously innovate. They are not subject to simply choosing the best counter-terrorism strategy from a set of strategies. They can create new ones. In doing so, the decision-maker may surprise others and they may also surprise themselves.

Only a decision theorist or computer scientist could come up with the idea of the 'problem space'. It would never occur to an ordinary person in a million years. Newell and Simon (1972) described what they mean by the problem space using the 'nine dot problem'. In this problem, there are nine dots and the task is to draw four straight lines that pass through all nine dots without raising the pencil from the paper:

```
•  •  •

•  •  •

•  •  •
```

If the individual approaches the problem by delineating the problem space as being 'within the boundary of the dots' (i.e. none of the drawn lines can go beyond the dots on the boundary), she will never solve the problem. If, however, the individual delineates the problem space such that lines can go beyond the boundary, then the problem can be easily solved (Newell & Simon 1972, p.90). As such, the problem space might not actually include the solution. In complex real-world problems, the problem space can be vast. The decision-maker tries to reduce this vastness by using new information or existing knowledge to limit the size of the problem space and delineate a suitable sub-space (Newell & Simon 1972, p.94). Of course, that sub-space too might not include the solution to the problem. Simple though it may be, this illustrates perfectly the idea that the individual in many ways creates a situation rather than just responds to a situation.

The playing field or social stage on which both the terrorist and the law enforcement agencies act is less structured than what it appears in analytical treatments. When a terrorist comes 'face-to-face' with law enforcement in this less structured everyday context, the progress from where both parties are now towards some ultimate conclusion is not a series of forks in the road where one side or the other is knocked 'off course'. At many points along the way, there are not even 'points' until the decision-makers create them. What is interesting about economic analysis, and why it has had any success at all, is that the structures it creates are not dissimilar to the structures that people try to create in order to better understand and cope with the world around them. People do not face complete nihilistic uncertainty because they seek and create order. Much of behavioural economics is about responding to given situations. Our discussion is about responding to situations that are not just given but where the situation itself is partly the product of one's own doing or one's own attempt to impose order on a situation and in which other people also try to do the same.

Evolving, interconnected reference points

Determining the complete set of such behaviours and interactions would require a very long book. Newell & Simon's (1972) *Human Problem Solving* is 920 pages long and something of the same scale would be needed. However, a very good start can be made using the central concept of prospect theory: the reference point. The way in which Kahneman & Tversky (1979) imagined the reference point was as the status quo. This interpretation has been broadened, as we have seen, to include goals and aspirations. In our work, we have used the reference point as a lever for copycat behaviour where a terrorist references his decisions against the outcomes achieved by a predecessor. Although the 'outside world' shapes the reference point in these broader interpretations, we can broaden the idea still further by loosening a little more the inward-looking nature of the reference point. Rather than depict the decision-maker as taking something from the outside world and forming a reference point and then making a choice, we can allow the reference points of different decision-makers to interact with each other. Many different examples could be used to frame this type of discussion but one that illustrates the interplay of reference points clearly enough is the case of Al-Qaeda.

The group was formed in the late 1980s by bin Laden and undertook its first attack in Yemen in 1992. The embassy bombings in East Africa in 1998 and the attack on the *USS Cole* in 2000 began to create wider public recognition for the group in the West. Within a few years, Al-Qaeda would be synonymous with terrorism. The 9/11 attacks were the most damaging of Al-Qaeda's six major attacks against Western targets. In hindsight, this seems surprisingly few really. In the mid-2010s, the group was overshadowed by the rise of Islamic State of Iraq and Syria (ISIS). The group's last attack on Western targets was the Charlie Hebdo shooting in Paris in early 2015 (carried out by AQAP, Al-Qaeda in the Arab Peninsula). Some people argue that the group is now more of an idea than a functioning organisation and that the decline the group experienced after 9/11 is permanent (e.g. Byman 2017; Jones 2017). However, Hoffman (2006) argues that the group reorganised itself considerably following 9/11 and strategically bided its time up until the end of the 2010s. Indeed, Hoffman believes that the group is more capable than ever (see Tiozek's 2019, interview with Hoffman).

'Spectacular attacks' is the type of attack associated with Al-Qaeda after 9/11. Although the history of 'spectaculars' arguably began much earlier (Arce & Sandler 2010), it was after 9/11 that law enforcement agencies across the world focused on preventing further 'spectaculars' while other terrorist groups aspired to perpetrate them (Cowen 2006). For example, Enders & Sandler (2005) found that logistically simple but more deadly bombings increased after 9/11, while hostage taking declined. The concept of a spectacular attack was the new reference point for terrorist groups and law enforcement agencies. Chermak, Freilich & Shemtob (2009, pp.1305–1306) summarise the situation:

> Policy concerns about terrorism have varied over time. Typically, a focusing event or a series of events—such as a bombing, hijacking, or assassination—opens a window of opportunity for policy development and change (Baumgartner & Jones 1993; Birkland 2004; Kingdon 1995; Sabatier & Jenkins-Smith 1993). Kingdon (1995) argues that such events create 'opportunities for advocates of proposals to push their pet solutions, or to push attention to their special problems' (p.173). For example, after Timothy McVeigh and Terry Nichols bombed the Alfred P. Murrah Federal Building in Oklahoma City, Oklahoma, and killed 168 people, law enforcement focused attention on homegrown terrorists in general and paramilitary militias in particular. Congressional hearings were held, and sweeping federal terrorism legislation was passed (Chermak, 2002). The power of a focusing event to set and shape the policy agenda was displayed after the attacks of September 11. These attacks widely affected society—especially, the political, public, private, and financial sectors—as well as terrorism scholarship....it is not surprising that law enforcement reinvented itself after September 11.

This was not dissimilar to a reference point 'switch' that arguably took place during the 1980s. Wilson & Lynxwiler (1988), writing with reference to abortion clinic bombings, identified a distinct shift in the treatment of these actions. First, the press coverage accorded to abortion clinic bombings declined markedly. Second, the FBI declared that these attacks should not be classed as terrorism. Third, this coincided with a shift from 'domestic terrorism' to 'international terrorism' in terms of law enforcement focus. For law enforcement, potential terrorists and the media, this change in reference point had tangible consequences.

If it were part of their objective to gain media attention, violent anti-abortion activists found their actions being accorded much less attention than before. Along with the move away from referring to abortion clinic bombings as terrorism, this might be partially attributed to the press deeming such attacks as no longer of being of interest (Wilson & Lynxwiler 1988). For law enforcement, the prestige shifted away from actions such as abortion clinic bombings to investigations with an international dimension. For the public, through the media, anti-abortion actions faded from attention and the 'real' terrorism threat was thought to reside elsewhere. Domestic terrorism rarely gained as much attention as it had before, with the Oklahoma City Bombing being one of the few exceptions. Following 9/11, of course, the spectacular attacks on the Twin Towers became a reference point for terrorists, academics, law enforcement agencies and the public, through a series of interconnected shifts in the reference points of all of these social actors.

It could be argued that 'lone wolf terrorism' replaced 'spectacular' attacks towards the later 2000s. With the emergence of ISIS, lone wolves inspired to action by the group's ideology were viewed as a significant threat, especially with 'returned foreign fighters' raising alarms in many circles. The risk of a spectacular attack perpetrated by ISIS or its followers was never far from consideration. Much to the concern of some, it took years before 'domestic terrorism' would start to regain attention. With the collapse of ISIS in Syria, the 'far right' began to occupy journalists just as much as Islamic fundamentalist terrorism had done a short time before. The rather complex composition of the 'far right' (see Durham 2003; Chermak, Freilich & Suttmoeller 2013) and the absence of a signature attack or attack type makes it somewhat difficult for the public to form a reference point based on any one of these groups. This is despite the considerable damage that domestic terrorist groups and lone wolves, on both sides of the political spectrum and motivated by various ideologies, have inflicted (Chermak, Freilich & Simone 2010).

The gradual shift towards mass casualty attacks beginning in the 1980s (see Quillen 2002) led almost inevitably to an increasing scale of terrorism as it became harder and harder to capture attention (e.g. Sandler 2003, p.781). If Bruce Hoffman is right, Al-Qaeda has deliberately avoided attacks that 'reference' 9/11. This precise possibility is why reference points are so important to our understanding of terrorist behaviour, public reactions and law enforcement decisions in the terrorism context. Could Al-Qaeda re-emerge in the West in a fundamentally different way, perhaps shunning civilian targets and focusing on infrastructure attacks? Most readers will experience a subtle or not-so-subtle resistance to this idea. Not the idea Al-Qaeda could re-emerge. That's debatable, of course, but the idea that if it did re-emerge it would not try to resume with a spectacular attack. Our existing reference points make it difficult for us to imagine other possibilities and prepare for them. The public, terrorist groups and law enforcement are connected by their reference points. No single actor sets a new reference point for all actors in one action. Reference points gradually evolve and the behaviour of all actors on the social stage of terrorism gradually evolve and change as these points of reference change.

Predictive policing

Since Snowden, everyone knows about the use of technology for surveillance. Law enforcement, counter-terrorism and intelligence agencies are constantly innovating. And many more innovations can be named. Among the most obvious are wiretaps (Bloss 2009), CCTV (Welsh & Farrington 2009) and surveillance cameras (Leman-Langlois 2002; Alexandrie 2017). Some of these methods were first introduced a long time ago but continue to evolve with technology and changes in society and the law. Wiretapping, for example, has been around since the 1890s and was widely used during the prohibition era (Berger 1938). Once it became widely known as a police surveillance technique, it immediately began to be the subject of intense public debate (see Brownell 1954). This debate, though on again off again, has never completely gone away.

A newer innovation is 'predictive policing'. Predictive policing refers to the use of different analytic tools, including algorithms and computer software, to forecast the location and timing of crimes (Moses & Chan 2018, p.806). These forecasts add to the stock of 'intelligence' used to allocate police resources. The essence of the idea is not really new. It is just the natural development of crime analysis, which promises to be able to direct police resources more effectively. A related approach, for example, is intelligence-led policing (ILP). ILP emerged during the 1990s in the UK, though its roots might be traced as far back as the 1970s. In response to high and increasing crime rates, there were calls for a more proactive approach to policing (Maguire 2000). Rather than responding to reports of crimes, police would try to pre-empt crimes. Information, including that derived from surveillance and the use of informants, would be interpreted and analysed to provide intelligence that could be used to better guide police activity. Following 9/11, ILP received a significant boost in popularity. Predictive policing is another step towards the integration of intelligence techniques and everyday policing (Moses & Chan 2018, p.808).

Predictive policing uses data and software. The software usually embeds an algorithm. The idea is to forecast location and timing for crimes and then direct police to patrol those areas. Sometimes the forecasts are driven purely by the algorithm. At other times, an analyst combines the algorithm's results with other information to form a more comprehensive intelligence assessment. An example of an algorithm is the 'self-exciting point process' applied to the predictive policing of residential burglaries by Mohler et al. (2011). The process was originally developed by seismologists. When there is an earthquake, seismologists use this type of mathematical model to predict the location and timing of 'nearby' earthquakes. Using data for past burglaries, the general idea is that the math can help identify crime hotspots on a city grid. It is essentially a contagion process. One crime in one location increases the chance of future crimes at the same location and at locations nearby. This should work reasonably well, at least in principle, for crimes such as burglaries, which do have characteristics that make them amenable to study by diffusion or contagion processes (e.g. Johnson 2008). Evidence remains mixed, however (Meijer & Wessels 2019).

Apart from the question, still unresolved, about whether predictive policing 'works', most researchers have been concerned with the possibility of bias and discrimination (e.g. Brantingham, Valasik & Mohler 2018). But there are plenty of other areas for debate. What is most interesting about predictive policing is that Gary Becker himself could have come up with it. The very vision of it is straight out of Becker (1968). That is, police resources are allocated seamlessly to problem areas on the city grid to deter crime. This deterrence effect works even without any arrests being made. Consider Brantingham, Valasik & Mohler's (2018, p.1) comments: 'The prevailing view, derived from experiments in hot spot policing, is that the presence of police in a given place removes opportunities for crime even without any direct contact with potential offenders'. Beneath the surface, we have Becker's (1968) narrative. Police officers are resources. Efficient allocation can reduce the costs. Predictive policing increases the efficiency of the allocation of police resources. Efficient allocation is something beyond sending police to arrest more criminals. Criminals respond to incentives and the deterrence effect of police presence. By picking the best spots to send police to, predictive policing spreads a deterrence effect over the locations where it will have the biggest impact per unit of cost. Classic Becker.

This leaves out a lot of agency, for the criminals, the police officers, the designers of the models and the assessors of the results. The crimes are treated as contagion processes rather than decision processes and the police response is treated as a resource allocation problem without a decision-making dimension. The impact of predictive policing on the decisions that officers make has been the implied concern of those researchers interested in the potential for predictive policing to introduce greater prejudice into police practice. Of course, we would also question the 'point prediction' nature of some applications of predictive policing. We have argued that pattern prediction is far sounder. Particular types of crime exhibit patterns because the offenders exhibit patterns in their choices. Contagion and diffusion processes capture none of the underlying behaviour. A particular location might be flagged as a hot spot because a crime was reported there. The reason why another crime might occur there is because the outcomes of crimes committed there are a reference point for local offenders. However, by this time, offenders are already expected to be 'on the move' because the chances of exceeding the reference point with another 'score' at the same location are slim and the offenders probably expect an increased police presence.[6] What is needed then is not a prediction of the offenders' (already outdated) reference point, but a geographic prediction of the direction of their domain of gains.

These weaknesses are apparent in the modelling undertaken by Mohler et al. (2011). Using the self-exciting point process model from seismology and data for 5,376 burglaries reported in an 18 × 18 kilometre grid for the San Fernando Valley in Los Angeles, Mohler et al. (2011) demonstrate that burglaries diffuse from a single point outwards along streets heading north-south, east-west (burglars do not travel at angles through backyards). Of these burglaries, however, 63 percent occurred in the same house and nearby houses during a 1–2-day period. The risk remains elevated for 7–10 days before a quick decline and gradual decay back to baseline. While the analysis seems impressive, the initial burglaries are most likely the work of a single offender or group and could not have been predicted before-hand. Their activity created a hot spot. The original offenders continue to work the same area for a week or so. It is possible that new offenders are initially attracted but not in great numbers and not for very long. Rather, we expect criminals to begin to drift, especially if they have been successful because they are in the domain of gains and, with the police closing in, are motivated by their risk aversion to protect the gains they have made.

Predictive counter-terrorism

Needless to say, the application of predictive policing to terrorist behaviour is much more challenging than its application to burglaries. Because the geographical clustering does not so readily apply to terrorism, the consequences of the omission of the decision processing dimensions that we have just been discussing become even more pronounced. If it can be used in counter-terrorism, predictive policing is more likely to be deployed indirectly, by targeting antisocial (or, possibly, social) behaviour that might be precursors to terrorist activity rather than terrorist activity itself. For example, racially charged vandalism, gang violence, gun offenses or drug dealing. In this regard, predictive policing in a counter-terrorism context may help to broaden some applications of ILP, which can sometimes be too narrowly focused on terrorism and fail to consider the terrorists' involvement in crime (McGarrell, Freilich & Chermak 2007, p.151). But the limitations of a contagion or diffusion process applied without consideration of decision-maker agency are clear and will need to be addressed.

We can offer a few suggestions based on both orthodox and behavioural economics. These suggestions can be used to guide the interpretation and use of the results of predictive policing algorithms by analysts whose task it is to generate intelligence used to guide the allocation of police resources. We do not think it feasible to build a full predictive 'profiling' model. Therefore, rather than add behav-ioural variables to predictive policing models, we think it better to concentrate on improving the interpretation of the results by consciously considering various aspects of the decision-making processes that are relevant in each case. This includes police, criminals, modellers and the analysts themselves. Even so, the prospects for using predictive policing (on its own) in a terrorism context are limited. Our suggestions are as follows. Remember, though, these are pattern predictions and are not expected to hold in every single case:

1.   Hot spots might be better interpreted as reference points. If the activities there have been successful, the offenders are likely in the domain of gains and risk averse. If the activities have been unsuccessful, the offenders are likely in the domain of losses and risk seeking. The first type of offender drifts away, the second type stays.
2.   The likelihoods determined by the analyst and embedded into directions for police resource allocations are subject to the analyst's probability weighting. High likelihoods have been underweighted and low likelihoods overweighted. This happens subconsciously without the analyst being aware of it. Even if the predictive policing algorithms gave absolutely correct probabilities about future offenses, the analyst would apply decision weights to those probabilities and distort them. Further distortion happens all the way down the line, including in the police cruiser doing its rounds on the dark, wet streets.
3.   Analysts who are invested in predictive policing will experience gains and losses from its success or failure. This shapes subsequent intelligence reports and adjustments that might be made to the underlying models, at times making the reports (and adjustments) too conservative while at other times too aggressive.
4.   Overconfidence in the use of predictive policing may lead to its overuse, beyond the point where its benefits begin to decline.

The key point is that predictive policing is not detached from decision-making processes. The fact that it *appears* to be is something that should be addressed before it is used more widely. The models, even the most basic ones, are based on choices. Human choices. Human decision-making processes have quirks. These quirks shape even the most basic choices. We value something more just because we have it. We overweight and underweight probabilities. We take more risk to avoid or recoup losses. We protect gains. We compartmentalise our resources into mental accounts. We assess gains and losses against a reference point rather than absolutely. Our reference points might be our status quo, an aspiration or goal or the product of our envy at what someone else has achieved and our desire to do better. We are overconfident, susceptible to information cascades and we can be pulled in various directions by our desires for career advancement and career stability. While analysts and researchers are often attracted to the big decisions and the spectacular events, it is in the everyday that all of these little decision-making quirks make themselves felt.

Four dot points to end the chapter

•   The economic analysis of terrorism has a tendency to focus on exceptional situations rather than the everyday of police work, law enforcement, intelligence and counter-terrorism.

- The exceptional situations are usually very structured and this fact makes highly structured theories, such as game theory and some orthodox models, appear to be far more relevant to the problem of terrorism and counter-terrorism than they really are.
- The everyday of human decision-making is much messier but still structured enough by frameworks, rules, laws and conventions that patterns of behaviour can be identified and used to make sense of even very complex situations.
- Innovations shape and re-shape the terrorism and law enforcement contexts. When new innovations appear, especially technological innovations, we must be careful not to overlook their very human roots. This is certainly the case for predictive policing.

Notes

1 Harvey (1968, p.8).
2 Ethnographies and other first-hand accounts of police work are available. See, for example, Baker (1985).
3 This refers to the case Terry v Ohio (1968), which set the legal standard for police stops.
4 Stop and frisk attracted much commentary during the 2016 presidential election (see Cassady 2017).
5 A game theorist might come up with a very clever proof that nobody will go to coffee at all.
6 If the crime was unsuccessful, say an interrupted burglary attempt, this might place the offender(s) in the domain of losses. Their risk-seeking behaviour will now prompt a repeat attempt at the same location or nearby. In fact, it is initial failure that might be more likely than initial success to prompt a repeat attempt.

References

Alexandrie, G. 2017. Surveillance Cameras and Crime: A Review of Randomised and Natural Experiments. *Journal of Scandinavian Studies in Criminology and Crime Prevention*, 18, 210–222.

Arce, D.G. & Sandler, T. 2010. Terrorist Spectaculars: Backlash Attacks and the Focus of Intelligence. *Journal of Conflict Resolution*, 54, 354–373.

Baker, M. 1985. Cops: *Their Lives in Their Own Words*. New York: Simon & Schuster.

Baumgartner, F. & Jones, B.D. 1993. *Agendas and Instability in American Politics*. Chicago: Chicago University Press.

Becker, G. 1968. Crime and Punishment: An Economic Approach. *Journal of Political Economy*, 76, 169–217.

Berger, M. 1938. Tapping the Wires. *The New Yorker*, June 18.

Birkland, T.A. 2004. 'The World Changed Today': Agenda-Setting and Policy Change in the Wake of the September 11 Terrorist Attacks. *Review of Policy Research*, 21, 179–200.

Bloss, W.P. 2009. Transforming US Police Surveillance in a New Privacy Paradigm. *Police Practice and Research*, 10, 225–238.

Bodner, R. & Prelec, D. 2002. Self-Signalling and Diagnostic Utility in Everyday Decision-Making. In I. Brocas & J. Carillo (Eds.), *Collected Essays in Psychology and Economics*. Oxford: Oxford University Press, 105–123.

Brantingham, P.J., Valasik, M. & Mohler, G.O. 2018. Does Predictive Policing Lead to Biased Arrests? Results from a Randomised Controlled Trial. *Statistics and Public Policy*, 5, 1–6.

Brownell, H. Jr. 1954. Public Security and Wiretapping. *Cornell Law Review*, 39, 195–212.

Byman, D. 2017. Judging Al-Qaeda's Record, Part 1. Is the Organisation in Decline? *Lawfare*, June 27. www.lawfareblog.com/judging-al-qaedas-record-part-i-organization-decline.

Cassady, A. 2017. Reintroducing Stop and Frisk or Revisiting It? *Minnesota Law Review*, 101, www. minnesotalawreview.org/2017/01/re-introducing-stop-and-frisk-or-revisiting-it/

Chermak, S.M. 2002. *Searching for a Demon: The Media's Construction of the Militia Movement*. Boston: Northeastern University Press.

Chermak, S.M., Freilich, J.D. & Shemtob, Z. 2009. Law Enforcement Training and the Domestic Far Right. *Criminal Justice and Behaviour*, 36, 1305–1322.

Chermak, S.M., Freilich, J.D. & Simone Jr, J. 2010. Surveying American State Police Agencies About Lone Wolves, Far-Right Criminality, and Far-Right and Islamic *Jihadist* Criminal Collaboration. *Studies in Conflict and Terrorism*, 33, 1019–1041.

Chermak, S.M., Freilich, J.D. & Suttmoeller, M. 2013. The Organisational Dynamics of Far-Right Hate Groups in the United States: Comparing Violent to Nonviolent Organisations. *Studies in Conflict & Terrorism*, 36, 193–218.

Cowen, T. 2006. Terrorism as Theatre: Analysis and Policy Implications. *Public Choice*, 128, 233–244.

Durham, M. 2003. The American Far Right and 9/11. *Terrorism and Political Violence*, 15, 96–111.

Enders, W. & Sandler, T. 2005. After 9/11. Is It all Different Now? *Journal of Conflict Resolution*, 49, 259–277.

Ferguson, A.G. 2012. Predictive Policing as Reasonable Suspicion. *Emory Law Journal*, 62, 261–325.

Gelman, A., Fagan, J. & Kiss, A. 2007. An Analysis of the New York City Police Department's 'Stop-and-Frisk' Policy in the Context of Claims of Racial Bias. *Journal of the American Statistical Association*, 102, 813–823.

Ghosh, S., Meijering, B. & Verbrugge, R. 2014. Strategic Reasoning: Building Cognitive Models from Logical Formulas. *Journal of Logic, Language and Information*, 23, 1–29.

Harvey, P. 1968. What Are Policemen Made Of? *FBI Law Enforcement Bulletin*, 37, 8.

Hastie, R. 2001. Problems for Judgement and Decision-Making. *Annual Review of Psychology*, 52, 653–683.

Hoffman, B. 2006. *Inside Terrorism*. New York: Columbia University Press.

Johnson, S.D. 2008. Repeat Burglary Victimisation: A Tale of Two Theories. *Journal of Experimental Criminology*, 4, 215–240.

Jones, S.G. 2017. Will Al-Qaeda Make a Comeback? *Foreign Affairs*, August 7.

Kingdon, J.W. 1995. *Agendas, Alternatives and Public Policies,* 2nd ed. New York: HarperCollins.

Leman-Langlois, S. 2002. The Myopic Panopticon: The Social Consequences of Policing through the Lens. *Policing and Society*, 13, 43–58.

Maguire, M. 2000. Policing by Risks and Targets: Some Dimensions and Implications of Intelligence-Led Crime Control. *Policing and Society*, 9, 315–336.

McGarrell, E.F., Freilich, J.D. & Chermak, S. 2007. Intelligence-Led Policing as a Framework for Responding to Terrorism. *Journal of Contemporary Criminal Justice*, 23, 142–158.

Meijer, A. & Wessels, M. 2019. Predictive Policing: Review of Benefits and Drawbacks. *International Journal of Public Administration*, 42, 1031–1039.

Mohler, G., Short, M., Brantingham, P., Schoenberg, F. & Tita, G. 2011. Self-Exciting Point Process Modelling of Crime. *Journal of the American Statistical Association*, 106, 100–108.

Moses, L.B. & Chan, J. 2018. Algorithmic Prediction in Policing: Assumptions, Evaluation and Accountability. *Policing and Society*, 28, 806–822.

Newell, A. & Simon, H.A. 1972. *Human Problem Solving*. Englewood Cliffs, NJ: Prentice Hall.

Quillen, C. 2002. A Historical Analysis of Mass Casualty Bomber. *Studies in Conflict and Terrorism*, 25, 279–292.

Sabatier, P. & Jenkins-Smith, H.C. 1993. *Policy Change and Learning: An Advocacy Coalition Approach*. Boulder, CO: Westview.

Sandler, T. 2003. Collective Action and Transnational Terrorism. *The World Economy*, 26, 779–802.

Schneider, F., Brück, T. & Meierrieks, D. 2015. The Economics of Counter-Terrorism: A Survey. *Journal of Economic Surveys*, 29, 131–157.

Shackle, G.L.S. 1961. *Decision Order and Time*. Cambridge: Cambridge University Press.

Sugden, R. 2001. The Evolutionary Turn in Game Theory. *Journal of Economic Methodology*, 8, 113–130.

Terry v. Ohio 1968. 392 U.S. 1, U.S. Supreme Court.

Tiozek, E. 2019. Al-Qaeda Was Forgotten during the Rise of Islamic State but the Terrorist Group Is More Dangerous than Ever. ABC News. July 31 2019. www.abc.net.au/news/2019-07-31/al-qaeda-was-forgotten-but-the-terror-group-is-more-dangerous/11365230

Tsebelis, G. 1990. Penalty Has No Impact on Crime: A Game-Theoretic Analysis. *Rationality and Society*, 2, 255–286.

Welsh, B.C. & Farrington, D.P. 2009. Public Area CCTV and Crime Prevention: An Updated Systematic Review and Meta-Analysis. *Justice Quarterly*, 26, 716–745.

Wilson, M. & Lynxwiler, J. 1988. Abortion Clinic Violence as Terrorism. *Studies in Conflict and Terrorism*, 11, 263–273.

14

REASON, STRATEGY AND DISCOVERY

It is cold at 6.40 in the morning of a March day in Paris, and seems even colder when a man is about to be executed by firing squad. At that hour on March 11, 1963, in the main courtyard of the For d'Ivry a French Air Force colonel stood before a stake driven into the chilly gravel as his hands were bound behind the post, and stared with slowly diminishing disbelief at the squad of soldiers facing him twenty metres away.[1]

Some people like to read. The idea that Carlos would be reading Frederick Forsyth's *The Day of the Jackal* certainly seemed plausible to the journalist who gave Carlos the name, The Jackal. And many people probably just assume that the book is about Carlos. On the other side of the fence, James Grady's *Six Days of the Condor*, a suspense novel about a CIA 'reader' that was made into the political thriller *Three Days of the Condor* starring Robert Redford, prompted the critic John Simon (1982, pp.195–198) to conclude, 'we must be grateful to the CIA: it does what our schools no longer do—engage some people to read books'. Reading, whether it's academic literature, fiction or non-fiction, is a matter of taste, chance, practice and timing. What we find to read, how we approach reading it and what we see in it are shaped by our decisions and our circumstances. That this might determine whether one has read Peter Wright's *Spycatcher* or John Le Carré's *Tinker, Tailor, Soldier, Spy* or Max Allan Collins' 'Quarry' novels is quite obvious. That it applies with equal force to our deliberate searching for relevant information is not quite obvious. And, it will surprise many people to learn that the core of behavioural economics research is still not that easy to find.

On New Year's Day 1980, there was no such thing as behavioural economics. Prospect theory had made its appearance just a few months before but it was just one of a number of 'generalisations' of expected utility theory. Herbert Simon had won the Nobel Prize for economics in 1978 for 'his pioneering research into the decision-making process within organisations' but despite the far-reaching implications of Simon's work, it was considered by most economists to be more business economics and administrative management than economics and psychology. In fact, Kahneman (2011) barely mentions Simon at all and obviously views the 'heuristics and biases' research program as something quite distinct. In 1980, Richard Thaler had only just completed a year at Stanford with Kahneman and Tversky, both of whom had only recently taken up posts in North America—Tversky at Stanford and Kahneman at the University of British Columbia. Jimmy Carter was president and the Iran hostage crisis was less than two months old. The first issue of the *American Economic Review* that year contained articles on unemployment, oligopoly, inflation, wages and monetary growth. There was one article with the word 'behavioural' in its title but it wasn't about human behaviour.

Kahneman & Tversky's (1979) prospect theory article was published in perhaps the most esoteric of places, in the journal *Econometrica*. Although there are some dedicated behavioural economics or behavioural finance journals, much of the work in behavioural economics is dispersed. As might be expected, then, there are many hidden gems that have not received wide attention and would not be easily spotted in searches of the literature. Although it is certainly far from complete, what we want to do here is provide a few roadmaps to the literature. Actually, these are more like subway maps. There is a redline running through the centre. It starts with prospect theory and follows the mainstream of behavioural economics research that was established by Richard Thaler. As we have alluded to a few times, prospect theory was not in such a good position early on. Other fountainheads might have prevailed. In this, our final chapter, we present several maps with significant waypoints. One of these starts with prospect theory. The other three start from other places. Sometimes the work intersects but mostly the pathways are distinct. We haven't the space to work through the pattern predictions that might be derived from these other streams of research but by charting some of the significant features of this literature, we hope that the relevant results will be less neglected than they otherwise might be.

The mainstream of the alternative

Behavioural economics is still not in the mainstream of economics so it feels strange to speak of a mainstream of behavioural economics. There is a mainstream though. Kahneman & Tversky (1979) did not come as a bolt from the blue. Not really. They had been working on their psychology experiments for years and Amos Tversky had published articles that were not only relevant to economic theory but also emulated the style of the prevailing orthodoxy. For example, 'The Intransitivity of Preferences' published in the *Psychological Review* in 1969 (Tversky 1969) and 'Elimination by Aspects: A Theory of Choice', which was published in the same journal in 1972 (Tversky 1972). It can be argued, too, that Ward Edwards, a long-time antagonist of Amos Tversky, had developed a similar functional form to prospect theory as early as the 1950s (see Edwards 1955, 1962). Kahneman and

Tversky's work, it seems, was already well known and many people had already seen its relevance for economics, not least among them the authors themselves. Indeed, apart from their grander vision of producing a descriptive model of choice to rival expected utility theory, Kahneman and Tversky knew that the best way to attract the economists' attention was to produce a model of decision-making under risk that could account for the Allais Paradox.

One of the axioms or rules that underpins expected utility theory is the independence axiom (Fishburn 1989). Remember (though we understand if you don't), the axioms of expected utility theory hold if and only if a utility function exists. And since there is mathematical proof that utility functions do exist and, in fact, there are lots of them, then the axioms hold. There is no problem. Because the theory is a prescriptive model, the actual decisions that people make are irrelevant. If they're silly enough not to use expected utility theory to guide them, using a calculator or computer if they cannot figure it out for themselves, then that is their problem. *However.* The axioms have come to be interpreted as rules of rational human decision-making. It became interesting, once this development had taken place, to see whether people's behaviour is in accordance with the axioms.[2] If so, then people are rational and we can use a utility function to represent their preferences and these preferences will be expressed as an ordering, highest to lowest, over the available alternatives. One of the first major contradictions between human choices and the axioms was the contravention of the independence axiom in Allais' Paradox.

The independence axiom says that mixing two alternatives, A and B, with a third, C, will make no difference to the original preferences for A and B. If A and B are two risky prospects and the probability is α that a third choice, C, is present then if A was preferred to B beforehand $(A \geq B)$, adding C to the set of choices does not change anything. The original choice is independent of the addition of a third choice:

$$A \geq B \Leftrightarrow \alpha A + (1 - \alpha)C \geq \alpha B + (1 - \alpha)C$$

Allais' Paradox refers to the finding that, contrary to the independence axiom, increases in the outcomes associated with risky prospect C do gradually begin to influence the ordering of A and B such that B and C might come to be preferred to A and C even though A is preferred to B. Prospect theory, along with most of the other generalisations of expected utility theory, can cope with this type of behaviour. In fact, problems with the first version of prospect theory required that it absorb a key part of one of the competing models, rank-dependent expected utility developed by Quiggin (1982). Instead of an adjusted version of prospect theory, why didn't we just adopt Quiggin's model in its place? Quiggin's (1982) theory, though obviously an important contribution, has none of the 'life' of prospect theory. His 1982 paper is standard economics and, rather than a model that might be useful in helping us to understand human action in different parts of life, he lists the main use to which his model may be put as the analysis of decisions that involve catastrophic (extremely unfavourable) outcomes. That does not sound like something that can be applied very widely.

The S-shaped utility function of prospect theory caught Richard Thaler's eye and imagination. During the 1980s, Thaler guided the development of behavioural economics based on the foundations provided by prospect theory. It was not easy. It was difficult getting articles published. One avenue that opened up was the opportunity to publish articles on 'anomalies' for the new *Journal of Economic Perspectives*. Thaler (2016) credits this as one of the keys to his success. However, the ongoing debate in finance over the informational 'efficiency' of financial markets also meant that there was a relatively receptive audience in finance for findings that questioned the 'rationality' of market participants. In other areas of economics, especially bargaining theory, researchers were also interested in adjusting their models to incorporate aspects of psychology that obviously shape actions and outcomes, including people's notions of fairness. Some of the main stepping-stones in the development of behavioural economics along this pathway, stretching from prospect theory in 1979 to contemporary developments in the field, may be listed as follows:

1. *People value something more when they possess it.* This is the endowment effect. It uses the concept of loss aversion from prospect theory (Knetsch & Sinden 1984; Kahneman, Knetsch & Thaler 1991).
2. *People partition their decisions, including gains and losses, into accounts with different labels (e.g. leisure, college fund etc.).* This is mental accounting. It uses the prospect theory concept of gains and losses from a reference point (Thaler 1985).
3. *People overreact to news.* This is a violation of Bayes' rule. In their study of overreaction by investors, De Bondt & Thaler (1985) use a number of concepts from Kahneman and Tversky's research program, including the representativeness heuristic.
4. *People depart from pure self-interest.* People will not always play strategic games with a ruthless objective of maximising outcomes for themselves. Often, they display sensitivity to notions of fairness. Kahneman, Knetsch & Thaler (1986a, 1986b) use the concept of reference point. It is against a reference 'transaction' that people assess the fairness of a proposed or actual choice.
5. *People's preferences are time inconsistent.* Our short-term tendency to pursue immediate gratification is inconsistent with our long-term preferences. While today we feel that it is best we do not overeat tomorrow, tomorrow we tend to overeat (Rabin 1998, p.38). This contravenes orthodox economics where people's preferences are time consistent. Interestingly, time inconsistency is different for gains and losses. Thaler (1981, p.202) explains:

> According to economic theory a person should be willing to pay the same amount to receive $100 a month sooner or to postpone paying $100 for a month ... [However], even someone who appears very impatient to receive a gain may nevertheless take a 'let's get it over with' attitude toward losses.

6. *People put in place various strategies to overcome time inconsistency.* The flipside of the time inconsistency coin is 'self-control'. Behavioural economists have been very interested in the degree to which people are aware that they will have self-control problems in the future and take steps to mitigate the problems. Many people believe that they will have the self-control necessary to quit an addiction tomorrow when in fact they will not and so they never quit. Others recognise this self-control problem and take steps, admittedly often very weak steps, such as throwing away their cigarettes today (Thaler & Shefrin 1981).

It is easy to see Thaler's influence over all of these ideas, which have become core parts of the mainstream of behavioural economics. It is surprising to see just how quickly he was able to develop these insights. Once he had prospect theory in hand, he was able to use it to ground each of his 'anomalies' in quick succession. Work on these themes has continued, steadily building in scale and scope, since the 1990s. Most of the applications have been directed towards financial decision-making and consumer choice. The financial markets are a natural laboratory for studying human decision-making. As such, the most highly developed part of the mainstream of behavioural economics is behavioural finance. The relevance of these results to the study of terrorism and other forms of violent behaviour is not completely obvious. However, take a look beneath the surface and one finds, for example, that procrastination that leads to time inconsistency and self-control problems has strong links with antisocial behaviour (e.g. Lyons & Rice 2014). The avenues for future research into terrorism and violence are open. Prospect theory is likely to remain the theoretical foundation, the reference point, for this research. Its place is well deserved. Of all the generalisations of expected utility theory published between 1979 and 1985, prospect theory attempted to do something different: *describe* the human decision-making process. It did so in a unique way with eye-catching features and open-ended interpretations. It had all of the features necessary for a successful theory.

Regret

Just after the publication of prospect theory and mixed in with the many new generalisations of expected utility theory that were designed, among other things, to deal with the Allais Paradox, was a theory that was every bit as original as prospect theory but not as eye-catching. This is 'regret theory'. It was developed simultaneously by Bell (1982) and Loomes & Sugden (1982). One of the puzzles that is usually associated with the Allais Paradox involves asking people to choose first between two alternatives, A and B:

A: $1,000,000 for sure (probability 1.00); or
B: $5,000,000 with probability 0.10, $1,000,000 with probability 0.89, and $0 with probability 0.01.

Most people choose A. Following this, they are presented with another problem. Choose between two alternatives, C and D:

C: $5,000,000 with probability 0.10 and $0 with probability 0.90; or
D: $1,000,000 with probability 0.11 and $0 with probability 0.89.

In round two, most people choose C but this set of choices, A and C, violates the independence axiom of expected utility theory. The 'trick' is that A and D are actually the same and so too are B and C, once the common elements are removed (which according to the independence axiom should make no difference). To see this, we can rewrite the options as:

A: $1,000,000 with probability of 0.89 and $1,000,000 with probability 0.11; or
B: $5,000,000 with probability 0.10, $1,000,000 with probability 0.89, and $0 with probability 0.01.
C: $5,000,000 with probability 0.10, $0 with probability 0.89 and $0 with probability 0.01; or
D: $1,000,000 with probability 0.11 and $0 with probability 0.89.

Let us now strike out the common elements:

A: ~~$1,000,000 with probability of 0.89~~ and $1,000,000 with probability 0.11; or
B: $5,000,000 with probability 0.10, ~~$1,000,000 with probability 0.89~~, and $0 with probability 0.01.
C: $5,000,000 with probability 0.10, ~~$0 with probability 0.89~~ and $0 with probability 0.01; or
D: $1,000,000 with probability 0.11 and ~~$0 with probability 0.89~~.

If the decision-maker says that she prefers A to B, then she reveals a preference for $1,000,000 with 0.11 probability over $5,000,000 with 0.10 probability and $0 with 0.01 probability. Then, in round two, if she says she prefers C, she reveals a preference for $5,000,000 with 0.10 probability and $0 with 0.01 probability over $1,000,000 with 0.11 probability. A complete preference reversal! While this is not universal behaviour or, indeed, the majority decision of people tested, it is the modal preference of decision-makers who participate in economics and psychology experiments (Raiffa 1968; Slovic & Tversky 1974). That is, the most likely preference to be observed from a random sample of subjects. While all of the generalisations of expected utility theory, including prospect theory, allow for this type of behaviour, regret theory provides a clear and straightforward *explanation* for it.

Bell (1982) and Looms & Sugden (1982) built an alternative to expected utility theory and prospect theory in which the decision-maker can anticipate feeling regret and this anticipation of a negative feeling in the future affects their decisions now. In the decision problem that we just discussed, the decision-maker anticipates the regret she will feel if she opts for B instead of A and the least likely outcome of receiving $0 eventuates when she could have had $1,000,000 for sure. In an interesting turning of the tables, it was this work by Bell, Loomes and Sugden, all economists writing for economics journals, which initiated the large research program in regret and disappointment in psychology. Of course, people feel regret after something happens but the idea that they can *anticipate* this regret during the decision-making process and that a rigorous model of choice could be built to incorporate it was new. In recent times, Bleichrodt & Wakker (2015) have argued that regret theory might just be the best alternative to the alternatives to expected utility theory. Despite the success of prospect theory as a fountainhead for the mainstream of behavioural economics, the richness of regret theory and the large volume of psychological results that have flowed from it mean that regret theory sits, albeit in the shadows, as a potential rival to prospect theory. We have taken some first steps towards showing how regret theory can help us understand terrorist behaviour (Phillips & Pohl 2020).

Fear and hope

Whereas prospect theory is firmly grounded in cognitive psychology, Lola Lopes (1987) introduced a competing model in which emotion rather than cognition plays the leading role. It is called SP/A theory. The S, P and A refer to 'security', 'potential' and 'aspiration'. Lopes describes a decision-maker who can be either hopeful or cautious. If the decision-maker is hopeful, he starts by evaluating risky prospects from the best outcomes and works 'down'. If he is cautious, he focuses on security and evaluates risky prospects starting with the worst outcomes and works 'up'. Whether he is 'security' or 'potential' minded shapes the way that his attention is drawn to particular outcomes. In addition to this evaluation of security and potential, each risky prospect is also assessed against an aspiration level. It is important to the decision-maker that the outcomes meet or exceed the aspiration level. It is possible for the decision-maker to become confused if the evaluation seems okay but the aspiration level is not met (or vice versa). For applications of decision theory where emotions are seen as an important part of any explanation of the behaviour involved, SP/A may turn out to be the best model to use. In Phillips & Pohl (2018) we use SP/A theory to explain why a terrorist group might delay its actions. This is just one possible application of SP/A theory to the study of terrorism.

Don't forget the orthodoxy

In 1947, von Neumann and Morgenstern set down expected utility theory as a mathematical, axiom based, prescriptive model of choice. The axioms were interpreted as rules of rational behaviour and the model treated more as a predictive or descriptive model than it was ever designed to be. Studies began to emerge to see whether people really did choose in accordance with 'rational choice' or whether the axioms were 'violated'. This activity helped to reconnect economics and psychology, a relationship that had been on again, off again but mostly off again. The Allais Paradox, along with the Ellsberg Paradox (Ellsberg 1961), gradually began to attract more and more attention. At first, nobody really knew what to make of Allais' (1953) results. What did they mean? Nothing, really, if you think of expected utility theory as a prescriptive model of choice. But if you want to view expected utility theory as something more than that, something that can describe or even predict human choices, then a violation of one of the axioms has more and more significance.

While Kahneman and Tversky worked on a descriptive model of choice and Loomes, Sugden and Bell worked on their regret theory, other economists attempted to adjust expected utility theory so that it could cope with rogue preferences. Apart from the obvious mission to 'save' expected utility theory,[3] there were good reasons not to throw the baby out with the bathwater. For one, people do tend to correct their preferences over time. For example, when subjects discussed their choices, they often changed their minds about the options presented in the standard Allais Paradox such that they agreed with the independence axiom (Moskowitz 1974). About one-quarter of people fall into this category, remembering that not everyone's choices violate the independence axiom in the first place. Even as a predictive model, expected utility does not perform too badly. If it could be adjusted in some way, we might keep everything that makes it a good prescriptive model and expand its applicability as a predictive model.

The generalisations of expected utility theory include (see Machina 1987, p.132):

1. Karmarkar's (1978, 1979) subjectively weighted utility;
2. Quiggin's (1982) rank dependent or 'anticipated' expected utility;
3. Chew's (1983) weighted utility; and
4. Yaari's (1987) dual expected utility.

All of these vary the form of the expected utility function from $\sum_{i=1}^{n} u(x_i) p_i$ to some other functional form that allows for behaviour that would lead to a violation of the independence axiom. Another approach has been to show that the departures from the independence axiom such as those associated with the Allais Paradox do not seriously impair the operation of expected utility theory. This was the approach taken by Machina (1982).

As this small sample of the literature shows, the task of generalising expected utility theory was a burgeoning research program. In many ways, this has been overshadowed by the mainstream of behavioural economics and because the mainstream draws primarily on prospect theory, the alternatives are not widely explored. This has not been a mistake because we had to proceed where we could and it was impossible to tell at the beginning where the behavioural economics research program would take us. Now we can survey the whole landscape of behavioural economics, orthodox economics and non-mainstream behavioural economics produced since 1979, and it would be a mistake to ignore the types of work that we have been discussing just now. The hidden value could be significant. After all, the way in which humans assess probabilities is central to prospect theory and mainstream behavioural economics. However, it is possible to develop models that abandon probabilities altogether. This is one of the more radical approaches that was identified during the 1980s as a way to avoid the problems associated with the Allais Paradox. Such models, which treat uncertainty without using probabilities, are based on 'state preference theory' (e.g. Hirshleifer 1966). But that is a subject for another day.

Ideas to take away

It will take a long time to work out the implications of everything that we have learned about human decision-making over the past three or four decades. In some areas, results continue to be published at faster rates than ever before. We may even miss some of the implications for the very reasons revealed and explained by this research! We started out, some time ago, to work through the narratives that could be built about terrorist decision-making from unorthodox applications of orthodox economics (e.g. Phillips 2009, 2013; Phillips & Pohl 2012). This has led us in some interesting and unanticipated directions because we have tried to keep an open mind or, more formally, we have tried to embrace methodological diversification. We added behavioural economics and set the reference point as the trigger for copycat behaviour. And we added the law enforcement and counter-terrorism decision-making processes to our list of things to analyse and, more recently, the information gathering and processing tasks that are undertaken by counter-terrorism and intelligence agencies. In the long history of terrorism studies, the connections between investigative psychology, psychology, economics, decision science and criminology wax and wane but new connections are always being formed. In some terrorism studies researchers have possibly been dismayed to see the 'avalanche' of new authors and new work tumble through or over 'their' field. We say, on the contrary, that there has never been a more exciting time. We end with a list of patterns and their roots in economics and decision theory. This is only the beginning of what we envisage to become a dynamic decision framework that can be applied to pre-empting and pursuing perpetrators.

1. Terrorists, being sensitive to changes to their resources and the resources required for particular attack types, will switch from one attack type to another under certain circumstances [**neoclassical consumer decision theory**].
2. If terrorists have expended considerable effort on their terrorist identity, including by certain signature attack methods, they will be very, very stubborn and exceedingly difficult to negotiate with [**loss aversion and the endowment effect**].

3. All actors in the terrorism context display some degree of loss aversion that leads them to take more risk when they face losses [**prospect theory**].

4. All actors in the terrorism context are prone to overweight unlikely outcomes and underweight more likely outcomes. This can distort the terrorists' preferences for attack types and locations just as easily as it can disrupt the ordering of suspects for a terrorism watch list [**probability weighting and prospect theory**].

5. Decision-makers assess outcomes against at least one reference point. For a terrorist group or a school shooter, this could be the number of victims associated with a rival or predecessor. For a counter-terrorism taskforce, this could be the recent successes of a rival taskforce [**reference points and prospect theory**].

6. Terrorists combine attack methods. This is a basic yet overlooked fact. The implications are stark. Terrorists generate higher expected outcomes (however measured) while bearing less risk than has been considered previously [**modern portfolio theory**].

7. Even naïve diversification works in the sense just described but terrorist groups can gain greater 'efficiency' by using some information about correlations. If that sounds unbelievable, then we could say that terrorists allocate their resources to various goals. As it happens, if they do this, they are likely to choose as efficiently as predicted by the orthodox model [**behavioural portfolio theory and mental accounting**].

8. The terrorists' share of payoffs is important to their survival, not their absolute payoffs. There is no need to use more resources once the nearest rival has been shaded out. Competition for share leads to spirals in terrorist activity [**evolutionary game theory**].

9. Expected utility is a measuring tool that can be used to measure terrorists' preferences. The terrorist's utility accelerates quickest at lower payoff levels and then declines. Even though it is a prescriptive model, many people choose in accordance with its prescriptions, initially or following feedback and further deliberation [**expected utility theory**].

10. Information cascades can start very easily and as early as the third decision-maker. It can influence suspect prioritisation and other aspects of an investigation. They can also flow across jurisdictions [**information cascades**].

11. The communication of ideas across fields of study and from the research community to practice and back again are subject to all of the decision-making biases that we have explored [**information, heuristics and biases**].

12. The everyday of policing and counter-terrorism is often overlooked in research that concentrates on big events, such as a hostage situation. Everyday law enforcement is not untouched by technology and innovation. When these innovations involve decision-making processes during development, operation, interpretation and implementation, their surface objectivity may be a mirage [**heuristics and biases in everyday decision-making**].

For those in search of useful ideas there has never been a better time for it. Within economics, behavioural economics is no longer the quirky cousin that nobody wants to dance with. Nor is it the case that 'mainstream' economics, perhaps the most misused term in the social sciences given the numerous competing schools of thought that constitute the orthodoxy, has been sent on its way. There has been a gelling of the two. This makes complete sense once one realises that the different models each capture something of the human decision process and the context in which decisions take place and each can be put to a different purpose. For one purpose, it is best to use expected utility theory. For another, prospect theory. For another, SP/A theory. For another, one of the orthodox generalisations of expected utility theory. And so on. The challenge is to search for the right model for the right purpose with an open mind.

Notes

1 Opening passage of Frederick Forsyth's *Day of the Jackal* (1971).
2 Though this actually has no real meaning for a prescriptive model and no meaning for a predictive model either. That is, if expected utility theory is used to predict (rather than prescribe) human choices, it also does not matter whether people choose in accordance with the axioms. All that matters is that the preference ordering computed using expected utility theory accords with the decision-maker's actual choices.
3 Remember, once more, it does not need saving if used as intended. As a prescriptive model, expected utility theory always gives us the right answers.

References

Allais, M. 1953. Le Comportement de l'Homme Rationnel devant le Risque, Critique des Postulats et Axiomes de l'Ecole Americaine. *Econometrica*, 21, 503–546.
Bell, D.E. 1982. Regret in Decision-Making under Uncertainty. *Operations Research*, 30, 961–81.
Bleichrodt, H. & Wakker, P.P. 2015. Regret Theory: A Bold Alternative to the Alternatives. *Economic Journal*, 125, 493–532.
Chew, S. 1983. A Generalisation of the Quasilinear Mean with Applications to the Measurement of Income Inequality and Decision Theory Resolving the Allais Paradox. *Econometrica*, 51, 1065–1092.
De Bondt, W.F.M. & Thaler, R. 1985. Does the Stock Market Overreact? *Journal of Finance*, 40, 793–805.
Edwards, W. 1955. The Prediction of Decisions among Bets. *Journal of Experimental Psychology*, 50, 201–214.
Edwards, W. 1962. Subjective Probabilities Inferred from Decisions. *Psychological Review*, 69, 109–135.
Ellsberg, D. 1961. Risk, Ambiguity and the Savage Axioms. *Quarterly Journal of Economics*, 75, 643–669.
Fishburn, P.C. 1989. Retrospective on the Utility Theory of von Neumann and Morgenstern. *Journal of Risk and Uncertainty*, 2, 127–158.
Forsyth, F. 1971. *The Day of the Jackal*. London, UK: Corgi Books.

Hirshleifer, J. 1966. Investment Decision under Uncertainty: Applications of the State-Preference Approach. *Quarterly Journal of Economics*, 80, 252–277.

Kahneman, D. 2011. *Thinking, Fast and Slow*. New York: Farrar, Straus, Giroux.

Kahneman, D. & Tversky, A. 1979. Prospect Theory: An Analysis of Decision under Risk. *Econometrica*, 47, 263–291.

Kahneman, D., Knetsch, J.L. & Thaler, R.H. 1986a. Fairness as a Constraint on Profit Seeking: Entitlements in the Market. *American Economic Review*, 76, 728–741.

Kahneman, D., Knetsch, J.L. & Thaler, R.H. 1986b. Fairness and the Assumptions of Economics. *Journal of Business*, 59, S285–S300.

Kahneman, D., Knetsch, J.L. & Thaler, R.H. 1991. The Endowment Effect, Loss Aversion and Status Quo Bias. *Journal of Economic Perspectives*, 5, 193–206.

Karmarkar, U. 1978. Subjectively Weighted Utility: A Descriptive Extension of the Expected Utility Model. *Organizational Behaviour and Human Performance*, 21, 61–72.

Karmarkar, U. 1979. Subjectively Weighted Utility and the Allais Paradox. *Organizational Behaviour and Human Performance*, 24, 67–72.

Knetsch, J.L. & Sinden, J.A. 1984. Willingness to Pay and Compensation Demanded: Experimental Evidence of an Unexpected Disparity in Measures of Value. *Quarterly Journal of Economics*, 99, 507–521.

Loomes, G. & Sugden, R.F. 1982. Regret Theory: An Alternative Theory of Rational Choice under Uncertainty. *Economic Journal*, 92, 805–824.

Lopes, L.L. 1987. Between Hope and Fear: The Psychology of Risk. *Advances in Experimental Social Psychology*, 20, 255–295.

Lyons, M. & Rice, H. 2014. Thieves of Time? Procrastination and the Dark Triad of Personality. *Personality and Individual Differences*, 61–62, 34–37.

Machina M. 1982. 'Expected Utility' Analysis without the Independence Axiom. *Econometrica*, 50, 277–323.

Machina, M.J. 1987. Choice under Uncertainty: Problems Solved and Unsolved. *Journal of Economic Perspectives*, 1, 121–154.

Moskowitz, H. 1974. Effects of Problem Representation and Feedback on Rational Behaviour in Allais and Morlat-Type Problems. *Decision Sciences*, 5, 225–242.

Phillips, P.J. 2009. Applying Portfolio Theory to the Analysis of Terrorism: Computing the Set of Attack Method Combinations from Which the Rational Terrorist Group Will Choose in Order to Maximise Injuries and Fatalities. *Defence and Peace Economics*, 20, 193–213.

Phillips, P.J. 2013. *In Pursuit of the Lone Wolf Terrorist*. New York: Nova.

Phillips, P.J. & Pohl, G. 2012. Economic Profiling of the Lone Wolf Terrorist: Can Economics Provide Behavioural Investigative Advice? *Journal of Applied Security Research*, 7, 151–177.

Phillips, P.J. & Pohl, G. 2018. The Deferral of Attacks: SP/A Theory as a Model of Terrorist Choice When Losses Are Inevitable. *Open Economics*, 1, 71–85.

Phillips, P.J. & Pohl, G. 2020. Anticipated Regret, Terrorist Behaviour and the Presentation of the Outcomes of Attacks in the Mainstream Media and in Terrorist Group Publications. *Aggression and Violent Behavior*, 51, Article 101394.

Quiggin, J. 1982. A Theory of Anticipated Utility. *Journal of Economic Behaviour and Organisation*, 3, 323–343.

Rabin, M. 1998. Psychology and Economics. *Journal of Economic Literature*, 36, 11–46.

Raiffa, H. 1968. *Decision Analysis: Introductory Lectures on Choices under Uncertainty*. Reading, MA: Addison-Wesley.

Simon, J. 1982. *Reverse Angle: A Decade of American Film*. New York: Crown.

Slovic, P. & Tversky, A. 1974. Who Accepts Savage's Axiom? *Behavioural Science*, 19, 368–373.

Thaler, R.H. 1981. Some Empirical Evidence on Dynamic Inconsistency. *Economics Letters*, 8, 201–207.

Thaler, R.H. 1985. Mental Accounting and Consumer Choice. *Marketing Science*, 4, 199–214.

Thaler, R.H. 2016. *Misbehaving: The Making of Behavioural Economics*. New York: W.W. Norton.

Thaler, R.H. & Shefrin, H.M. 1981. An Economic Theory of Self-Control. *Journal of Political Economy*, 89, 392–406.

Tversky, A. 1969. Intransitivity of Preferences. *Psychological Review*, 76, 31–48.

Tversky, A. 1972. Elimination by Aspects: A Theory of Choice. *Psychological Review*, 79, 281–299.

Von Neumann, J. & Morgenstern, O. 1947. *Theory of Games and Economic Behaviour*, 2nd ed. Princeton, NJ: Princeton University Press.

Yaari, M. 1987. The Dual Theory of Choice under Risk. *Econometrica*, 55, 95–115.

INDEX

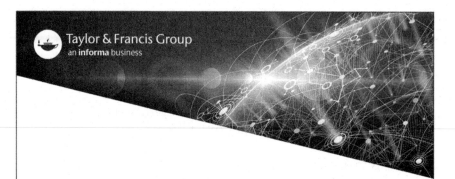

Printed in the United States
By Bookmasters